The Money Supply Process

Brooks/Cole Publishing Company   Charles A. Jones Publishing Co.,   Duxbury Press

4505 South 5600 West   Salt Lake City, Utah 84120

Purchase Order No. 480060

FULL CARTONS SHIPPED	LESS THAN CARTON QUANTITY	TOTAL BOOKS SHIPPED	TITLE CODE	BOOK TITLE	LIST PRICE
		✓1	04W5000	MONEY SUPPLY PROCESS	6.95

PACKING LIST

PACKING LIST

PAGE NO. 1

ALL SHIPPING ERRORS MUST BE REPORTED WITHIN 10 DAYS TO:

CUSTOMER SERVICE DEPARTMENT
BELMONT, CA. 94002 (415) 592-1300

The Money Supply Process

Albert E. Burger

Economist, Federal Reserve Bank of St. Louis
and
Assistant Professor of Economics
Southern Illinois University

Wadsworth Publishing Company, Inc.,
Belmont, California

ISBN-0-534-00037-1
L. C. Cat. Card No. 71-166408
Printed in the United States of America

1 2 3 4 5 6 7 8 9 10—76 75 74 73 72 71

Preface

A thorough understanding of the money supply process is equally important, both for economists and noneconomists. In the last 10 or 15 years an expanding volume of empirical and theoretical work on monetary theory and policy has developed. This research supports the conjecture that changes in the growth rate of money have an important influence on economic activity. The trend and fluctuations in the growth rate of money affect the prices we pay for goods and services, the level of unemployment, and the level of market interest rates. Therefore, a clear blueprint of the money supply process is essential so that monetary policymakers can understand how their policy actions affect the money supply process; so economists can advise the policymakers on the most efficient way of controlling money; and so other individuals can evaluate the responsibility of the monetary authorities for the growth of money and how they carry it out.

Most money and banking texts devote some space to the money supply process. This book differs from others in the field by concentrating exclusively on the money supply process and giving a complete framework for analyzing this process. It explains how policy actions by the Federal Reserve, portfolio decisions by the public and the banks, actions by the Treasury, and changes in institutional conditions affect the growth of the money stock. It also analyzes the relationship between money and bank credit and the relationship between money and interest rates.

A basic knowledge of economics, equivalent to a principles course in micro- and macroeconomics, is assumed. All mathematical notation is explained; after the reader becomes used to a few general forms, he should have no difficulty in following the text. The book can be used at several levels, from an intermediate course in money and banking to one at the graduate level. However, it requires some study and thought on the part of the reader. Although the general reader can understand the material without working out all steps in the analysis, each stage in the analysis is developed in considerable detail so that the advanced reader can follow the stages of deduction and critically analyze the conclusions.

Much work remains to be done to analyze the money supply process. This book develops the present state of the art. Some of the material is preliminary, especially in Chapter 10 on controlling the growth of the money stock.

The Money Supply Process is meant to inform as well as to generate comment, criticism, and future research.

The incentive for writing this book came primarily from my association with the Research Department of the Federal Reserve Bank of St. Louis. The continued logical and empirical analysis of existing economic theory and the development of new ideas within the Research Department were basic ingredients. Darryl R. Francis, president of the Bank, and Homer Jones and Leonall C. Andersen, directors of research, through their efforts to involve the research staff in monetary policy, encouragement of basic research, and close contact with each economist created this atmosphere conducive to basic research. All of the economists on the research staff, at one time or another, read parts of this book. Their criticisms have been invaluable. In this regard, a specific acknowledgment is due Jerry L. Jordan, whose criticisms and discussions with the author were most helpful.

The framework of analysis developed in this book is based on the studies of Karl Brunner, University of Rochester, and Allen H. Meltzer, Carnegie-Mellon University. Professors Brunner and Meltzer read drafts of the book, offered many suggestions, and spent several working sessions with the author. Much of the merit of this book is the result of their comments, and their assistance is gratefully acknowledged. The author also received useful comments from Professors J. Richard Zecher, The University of Chicago, Harland W. Whitmore, Jr., University of Cincinnati, William P. Yohe, Duke University and Manfred Willms, The University of Kiel, Germany.

Mrs. Connie Parham was a great help in collecting and organizing the data and editing the numerous drafts of the manuscript. The author is deeply indebted to her. Miss Marie Wahlig, through her understanding of the detailed composition of the data, provided valuable technical assistance. Mrs. Betty Yerlikaya was responsible for rapid and efficient typing. At one time or another, the author also received technical, editorial, and typing assistance from most of the other members of the Research Department. Their aid is gratefully acknowledged. A special acknowledgment must go to my wife, Linda, and to my children. They patiently and in good humor endured my periods of frustration and gave up many evenings and weekends for the sake of this book.

Any opinions expressed in the book, as well as any conclusions or analytical errors, are the sole responsibility of the author. In no way should any conclusions or other statements in the book be taken as representing the views or policy position of the Federal Reserve Bank of St. Louis or anyone else in the Federal Reserve System.

A. E. B.
September, 1971

Contents

Chapter One Introduction

In recent years an approach to monetary theory that might be labeled "The Portfolio Theory of Monetary Policy" has gained wide acceptance in the economics profession. Within this approach, monetary theory is considered to be part of the broader theory of asset choice and portfolio management of economic units. A monetary disturbance such as an injection of base money into the economic system is viewed as changing the existing conditions under which wealthholders are willing to hold current assets. A policy-induced change in the amount of the existing stock of any one asset (such as the amount of reserves that banks hold) lead to a behavioral reaction on the part of economic units as they attempt to readjust their stocks of both real and financial assets to the amounts desired under these new conditions. The attempt by individual economic units—households, commercial banks, nonbank financial institutions, other business firms, and government units—to reallocate their nonhuman wealth to a different set of assets appears in the real sector via a change in the quantity demanded of real assets (such as capital goods and consumer goods) and thus affects real output and prices.

One of the consequences of this approach has been to view the money stock as being determined both on the supply and demand side by the behavioral actions of economic units. Money is considered as only one of many assets that economic units hold. The money stock is no longer considered to be completely exogenously determined, but is viewed as a quantity whose magnitude is partly determined by the policy actions of the central bank and partly endogenously determined within the economic system by rational portfolio decisions of the commercial banks and the public.

This book is an attempt to explain the money supply and bank credit processes and their dependence and influence on credit market interest rates; more precisely, it develops a hypothesis.

What exactly is a hypothesis? Especially, what is the purpose of devoting time and energy to developing a money supply hypothesis? First, let us consider what "hypothesis" means. It is a carefully formulated attempt to explain some phenomena of the real world. A hypothesis, or a mathematical formulation of the hypothesis, is not the "real world," but is only a representation of the real world. Of necessity it must abstract from many facets of the real world situation that it is attempting to represent, and it can include only those aspects that are considered crucial to the explanation of the phenomena which it is designed to explain.

From a carefully designed hypothesis, logical consequences can be derived which may be confronted with empirical observations. Such a confrontation is called a "test" of the hypothesis. A hypothesis that has been tested, and found repeatedly to have its logically derivable consequences in agreement with empirical observations may serve as a valuable aid in understanding a part of the real world.

Some persons, including some economists, question the importance of explaining changes in such quantities as money and bank credit. They argue that what is really important are changes in money income, real income, prices, and employment. In the extreme form of this assertion, they argue that "money doesn't matter." However, a substantial body of economic theory and empirical evidence strongly indicates that changes in the money stock can have and have had an important impact on changes in the aggregate price level, money income, and employment. One of the most comprehensive studies of the relationship between changes in money (defined to include time deposits), money income, and prices is the work of Milton Friedman and Anna Schwartz. From a study of the period 1867–1960, their major conclusions were as follows:

> 1. Changes in the behavior of the money stock have been closely associated with changes in economic activity, money income, and prices.
>
> 2. The interrelationship between monetary and economic change has been highly stable.
>
> 3. Monetary changes have often had an independent origin; they have not been simply a reflection of changes in economic activity.[1]

There is still considerable disagreement about how to discuss the relationship between money and income. Should money be defined as just demand deposits and currency held by the nonbank public or should money include time deposits? Should income be defined as permanent income rather than measured income? In any case, several studies have substantiated the close relationship between changes in "money" and changes in "income."

Leonall C. Andersen and Jerry L. Jordan have presented evidence that supports the class of hypotheses whose derivable consequences contain assertions that the influence of changes in the money stock (M^1) have a strong, rapid and predictable effect on the rate of change of economic activity.[2] Michael W. Keran has extended the Andersen–Jordan work over the longer period 1919–1969.[3] Keran's results support the conclusion that monetary influences have

---

[1] Milton Friedman and Anna Schwartz, *A Monetary History of the United States: 1867–1960*, (Princeton, N.J.: Princeton University Press, 1963) p. 676.

[2] Leonall C. Andersen and Jerry L. Jordan, "Monetary and Fiscal Actions: A Test of their Relative Importance in Economic Stabilization," Federal Reserve Bank of St. Louis *Review* November 1968, pp. 11–24.

[3] Michael W. Keran, "Monetary and Fiscal Influences on Economic Activity—The Historical Evidence," Federal Reserve Bank of St. Louis *Review*, November 1969, pp. 5–24.

dominated economic activity in periods when financial and institutional factors were substantially different.[4]

If, as an increasing body of empirical evidence indicates, monetary influences exert an important and predictable influence on economic activity, then such questions as "How is the supply of money determined" and "Can the Federal Reserve control the money supply process?" become very pertinent.

The policy actions of the central bank are limited to procedures such as purchase or sale of government securities, changes in the legal reserve requirements on member bank demand and time deposits, changes in the discount rate, and changes in the Regulation *Q* ceiling rates on time deposits. If policymaking groups such as the Federal Open Market Committee and Board of Governors are told they should control the level of market interest rates or the money stock, this advice is of little use to them unless they are also advised how the policy actions they may perform will result in the desired levels or rates of changes of interest rates or the stock of money.[5]

People who have asserted that expanding the Federal Reserve System's holdings of government securities would decrease the level of market interest rates have in recent years found to their dismay that the opposite effect occurred. Advisors who have assumed that the money stock is a simple expansion of bank reserves have also on occasion been dismayed by the results of their policy recommendations. In the proverbial phrase, "there's many a slip 'twixt the cup and the lip," even when the objective of policy actions has not been employment or prices but a more intermediate objective, such as money or interest rates.

Three of the minimum requirements that a hypothesis concerning the determination of the money stock must satisfy, if it is to be useful to policymaking groups such as the Board of Governors and the Federal Open Market Committee, are as follows:

1. It must explicitly include the policy variables under the direct control of the monetary authorities.
2. It must establish a definite link between these control variables and the monetary aggregates.
3. It must take into account the existing institutional framework within which the policymakers must operate, and it must be able to demonstrate the effects of a change in one of these institutional conditions upon the impact of changes in policy variables.

The hypothesis developed in this book is based on the work of Professors Karl Brunner and Allan Meltzer. The framework of the hypothesis is essentially what Brunner and Meltzer have called their Non-Linear Money

---

[4] For further discussions of the monetary influences on economic activity, see: Anna Schwartz, "Why Money Matters," *Lloyd's Bank Review*, October 1969, pp. 1–16; and Karl Brunner and Allan Meltzer, "Predicting Velocity: Implications for Theory and Policy," *Journal of Finance*, Vol. XVIII (May 1963), pp. 319–354.

[5] See Albert E. Burger and Leonall C. Andersen, "The Development of Explanatory Economic Hypotheses for Monetary Management," *Southern Journal of Business*, Vol. IV (October 1969), pp. 140–164.

Supply Hypothesis.[6] The Brunner–Meltzer work is more than an attempt to forecast the magnitudes of the economic quantities: money, defined to include demand deposits and currency held by the nonbank public; money, defined to include time deposits; and bank credit. It is an attempt to explain the process by which the stocks of money and bank credit are determined.[7]

No claim is made that the method presented in this book is the only way to formulate an explanation of the money supply process. There are many possible ways in which the basic balance sheet items could be combined to form a framework for analyzing the money supply process. The Brunner–Meltzer Non-Linear Money Supply Hypothesis was chosen because it meets all three of the basic criteria listed above. Within this framework we are able to analyze the influence of Federal Reserve policy actions, behavioral actions of the banks and the public, and to consider institutional conditions and changes in these conditions as they influence the money supply and bank credit processes. Also, the development of this hypothesis permits an analysis of the influence of these factors on credit market interest rates and the influence of credit market interest rates on the money supply and bank credit processes.

The analysis begins with an item called the source base (B) which is derived from the consolidated balance sheets of the Treasury and Federal Reserve. Member bank borrowings from the Federal Reserve are then subtracted from the source base to obtain an item called the net source base (B^a). This net source base may be viewed from the sources side or from the uses side. The total is the same regardless of which way is chosen to discuss the base. However, for purposes of discussing operating strategies for monetary policy, the distinction between sources and uses is extremely useful and important. The major component, from the sources side of B^a, is the Federal Reserve System's holdings of government securities. Hence, the amount of net source base supplied to the economy is partly dependent upon open market actions by the Federal Reserve System.

From the consolidated balance sheets of the monetary authorities and the commercial banks, relations are derived between the money stock (M^1), money defined to include time deposits (M^2), bank credit (E), and the net source base (B^a). These relations are expressed as

$$M^1 = m^1 B^a,$$
$$M^2 = m^2 B^a,$$
$$E = (m^2 - 1)B^a.$$

The items m^1, m^2, and $m^2 - 1$ are referred to as multipliers. The multipliers express the amount of M^1, M^2, and E that will be supplied to the public given the magnitude of B^a. The numerical values of the multipliers depend upon portfolio decisions by the banks and the public, Federal Reserve policy actions, institutional factors such as the distribution of deposits between

---

[6] See Karl Brunner and Allan H. Meltzer, "Liquidity Traps for Money, Bank Credit, and Interest Rates," *Journal of Political Economy*, Vol. 76, No. 1 (January/February 1968), pp. 1–37.

[7] For an elementary discussion of the difference between forecasting and explanation see Stephen Toulmin, *Foresight and Understanding* (Bloomington: Indiana University Press, 1961).

member and nonmember banks, actions by the Treasury, and credit market interest rates.

Within the hypothesis of this book the equilibrium values of money and bank credit are determined jointly by the policy actions of the Federal Reserve System and the portfolio decisions of the commercial banks and the public. Federal Reserve open market actions are incorporated in changes in the net source base. Federal Reserve discount rate changes, reserve requirement actions, and Regulation Q ceiling rates are incorporated via behavioral reactions by the banks and the public in the money and bank credit multipliers. The hypothesis takes into consideration not only the impact of a given policy action by the central bank, but also how changes in the decisions of the banks and the public to acquire assets and emit liabilities affects the equilibrium stocks of money and bank credit. The partial-equilibrium responses of money and bank credit to changes in market interest rates are also analyzed.

This book does not attempt to discuss fully all of the implications and applications of Brunner and Meltzer's studies of the monetary process. For detailed discussions and mathematical derivations, the reader should consult the articles by Brunner and Meltzer cited in the references. This book attempts to give a basic framework for analyzing the money supply and bank credit process and their interaction with credit market interest rates.

Chapter 2 gives a general view of this book's procedure and relates the entire book to what the reader may already know from money and banking courses. Some basic terminology is also introduced. In Chapter 3, development of the hypothesis begins; the basic relations underlying the hypothesis are presented, and the multipliers are derived. Chapter 4 presents the complete specification of the dependence of the parameters of the multipliers. Chapter 5 analyzes the dependence of the multipliers on interest rates. Chapter 6 combines the banks' demand for earning assets and the public's supply of earning assets to banks and discusses the partial equilibrium solutions for money, M^2, and bank credit. Chapter 7 is an analysis of the influence of policy actions. The last three chapters are concerned with the problem of implementing monetary policy and the implications of the hypothesis for this problem.

The author hopes the nonmathematically inclined reader will not be dismayed by the abundance of mathematical equations that appear in the first part of this book. Mathematical notation and functional expressions are used as a convenient notational device that permits many ideas to be written in a condensed form. Also, using the analytical system of mathematics allows us to proceed carefully and to check the deductions arrived at in different stages of the analysis. Each introduction of a mathematical form will be carefully explained and discussed.

Chapter Two — What This Book Is All About

This chapter presents a brief, general treatment of the basic content of this book. No attempt is made to consider details. The purpose of the chapter is to drive home a few basic points and to give the reader a bird's-eye-view of the material before undertaking a detailed analysis. Those who are already familiar with monetary analysis may want to omit this chapter and go directly to Chapter 3.

To begin, let us assume there are three economic sectors in the economy: (1) the monetary authorities, which include the Treasury and the Federal Reserve System, (2) the commercial banks, and (3) the nonbank public. Each sector has a balance sheet of assets and liabilities which are presented in simple *T*-account form as shown below.

MONETARY AUTHORITIES

Assets	Liabilities
Gold	Currency held by the public (C^p)
Government securities	Deposits of banks at the Federal Reserve Banks (R)

BANKS

Assets	Liabilities
Deposits at Federal Reserve Banks (R = reserves)	Demand deposits of the nonbank public (D^p)
Earning assets (E) = Loans to the public (L) and securities (S)	

NONBANK PUBLIC

Assets	Liabilities
Currency (C^p) Demand deposits (D^p) Securities (S)	Loans from banks (L)

In the above balance sheets some shorthand notation is introduced to avoid writing out these terms each time they are used. For example, currency held by the nonbank public is written as C^p. The reader will note that these balance sheets are very incomplete representations of the actual balance sheets of these sectors. Again we emphasize that our purpose is to make the analysis as simple as possible so that a few basic principles can be illustrated.

First, let us define base money, a term that is used frequently in the following analysis. Base money (sometimes called high-powered money) is defined as the net monetary liabilities of the government (monetary authorities) held by the commercial banks and the nonbank public. For the balance sheets above, base money (B) consists of deposits of banks at the Federal Reserve Banks (R) and currency held by the nonbank public (C^p):

$$B = R + C^p.$$

In Chapter 3, the definition of the base is broadened to take into account the fact that banks also hold currency (vault cash). Hence the base must also include vault cash holdings of banks. In this chapter, to keep the analysis as simple as possible, reserves are not divided into member bank deposits at the Federal Reserve and vault cash. For simplicity it is assumed that all of the banks' holdings of base money consist of deposits at Federal Reserve Banks.

Total bank reserves plus currency held by the public reflect the *uses* of the base. To compute the base from the *sources* side, we turn to the balance sheet of the monetary authorities. In our example, to compute the base from the sources side we add the gold stock plus government securities held by the monetary authorities plus currency. If the monetary authorities buy gold or securities, they are supplying more base money to the banks and public. When the monetary authorities issue more currency to the banks and public, the amount of base money held by the banks and the public increases.[1]

Actual computation of the base from the sources side requires consideration of a number of items besides securities, gold, and currency in the consolidated balance sheet of the monetary authorities. A complete analysis of the sources of the base is presented in the following chapter. The important distinction between sources and uses of the base is the basic point of this simplified discussion.

The purpose of this book is to explain the process by which the amount

[1] For this example the only form of currency is assumed to be that issued by the Treasury. In an expanded balance sheet currency issued by the Federal Reserve (Federal Reserve notes) would be included. When the Federal Reserve issues currency to the banks, who in turn issue the Federal Reserve notes to the public, there is an offsetting debit to the banks' reserve accounts at the Fed.

of money ($D^p + C^p$) supplied to the nonbank public is determined. Since the largest portion of the money stock is produced by commercial banks, let us turn first to the behavior of banks. From the balance sheet of the banks in our example, we start with the following basic balance sheet identity, deposit liabilities (D^p) equal reserves (R) plus earning assets (E):

$$D^p = R + E.$$

Now, some high school algebra is performed on this relation:

$$\frac{D^p}{R} = 1 + \frac{E}{R}.$$

Let us denote the ratio of banks' holdings of base money (reserves) to their deposit liabilities by r and call this the reserve ratio. Then,

$$r = \frac{R}{D^p}.$$

Substituting equals for equals yields

$$\frac{1}{r} = 1 + \frac{E}{R}.$$

Multiplying by R, we have

$$\frac{1}{r}R = R + E;$$

and substituting $R + E = D^p$ gives

$$\boxed{\frac{1}{r}R = D^p.}$$

This expression gives a relationship between the amount of base held by banks (R) and the amount of bank money supplied to the public (D^p). The connecting link ($1/r$) is called the *bank money multiplier*. The bank money multiplier gives the amount of D^p associated with each dollar of base held by banks.

The bank money multiplier, in our simple example, is the reciprocal of the reserve ratio. What factors operate to determine the reserve ratio? To keep the exposition as simple as possible, let us assume that there are only two factors:

1. Banks are required to hold reserves equal to a percentage of their outstanding deposit liabilities. These reserves are called legal reserves (R_L), and this requirement can be expressed as a ratio:

$$r^d = \frac{R_L}{D^p} \quad \text{legal reserve ratio.}$$

2. Banks desire to hold some reserves over and above what they are legally required to hold. These reserves are called excess reserves (R^e). Let us express banks' holdings of excess reserves relative to deposits as a ratio:

$$e = \frac{R^e}{D^p} \qquad \text{excess reserve ratio.}$$

The sum of the legal reserve ratio and the excess reserve ratio equals the reserve ratio:

$$R = R_L + R^e,$$

$$\frac{R}{D^p} = \frac{R_L}{D^p} + \frac{R^e}{D^p},$$

$$r = r^d + e.$$

Hence, the bank money multiplier may be written as

$$\frac{1}{r} = \frac{1}{r^d + e}.$$

Two important factors that will influence the relation between reserves and bank money are now evident—first, the legal reserve ratio set by the Federal Reserve System and, second, the excess reserve ratio which is determined by the portfolio preference of the banks.

Numerical Example

As a very simple example, let us assume the following:[2]

$$r^d = .1 \qquad e = .1.$$

The banks are required to hold one dollar of reserves for each \$10 of deposit liabilities. In addition to their required reserves, banks desire to hold one dollar of base (excess reserves) for each \$10 of deposit liabilities.

In this example the balance sheets of the monetary authorities, banks, and the public appear as follows:

Monetary Authorities

Gold = 10,000	C^p = 100,000
S = 90,000	R = 100,000

[2] In this example we shall assume that a change in the base has no effect on the equilibrium value of the multiplier. As we shall see in later chapters, this is a highly artificial assumption under most conditions.

BANKS

$R = 100{,}000$	$D^p = 500{,}000$
$E = 400{,}000$	
$L = 300{,}000$	
$S = 100{,}000$	

PUBLIC

$D^p = 500{,}000$	Bank loans $= 300{,}000$
$C^p = 100{,}000$	
$S = 100{,}000$	

Checking through the balance sheets, the following results hold:

1. Base equals $200,000. One half of the stock of base is used as currency by the public, and one half is used as reserves by the banks.
2. The total stock of securities held by the public and banks equals $200,000.
3. The public's loan liabilities to the banks are $300,000.

Examining the balance sheet for the banks, given the assumption we have made and assuming that the banks have distributed their earning assets between loans and investments in the manner they desire, the banking system is in equilibrium. The amount of reserves the banks hold equals the amount they desire to hold, given that the demand deposit liabilities to the public are $500,000.

Federal Reserve Open Market Actions

Suppose the Federal Reserve now purchases $10,000 of government securities from the commercial banks. After the transaction the balance sheets appear as follows; an asterisk is used to indicate the components of the balance sheets that change:

MONETARY AUTHORITIES

Gold $= 10{,}000$	$C^p = 100{,}000$
$S^* = 100{,}000$	$R = 110{,}000^*$

BANKS

$R^* = 110{,}000$	$D^p = 500{,}000$
$E^* = 390{,}000$	
$L = 300{,}000$	
$S^* = 90{,}000$	

As a result of the open market purchase by the Federal Reserve System, banks are no longer holding the portfolio of assets they desire to hold, given their deposit liabilities. Although banks hold the same amount of total assets as before, their holdings of nonearning assets (R) are greater than they desire to hold given the dollar amount of their deposit liabilities. The banks now begin to adjust their portfolios of assets. In the process of portfolio adjustment they expand their holdings of earning assets by acquiring securities and making loans. The banks pay for these assets with bank money (D^p). To induce the public to supply securities, banks bid up the price of securities. To induce the public to increase its indebtedness to the banks, the banks lower the interest rate they charge on bank loans. The market interest rate falls.

For our example, let us assume that the banks purchase $10,000 of securities from the public and that the public increases its debt to the banks by $40,000.

The balance sheets for the banks and the public now appear as follows:

BANKS

R = 110,000	D^p = 550,000*
E^* = 440,000	
L^* = 340,000	
S^* = 100,000	

PUBLIC

D^{p*} = 550,000	Bank loans = 340,000*
C^p = 100,000	
S^* = 90,000	

The banking system is back in equilibrium. The banks are holding the amount of reserves they desire to hold given their deposit liabilities. In the process by which the banks adjusted their portfolios to the initial increase in the base, the banks bid up the price of securities and lowered the interest rate they charged on loans. The public, responding to the lower interest rate, increased the quantity of earning assets it supplied to the banks by $50,000—increased loan liabilities to banks by $40,000 and sold $10,000 of securities to the banks. The banks paid for the additional $50,000 of earning assets they acquired with bank money (D^p); hence the money stock rose by $50,000.

The Public and Currency

So far only bank money has been discussed. However, the public has a choice as to how to hold its money balances. The alternative to money produced by the banks (D^p) is government money (currency). The money stock consists of demand deposits and currency:

$$M = D^p + C^p.$$

The public decides what portion of its money balances it wants to hold in D^p and what portion in currency. Since the existing stock of base is given to the banks and the public, if the public decides to hold a larger amount of base (currency), this means that there is less base (reserves) held by the banks. Such decisions by the public affect the money supply and bank credit processes.

The first balance sheet for the public shows that the public holds $1 of currency for every $5 of D^p. The public's allocation of its money balance between demand deposits and currency is expressed by the ratio

$$\frac{C^p}{D^p} = k \qquad \text{currency ratio.}$$

In the example, the k-ratio equals

$$\frac{C^p}{D^p} = \frac{\$100{,}000}{\$500{,}000} = .2.$$

However, after the Federal Reserve's purchase of securities from the banks and the banks' portfolio adjustment, the public is no longer holding the ratio of currency to demand deposits that it desires to hold. The public's holdings of bank money have risen to $550,000, but the public is still holding only $100,000 in currency. The public now attempts to increase its holdings of currency. To do so the public exercises its instant repurchase agreement with the banks. They require the banks to buy back bank money with currency. As a result, base is drained out of the banks.

This effect appears in the balance sheet of the banks as follows:

BANKS

R^* = 105,000	D^p = 545,000*
E = 440,000	

As a result of the currency drain, the banks' holdings of reserves is smaller than they desire, given their deposit liabilities of $545,000.

The banks attempt to adjust their portfolio of assets. Let us assume that this adjustment is carried out by the banks selling securities to the public. The balance sheet results of this process are given below:

BANKS

R = 105,000	D^p = 525,000*
E^* = 420,000	
L = 340,000	
S^* = 80,000	

PUBLIC

D^{p*} = 525,000	Bank loans = 340,000
C^{p*} = 105,000	
S^* = 110,000	

In the adjustment process the banking system sells \$20,000 of securities to the public, and the public pays for these securities by drawing down its demand deposits at banks. The money stock rises by \$30,000 (25,000 D^p +5,000 C^p), instead of \$50,000, as our first partial equilibrium result indicated.

In summary, the result of the open market purchase of securities by the Federal Reserve, at this stage of the analysis, is as follows:

1. The base has risen by \$10,000—the amount of government securities purchased by the Federal Reserve System.
2. The increase in the base has been allocated, by the actions of the banks and the public, to \$5,000 more in bank reserves and \$5,000 more in currency held by the public.
3. The stock of securities held by the banks and public has decreased from \$200,000 to \$190,000—the amount of government securities purchased by the Federal Reserve.
4. The public has increased its loan liabilities to the banks by \$40,000, sold \$10,000 of securities to the banks, and has purchased \$20,000 of securities from the banks and exchanged \$5,000 of demand deposits for currency. Hence the net change in bank money (D^p) is \$25,000.

Expansion of the Multiplier

It is clear from the foregoing example that a multiplier of the form $1/r$ gives only an incomplete means of analyzing the money supply and bank credit processes. Given that the public has a choice as to how to hold its money balances, the multiplier must be broadened to this form:

$$\text{money multiplier} = \frac{1+k}{(r^d+e)+k}.$$

The full expression for the money supply (M^1) then becomes

$$\frac{1+k}{(r^d+e)+k}B = M^1,$$

where

$$B = R + C^p.$$

Base (B) is used, rather than only reserves, because the money stock consists of bank money *and* currency. Also the public's desire to hold currency relative to bank money affects the amount of reserves held by banks and hence demand deposits held by the public, bank credit, and the money stock.

Although still at a very primitive level of analysis, examples of the three major factors that determine the amount of money and bank credit supplied to the public have been introduced. The first factor is Federal Reserve actions such as changes in legal reserve requirements and open market operations. The second factor is portfolio decisions by the banks expressed in the *e*-ratio. The third is portfolio decisions by the public, impounded in the *k*-ratio.

This brief outline has provided an overview of what the rest of the book will develop. To make the analysis of the money supply and bank credit processes useful for policy purposes, many other factors must be included. Bank deposits must be broadened to include time deposits and government demand deposits. The other policy instruments of the Federal Reserve—such as the discount rate, reserve requirements on time deposits, and Regulation *Q*—must be added. Institutional factors (such as the fact that all banks are not members of the Federal Reserve System and that reserve requirements differ according to class of member banks) must also be considered. In addition, the dependence of the behavioral actions of the public and banks on interest rates and other factors needs to be taken into account, and the assumption of the independence of the multipliers and changes in the base must be relaxed.

Chapter Three

Basic Definitions and Derivation of the Multipliers

The explanation of the process by which the stocks of money (M^1), money plus time deposits (M^2), and bank credit (E) are determined begins with a definition of an economic quantity called the *net source base*, which is denoted as (B^a). Relationships between B^a and M^1, M^2, and E are then derived. These derived quantities are called multipliers. The multipliers summarize those factors, other than changes in B^a, that influence the money supply and bank credit processes.

In this chapter the net source base is defined and discussed. Following the discussion of B^a the parameters of the multipliers are introduced. These parameters are defined and the way in which they are measured is discussed. After the introduction of all of the ratios that enter the multipliers, the multipliers are derived.

In this chapter, only the definition and measurement of the parameters (the ratios) in the multipliers are discussed. In the following chapter we shall specify the functional dependence of the parameters of the multipliers. The reader should keep in mind the key distinction between definition, measurement, and behavioral assumptions about the determination of the equilibrium values of the ratios that enter the multipliers.

Monetary Aggregates and Bank Credit

The basic monetary aggregates and bank credit are defined as follows:

$$M^1 = D^p + C^p \qquad \text{money,} \tag{3.1}$$

$$M^2 = M^1 + T \qquad \text{money plus time deposits,} \tag{3.2}$$

$$E = L + S - (N + D^t) \qquad \text{bank credit,}^1 \tag{3.3}$$

[1] This definition of bank credit is a modified definition of what is usually referred to as bank credit. The reason for this change and the relationship between E and bank credit defined as loans and securities held by banks will be discussed later.

where:

D^p = net demand deposits held by the public
C^P = currency held by the public
T = time deposits
L = loans held by commercial banks
S = security holdings by commercial banks
N = capital accounts of commercial banks
D^t = Treasury deposits at commercial banks.

Net Source Base

The basic concepts of the source base and the net source base are introduced in relations (3.4) through (3.7):

$$B = A + B^a \quad \text{source base,} \tag{3.4}$$

$$B^a = B - A \quad \text{net source base,} \tag{3.5}$$

$$B^a = F^s + U + C^T + Fl - (g + f + o + c) \quad \text{sources of } B^a, \tag{3.6}$$

$$B^a = (R^m - A) + V + C^P \quad \text{uses of } B^a, \tag{3.7}$$

where:

A = sum of discounts and advances to member banks by the Federal Reserve Banks
F^s = earning assets of the Federal Reserve net of discounts and advances
U = gold stock
C^T = total Treasury currency outstanding
Fl = float
g = Treasury deposits at Federal Reserve
f = foreign deposits at the Federal Reserve
c = Treasury cash
o = other deposits at Federal Reserve plus other Federal Reserve liabilities and capital minus other Federal Reserve assets[2]
R^m = member bank reserves
V = vault cash of nonmember banks.

Relation (3.6) defines the net source base in terms of its sources, which are (1) Federal Reserve holdings of government securities, (2) the nation's

---

[2] Prior to April 1969, this item appeared in the Federal Reserve *Bulletin* as other deposits at Federal Reserve and other accounts "net."

gold stock including, beginning January 1970, Special Drawing Rights Certificates, and (3) Treasury currency and float outstanding less Treasury deposits at the Federal Reserve Banks, Treasury cash balances, and other deposits and accounts at the Federal Reserve Banks (see Table 3.1).

The base may be viewed as an asset supplied by the Federal Reserve and the Treasury to the economic units that make up the economy. The uses of B^a reflect member banks' demands for nonborrowed reserves $(R^m - A)$, the nonmember banks' demand for vault cash (V), and the public's demand for currency (C^p). Given the amount of net source base supplied by the monetary authorities, the banks and the public determine its allocation between reserves held by banks and currency held by the public. The monetary authorities by their actions determine the size of the stock of the base and the rate at which it is supplied. The banks and the public determine the uses of the base.

Since the supply of the asset B^a is under control of the monetary authorities, banks and the public must adjust their holdings of both real and financial assets so that the amount of base they desire to hold is equal to the amount supplied by the actions of the monetary authorities. The process by which the quantity of B^a demanded is adjusted to the quantity supplied leads to a change in the prices of real assets and a change in interest rates.

As can be seen by examining Table 3.1, regardless of whether the net source base (or any other variant of the base concept) is calculated from the sources side or from the uses side, the total is the same. However, the choice between examining the base from the uses side or the sources side becomes very significant in discussions of the Federal Reserves' control over the money supply process.

From the sources side, the amount of net source base supplied to the economy can be controlled by the Federal Reserve System. Federal Reserve holdings of government securities, which account for over 70 per cent of the sources of B^a, are completely under the control of the Federal Reserve System. The size of the gold stock depends primarily upon past movements in the balance of payments. Treasury deposits at Federal Reserve banks are under the control of the Treasury, but are known by the Federal Reserve. Treasury currency and Treasury cash balances, although not under the direct control of the Federal Reserve, are known by them. The volume of float depends primarily upon seasonal and weather factors, and information on changes in the level of float is available to the Federal Reserve.

Federal Reserve control over the size of the stock of B^a and the rate at which it is supplied does not imply that the Federal Reserve can control each of the individual items on the sources side; it can directly and completely control only its holdings of government securities. By buying and selling government securities, the Federal Reserve can control the total amount of the base. This concept of control does not imply in any way that the Federal Reserve exercises control over the other individual components of the source base. Control over B^a does not mean that the Federal Reserve System has in the past, or does at present, consciously attempt to control the net source base. Also, control does not mean dollar-for-dollar control on a daily basis.

The Federal Reserve has reliable information on a weekly basis about changes in the factors supplying the base. If the Federal Reserve System desires to do so, it has the power to control, within narrow limits, the amount and growth rate of the net source base.

TABLE 3.1

SOURCES AND USES* OF THE SOURCE BASE, JANUARY 1970 (MILLIONS OF DOLLARS)

Sources		Uses	
Federal Reserve holdings of government securities	\$56,346†	Member bank deposits at the Federal Reserve	\$23,580
Gold stock plus special drawing rights	11,296‡	Currency held by banks‖	6,622
Treasury currency outstanding	6,856	Currency held by the nonbank public#	46,100
Federal Reserve float	3,442		
Other Federal Reserve assets	2,114§		
Less:		Less:	
Treasury cash holdings	655	Member bank borrowings from Federal Reserve Banks	965
Treasury deposits at the Federal Reserve Banks	1,206		
Foreign deposits at Federal Reserve Banks	170		
Other deposits at F. R. plus F. R. liabilities and capital	2,686		
Equals:		Equals:	
Adjusted Monetary Source Base (B^a)	\$75,337	Net Source Base (B^a)	\$75,337

* Source, F. R. *Bulletin*, April 1970, pp. A4, A5, A17. Data are not seasonally adjusted, monthly averages of daily figures.

† Includes \$73 million of acceptances not shown separately.

‡ On January 8, 1970, the Exchange Stabilization Fund issued \$1 billion in gold certificates and \$200 million in "Special Drawing Rights" certificates to the Federal Reserve in exchange for dollars. Therefore, these amounts became "monetized" as sources of the base.

§ For a complete listing of "other assets" see the "Detailed Statement of Condition of All Federal Banks Combined" in *Annual Report*, Board of Governors of the Federal Reserve System. For example, in the 1968 *Annual Report*, this statement appears on pp. 364–365.

‖ Vault cash.

Currency component of the money supply.

Data for Calculating the Sources and Uses of the Base

The data necessary for calculating the net source base (B^a) may be found in the table "Member Bank Reserves, Federal Reserve Bank Credit, and Related Items" in the monthly Federal Reserve *Bulletin*. From the uses side, the source base may be calculated from the two tables "Member Bank Reserves, Federal Reserve Bank Credit and Related Items" and "Money Supply and Related Data" appearing in the *Bulletin*. From the *uses side* the source base consists of the sum of two items: (1) member bank reserves with Federal Reserve Banks, and (2) total currency in circulation. Total currency in circulation includes currency held by the nonbank public and vault cash of banks. The net source base may then be obtained by subtracting discounts and advances by Federal Reserve Banks from the total source base.

Public Behavior

The third basic set of definitions expresses portfolio decisions by the public that affect the money supply and bank credit processes. First, the public has a choice as to how to hold its money balances. The public may choose either currency (government money) or demand deposits (bank money). Relation (3.8) describes the public's decision as to the allocation of monetary wealth between currency and demand deposits:

$$k = \frac{C^P}{D^P} = \text{currency ratio,} \tag{3.8}$$

where

$$C^P = \text{currency held by the public,}$$
$$D^P = \text{demand deposits held by the public.}$$

Second, the public makes a decision as to what portion of bank deposits it wishes to allocate to demand deposits and what portion to time deposits. Relation (3.9) describes this portfolio decision by the public:

$$t = \frac{T}{D^P} \qquad \text{time deposit ratio,} \tag{3.9}$$

where

$$T = \text{time deposits held by the public.}$$

Treasury Behavior

Although the Federal Reserve System has the major responsibility and policy instruments to control the monetary process, certain monetary actions by the Treasury can have important influences on the process by which credit market interest rates and the stocks of money and bank credit are determined.[3] Treasury actions which affect the monetary process are (1) Treasury

---

[3] During the 1933–1939 period, Treasury actions, relating to the rate at which the large gold inflows of this period were monetized, were the dominant effect on monetary influences. See Michael Keran and Christopher Babb, "An Explanation of Federal Reserve Actions," Federal Reserve Bank of St. Louis *Review*, July 1969, p. 15.

purchase and sale of gold and (2) the Treasury's role in collecting and spending cash balances resulting from tax and expenditure decisions of the federal government.

The Treasury's purchases and sales of gold are reflected in changes in the stock of base money. The effects of the Treasury's management of its cash balances on the money supply process are incorporated in the hypothesis in the following manner:

$$d = \frac{D^t}{D^p} = \text{Treasury deposit ratio,} \tag{3.10}$$

where

$$D^t = \text{Treasury deposits at commercial banks.}^4$$

The Treasury deposits the revenue from tax collections and from the sale of government securities either in the Treasury tax and loan accounts at commercial banks (D^t) or in its accounts at the Federal Reserve Banks. When the Treasury pays for government expenditures it draws checks on its deposits at Federal Reserve Banks.

As individuals and corporations pay taxes and purchase new securities issued by the government, private demand deposits (D^p) decrease. Assuming that the Treasury channels these proceeds into its tax and loan accounts, Treasury deposits at commercial banks rise and hence the d-ratio rises. When the Government prepares to spend, the Treasury makes a "call" on its tax and loan accounts and transfers funds from the banks to its accounts at the Federal Reserve Banks. The d-ratio falls and the amount of base (reserves) held by the banks decreases, and the amount of source base also decreases since the item "Treasury deposits at the Federal Reserve" in Table 3.1 increases. When the Government spends, the Treasury issues checks drawn on its account at the Federal Reserve Banks; and demand deposits of the public rise, the d-ratio falls, the amount of base held by banks increases, and the total source base rises.

The hypothesis takes into consideration the effect on the money supply process of a shift in demand deposit liabilities of the banks from the public (D^p) to the Treasury (D^t) in the d-ratio. In the d-ratio it is D^t that is determined by the Treasury. Private demand deposits (D^p) are primarily determined by the public, banks, and institutional factors such as the different reserve requirements among different classes of banks. D^p is little affected, except in short periods of time by changes in D^t. Changes in D^t dominate short-run movements in the d-ratio. The short-run dominance of changes in D^t on the d-ratio can be seen in Figure 3.1.

Over a period of time, these sharp short-run fluctuations in the d-ratio are averaged out. However, in short periods of time, changes in the Treasury's allocation of its deposits between commercial banks and the Federal Reserve may have an important short-run influence on the growth rates of the monetary aggregates.[5]

---

[4] Referred to as U.S. Government demand deposits in the Federal Reserve *Bulletin*.

[5] See Jerry L. Jordan, "Relations among Monetary Aggregates," Federal Reserve Bank of St. Louis *Review*, March 1969, pp. 8–9.

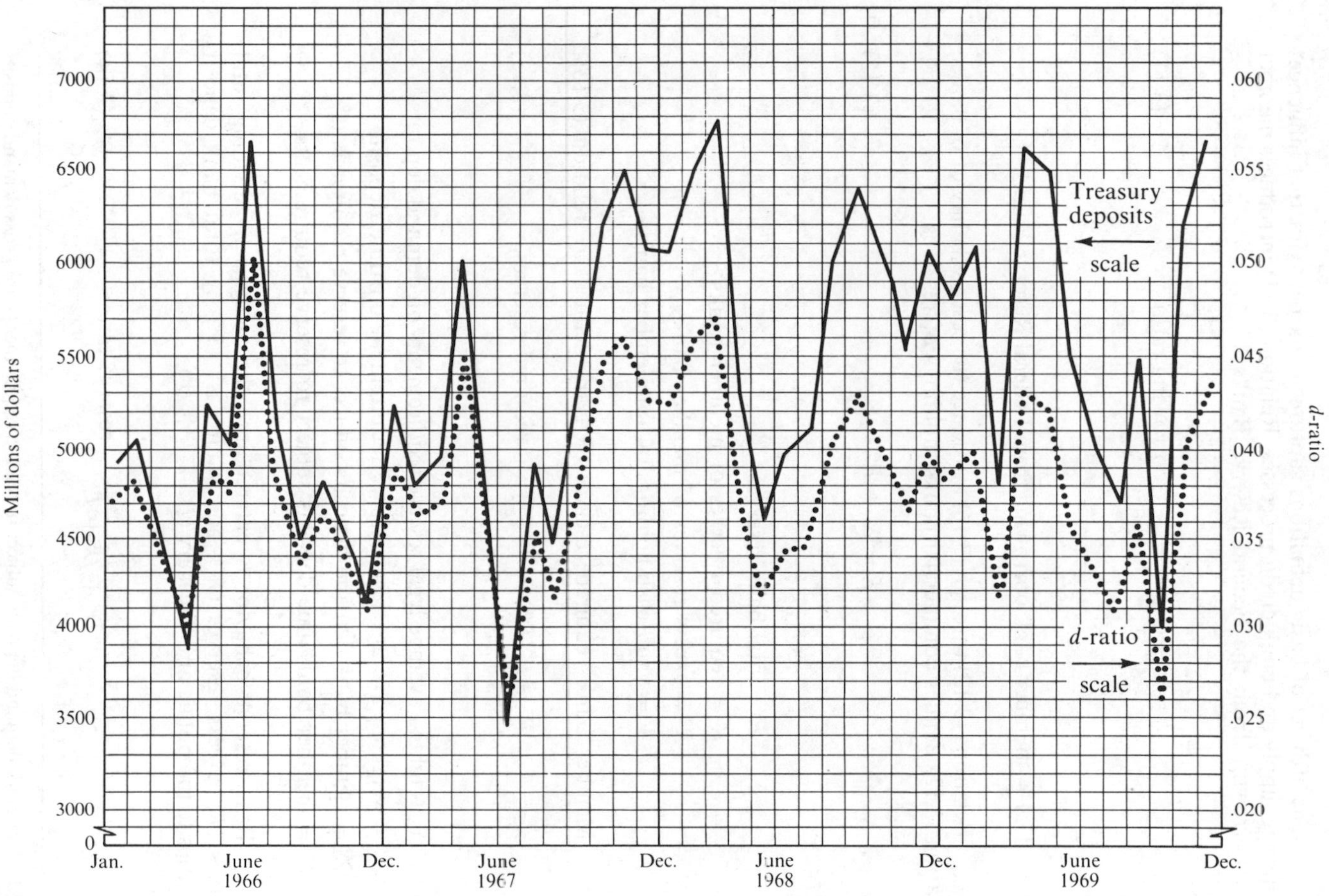

Figure 3.1 Treasury Deposits and the Treasury Deposit Ratio (Seasonally Adjusted)

Bank Behavior

The fifth set of basic definitions captures bank behavior that influences the money supply and bank credit processes. Relation (3.11) introduces member bank borrowing from the Federal Reserve Banks:

$$b = \frac{A}{D^p + D^t + T} \qquad \text{borrowing ratio} \tag{3.11}$$

where

A = member bank borrowing from Federal Reserve Banks.

Relations (3.12) through (3.16) introduce the reserve behavior of banks. Relation (3.12) defines commercial banks' holdings of reserves:

$$R = R^r + R^e + V. \tag{3.12}$$

where

R = total bank reserves
R^r = required reserves of member banks
R^e = excess reserves of member banks
V = vault cash holdings of nonmember banks.

Member bank required reserves (R^r) are defined by relation (3.13):

$$R^r = r^d\,(D^m) + r^t\,(T^m) \qquad \text{required reserves,} \tag{3.13}$$

where

r^d = weighted average legal reserve requirements on demand deposits
r^t = weighted average legal reserve requirement on time deposits
D^m = member bank demand deposits subject to reserve requirements[6]
T^m = member bank time deposits subject to reserve requirements.

Bank reserve behavior is entered into the analysis by dividing total reserves (R), excess reserves (R^e), and vault cash (V) by total bank deposit liabilities to the public and Treasury ($D^p + T + D^t$).

$$r = \frac{R}{D^p + D^t + T} \qquad \text{reserve ratio,} \tag{3.14}$$

[6] Member bank demand deposits subject to reserve requirements are gross demand deposits minus cash items in process of collection and demand balances due from domestic banks. See the table "Deposits, Cash, and Reserves of Member Banks," in any issue of the Federal Reserve *Bulletin*.

$$e = \frac{R^e}{D^p + D^t + T} \quad \text{excess reserve ratio,} \tag{3.15}$$

$$v = \frac{V}{D^p + D^t + T} \quad \text{nonmember bank vault cash ratio.} \tag{3.16}$$

The reserve ratio (r) is the ratio of the holdings of reserves by banks (R) to their total net deposit liabilities to the public and Treasury. Banks' holdings of reserves (R) include total reserves for member and nonmember banks. It *does not* solely include member bank reserves with the Federal Reserve Banks. The r-ratio may conveniently be calculated as follows:

$$r = \frac{B - C^p}{D^p + D^t + T} = \frac{B^a + A - C^p}{D^p + D^t + T}.$$

The nonmember bank vault cash ratio (v) is defined in relation (3.16). The v-ratio is the ratio of holdings of vault cash by nonmember banks (V) to the sum of demand deposits held by the public at all commercial banks (D^p), of Treasury deposits at commercial banks (D^t), and of time deposits (T). The nonmember banks' holdings of vault cash may be calculated in the following way by using data available in monthly issues of the Federal Reserve *Bulletin* in the tables entitled "Member Bank Reserves, Federal Reserve Credit, and Related Items," and "Money Supply and Related Data":

> Total currency in circulation less the currency component of the money supply (C^p) less currency and coin held by member banks equals vault cash holdings of nonmember banks.

The nonmember banks' holdings of vault cash amounted to \$1.3 billion in January 1970.

The condition that the reserve ratio also depends upon the distribution of deposits between member and nonmember banks is introduced by definitions (3.17) and (3.18):

$$\delta = \frac{\text{member bank demand deposits}}{\text{total bank demand deposits}} = \frac{D^m}{D^p + D^t}, \tag{3.17}$$

$$\tau = \frac{\text{member bank time deposits}}{\text{total bank time deposits}} = \frac{T^m}{T}, \tag{3.18}$$

where

D^m = member bank demand deposits subject to reserve requirements,

T^m = member bank time deposits subject to reserve requirements.

Using relations (3.12) through (3.16) the reserve ratio may be expressed in terms of the e-ratio, v-ratio, reserve requirements, and the distribution of deposits between member and nonmember banks. To proceed, we first use (3.12) and divide by bank deposits:

$$\frac{R}{D^p + D^t + T} = \frac{R^r}{D^p + D^t + T} + \frac{R^e}{D^p + D^t + T} + \frac{V}{D^p + D^t + T}.$$

Then, using definitions (3.14), (3.15), and (3.16) we may write

$$r = \frac{R^r}{D^p + D^t + T} + e + v\,.$$

Returning to (3.13) gives the following result:

$$\frac{R^r}{D^p + D^t + T} = r^d\left(\frac{D^m}{D^p + D^t + T}\right) + r^t\left(\frac{T^m}{D^p + D^t + T}\right).$$

We now make use of the following substitutions:

$$\left(\frac{D^m}{D^p + D^t + T}\right)\cdot\left(\frac{D^p + D^t}{D^p + D^t}\right) = \left(\frac{D^m}{D^p + D^t}\right)\cdot\left(\frac{D^p + D^t}{D^p + D^t + T}\right),$$

$$\left(\frac{T^m}{D^p + D^t + T}\right)\cdot\left(\frac{T}{T}\right) = \left(\frac{T^m}{T}\right)\cdot\left(\frac{T}{D^p + D^t + T}\right).$$

Using the previous definitions of the *t*-ratio and *d*-ratio, the further substitution follows:

$$\frac{D^p + D^t}{D^p + D^t + T} = \frac{1 + d}{1 + t + d}$$

We shall denote this expression by:

$$u = \frac{1 + d}{1 + t + d}.$$

The reader may check that:

$$\frac{T}{D^p + D^t + T} = 1 - u\,.$$

Now, using definitions (3.17) and (3.18) for δ and τ the following expressions result:

$$\left(\frac{D^m}{D^p + D^t}\right)\left(\frac{D^p + D^t}{D^p + D^t + T}\right) = \delta\, u\,,$$

$$\left(\frac{T^m}{T}\right)\left(\frac{T}{D^p + D^t + T}\right) = \tau\,(1 - u)\,.$$

Therefore we may write

$$\frac{R^r}{D^p + D^t + T} = r^d\delta u + r^t\tau(1 - u).$$

The full expression for the reserve ratio then becomes

$$r = r^d \delta u + r^t \tau(1-u) + e + v. \tag{3.19}$$

The introduction of the δ-ratio and τ-ratio into the hypothesis permits explicit recognition of the institutional condition that reserve requirements differ between member and nonmember banks. The δ and τ-ratios are determined by the decision of holders of bank deposits to allocate such deposits between member and nonmember banks. For example, other factors remaining constant, a shift of demand deposits from member to nonmember banks causes a decline in δ and hence a decline in the reserve ratio.

With this developed form of the reserve ratio, the hypothesis permits explicit analysis of the influence of factors such as shifts in the distribution of member bank deposits between demand and time deposits and changes in the relative size of member banks versus nonmember banks on the levels and rates of change of the monetary aggregates and bank credit.

Relationships between the Net Source Base, Money, Money plus Time Deposits, and Bank Credit

In this section, using the basic definitions set forth above, we will derive definite relationships between the net source base (B^a), and the monetary aggregate (M^1 and M^2) and bank credit. The source base, M^1, M^2, and bank credit are definite economic quantities. For example, to determine the magnitude of the money stock (M^1) at any point in time, one proceeds to count the amount of currency held by the nonbank public and the volume of outstanding net demand deposit liabilities of banks held by the nonbank public. The unit of measurement is the dollar. We shall now develop derived quantities, called multipliers, that express definite relationships between B^a and the monetary aggregates and bank credit.

Money Multiplier

The first step will be to develop the money multiplier. The relationship we are seeking has the following form:

$$M^1 = m^1 B^a.$$

The symbol (m^1) denotes the money multiplier and expresses the condition that M^1 is related to B^a by the derived quantity (m^1).

If m were a constant, then an explanation of the money supply and bank credit processes would only require a well formulated and tested explanation of the determination of B^a. However, a look at empirical data on M^1 and B^a reveals that the multiplier cannot be considered a constant. Different magnitudes of M^1 are associated with the same magnitude of B^a. To give a full explanation of the money supply and bank credit processes it is necessary to explicitly develop the form of the multipliers.

The following basic definitions are used:

$$B^a = R - A + C^P,$$
$$M^1 = D^P + C^P,$$

where

$$R = \text{total bank reserves} = R^r + R^e + V$$
$$C^P = \text{currency held by the public}$$
$$A = \text{member bank borrowings}$$
$$D^P = \text{demand deposits of the public.}$$

From definitions (3.14) and (3.11) we may write

$$R = r(D^P + T + D^t),$$
$$A = b(D^P + T + D^t).$$

Substituting these expressions in the definition of B^a results in the following:

$$B^a = (r - b)(D^P + T + D^t) + C^P.$$

Dividing this expression by D^P gives

$$\frac{B^a}{D^P} = (r - b)\left(\frac{D^P}{D^P} + \frac{T}{D^P} + \frac{D^t}{D^P}\right) + \frac{C^P}{D^P}.$$

Referring to the definitions of the k, t, and d-ratios given in definitions (3.8), (3.9), and (3.10), the above expression may be written as

$$\frac{B^a}{D^P} = (r - b)(1 + t + d) + k.$$

Rearranging the above expression gives the following:

$$D^P = \frac{1}{(r - b)(1 + t + d) + k} B^a.$$

Our interest is, however, in a relationship between the money stock and B^a, not just between money produced by the banks (D^P) and B^a. To expand this relation to a relation between M and B^a, we proceed as follows:

$$M^1 = D^P + C^P,$$

since

$$1 + k = \frac{D^P + C^P}{D^P},$$

$$\frac{1}{1 + k}(M^1) = D^P.$$

Therefore, substituting this expression for D^P in the derived relationship between D^P and B^a yields:

$$M^1 = \frac{1 + k}{(r - b)(1 + t + d) + k} B^a,$$

$$M^1 = m^1 B^a.$$

Hence, the full explicit form for the money multiplier, which will be denoted by m^1, is as follows:

$$m^1 = \frac{1 + k}{(r - b)(1 + t + d) + k} \quad \text{money multiplier.}$$

M^2 Multiplier

To derive the multiplier that expresses the relationship between M^2 (money more broadly defined to include time deposits), and the net source base, the following basic definition is used:

$$M^2 = D^P + C^P + T.$$

The explicit form of the derived relation between B^a and money (M^2) may be derived by using the result obtained previously:

$$D^P = \frac{1}{(r - b)(1 + t + d) + k} B^a.$$

since

$$1 + k + t = \frac{D^P + C^P + T}{D^P},$$

then

$$\left(\frac{1}{1 + k + t}\right) M^2 = D^P.$$

Therefore, proceeding as before and substituting this expression for D^P into the relation between D^P and B^a,

$$M^2 = \frac{1 + k + t}{(r - b)(1 + t + d) + k} B^a.$$

The derived expression between M^2 and B^a is called the "money defined to include time deposits multiplier" and is denoted by m^2.

$$m^2 = \frac{1 + k + t}{(r - b)(1 + t + d) + k} \qquad \text{money including time deposits multiplier.}$$

Bank Credit Multiplier

The relationship of bank credit (E), which is the earning assets of banks' net of capital accounts and Treasury deposits at commercial banks, to the net source base (B^a) is expressed by[7]

$$E = (m^2 - 1)\, B^a.$$

Thus $m^2 - 1$ is the bank credit multiplier. Since

$$m^2 = \frac{1 + k + t}{(r - b)(1 + t + d) + k},$$

the bank credit multiplier may be expressed as follows:

$$m^2 - 1 = \frac{1 + k + t}{(r - b)(1 + t + d) + k} - \frac{(r - b)(1 + t + d) + k}{(r - b)(1 + t + d) + k}$$

$$= \frac{(1 + k + t) - (r - b)(1 + t + d) - k}{(r - b)(1 + t + d) + k}.$$

Cancelling k results in the following:

$$m^2 - 1 = \frac{(1 + t) - (r - b)(1 + t + d)}{(r - b)(1 + t + d) + k} \qquad \text{bank credit multiplier.}$$

Total Bank Credit Multiplier

The net source base can also be related to total bank credit, which consists of total loans and investments (BC). This relationship may be expressed as

$$BC = aB^a,$$

[7] See Appendix II at the end of the chapter.

where the total bank credit multiplier a is defined[8] as

$$a = \frac{(1 + t + d)\,[1 + n - (r - b)]}{(r - b)\,(1 + t + d) + k},$$

$$n = \frac{\text{capital accounts}}{\text{total bank deposits}}.$$

Relationship of the Values of the Multipliers

Rewriting the expression for the m^2 multiplier as

$$m^2 = m^1 + \frac{t}{(r - b)\,(1 + t + d) + k},$$

we see that

$$m^2 > m^1.$$

The bank credit multiplier $m^2 - 1$ may be rewritten as

$$m^2 - 1 = m^1 + \left[\frac{t}{(r - b)\,(1 + t + d) + k} - 1\right].$$

If $t > (r - b)\,(1 + t + d) + k$, then the expression in the brackets is positive and:

$$m^2 - 1 > m^1.$$

The relationship $m^2 > m^1$ is derivable from the hypothesis. The relationship between m^1 and $m^2 - 1$ is not derivable from the hypothesis, but is dependent on the empirical relationship between the magnitude of the t-ratio and the magnitude of the denominator of the multipliers.

The total bank credit multiplier a is larger than $m^2 - 1$ by a factor:

$$\frac{d + n(1 + t + d)}{(r - b)\,(1 + t + d) + k}.$$

The notation n introduces another bank behavioral relation. The use of the total bank credit multiplier (a) requires an extension of the hypothesis to include banks' behavior with regard to capital accounts. Therefore, the variability of the bank credit multiplier may be increased, and hence divergent movements of M^1 and bank credit, discussed later, may be amplified.[9]

---

[8] See Appendix III at the end of the chapter.

[9] See Appendix III at the end of the chapter.

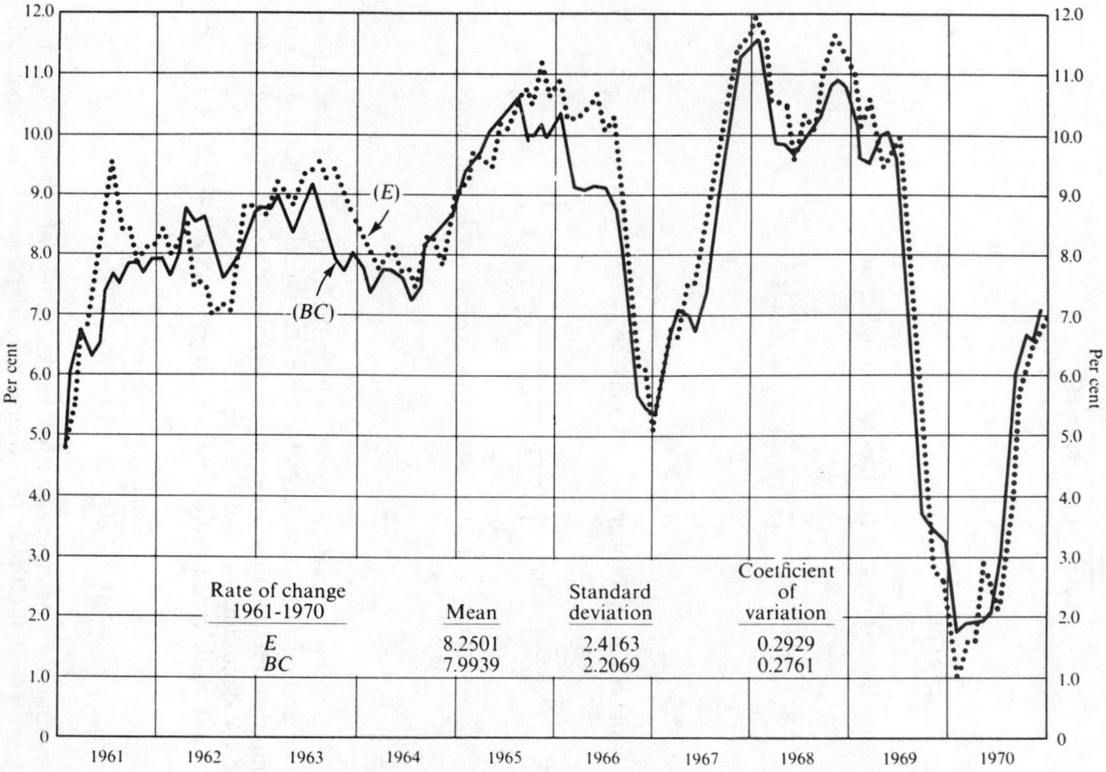

Rate of change 1961-1970	Mean	Standard deviation	Coefficient of variation
E	8.2501	2.4163	0.2929
BC	7.9939	2.2069	0.2761

***Figure 3.2** Adjusted Bank Credit (E) and Bank Credit (BC) Annual Rates of Change**

* Rates of change are based on first differences of corresponding months. For example, the rate of change of $E_t = \dfrac{E_t - E_{t-12}}{E_{t-12}}$. Beginning July 1969, data includes valuation reserves on loans and securities, however rates for one year were computed using adjusted amounts.

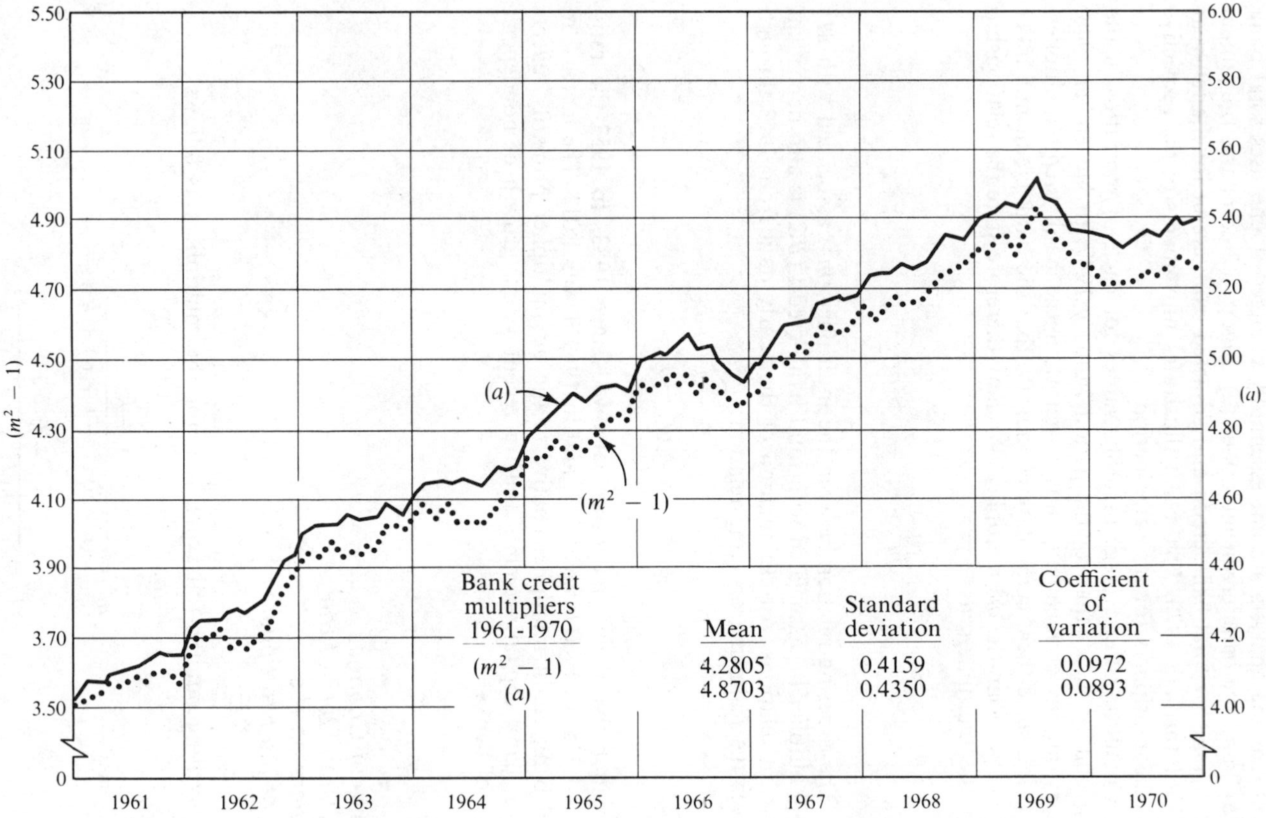

Figure 3.3 Adjusted Bank Credit Multiplier ($m^2 - 1$), and Total Bank Credit Multiplier (a)

To avoid further complications of our exposition of the hypothesis, we shall, in the remainder of the paper, work with bank credit adjusted (E). The results of the analysis are not essentially changed if one uses total bank credit (BC) and the bank credit multiplier (a). Figure 3.2 compares the annual rates of change for total bank credit and adjusted bank credit for the ten-year period 1961 through 1970. Figure 3.3 illustrates movements of the respective bank credit multipliers for the same period.

Computing the average monthly values for each of the ratios in the above inequality shows that for the period January 1947, to November 1948, the money multiplier inequality was larger than the bank credit multiplier. In the period since then, computations indicate that the bank credit multiplier has been larger than the m^1 multiplier. We may therefore state the relationship between the multipliers as

$$m^2 > m^2 - 1 > m^1.$$

The ordering relation between the multiplier (m^2) associated with M^2 and the multiplier (a) associated with total bank credit (BC) is also dependent on empirical relations. An examination of the yearly data from 1953 through 1969 gives the following ordering relation:

$$m^2 > a > m^2 - 1.$$

The spread between m^2 and a has narrowed since 1953. In 1953 the ratio m^2/a was 1.215, in 1960 it was 1.117, and in 1969 it was 1.011. The increase in the total bank credit multiplier relative to the m^2 multiplier primarily reflects growth in bank capital accounts and, in recent years, growth of nondeposit liabilities of banks.

Influence of Changes in the Parameters of the Multipliers on the Values of the Multipliers

Writing out the full expressions for the multipliers as follows

$$m^1 = \frac{1 + k}{(r - b)(1 + t + d) + k},$$

$$m^2 = \frac{1 + k + t}{(r - b)(1 + t + d) + k},$$

the effect on the multipliers of changes in each of the parameters may be analyzed.

An increase in the reserve ratio lowers the values of the multipliers.

Expressing in terms of elasticities[10] the response of the multipliers to changes in parameters of the multipliers, the following holds:

$$\varepsilon\,(m, r) < 0.$$

Since an increase in the excess reserve ratio raises the *r*-ratio, we may also write

$$\varepsilon\,(m, e) < 0.$$

An increase in the borrowing ratio raises the values of the multipliers; hence

$$\varepsilon\,(m, b) > 0.$$

The *d*-ratio appears in the denominator of all three multipliers, hence a rise in the *d*-ratio lowers the values of the multipliers. In elasticity terms this is expressed as follows:

$$\varepsilon\,(m, d) < 0.$$

The change in the money multiplier resulting from a change in the currency ratio may be expressed as follows:[11]

$$\frac{\partial m^1}{\partial k} = \frac{[(r-b)(1+t+d)+k-(l+k)]}{[(r-b)(1+t+d)+k]^2}.$$

Reducing the numerator of this expression by canceling *k* gives the following expression for the numerator:

$$(r-b)(1+t+d)-1.$$

Since, by using empirical data, it can be shown that

$$(r-b)(1+t+d) < 1,$$

---

[10] When the magnitude of one economic quantity is dependent upon the magnitude of another quantity, economists frequently express the relationship between the dependent quantity and independent quantity in terms of elasticities. The concept of elasticity takes into account the fact that magnitudes of the two quantities may not be measured in the same units. Elasticity, instead of referring to absolute changes, refers to percentage changes. For example, the elasticity of the *e*-ratio with respect to the interest rate (i) denoted by $\varepsilon(e, i)$ expresses the percentage change in the *e*-ratio (the dependent variable) given a one per cent change in the interest rate (the independent variable). The formula for the partial elasticity of the *e*-ratio with respect to i may be written as

$$\frac{\partial e}{\partial i}\frac{i}{e} = \varepsilon\,(e, i).$$

The notation $\partial e/\partial i$ is a partial derivative. It denotes the change in the *e*-ratio given a change in the interest rate when all other factors which influence the *e*-ratio are held constant. For a discussion of the concept of elasticity see R. H. Leftwich, *The Price System and Resource Allocation*, rev. ed. (New York: Holt, Rinehart and Winston, 1960), pp. 34–47.

[11] The partial derivative of m^1 with respect to the *k*-ratio.

the following result holds:

$$\frac{\partial m^1}{\partial k} < 0.$$

Since from our previous discussion

$$m^2 = m^1 + \frac{t}{(r - b)(1 + t + d) + k},$$

it follows that

$$\frac{\partial m^2}{\partial k} < 0.$$

An increase in the k-ratio reduces the multipliers, and a reduction in the k-ratio increases the multipliers. In elasticity terms this result is expressed in the following manner:

$$\varepsilon\,(m, k) < 0.$$

For the t-ratio, looking at the expression for m^1, we see that

$$\varepsilon\,(m^1, t) < 0.$$

A change in the t-ratio involves a change in the proportion of demand deposits to time deposits. Since the reserve requirements against these two classes of bank deposits are not the same, a change in the t-ratio involves a change in the ratio of reserves to deposits (r-ratio). This change is reflected in the notation u as

$$u = \frac{1 + d}{1 + t + d},$$

which appears in the r-ratio. The change in the reserve ratio for a given change in the u-ratio is:

$$\frac{\partial r}{\partial u} = r^d\delta - r^t\tau$$

Since $r^d\delta$ is greater than $r^t\tau$, then[12]

$$\frac{\partial r}{\partial u} > 0$$

[12] For 1969 the average values of these parameters were, $r^d = 15.39$, $r^t = 4.23$, $\delta = 0.75$ and $\tau = 0.79$.

An increase (decrease) in u raises (lowers) the reserve ratio and hence the multipliers are decreased (increased).

The effect of the change in t-ratio on the r-ratio is to decrease, but not to completely offset, the numerical value of the change in the denominators of the multipliers resulting from a change in the t-ratio. When estimating the elasticities of m^1 and m^2 with respect to t, this dependence of the r-ratio on the t-ratio must be considered. For example, in the m^1 multiplier, the dependence of the reserve ratio on the time deposit ratio reduces the absolute value of the elasticity of m^1 with respect to t. Having noted this point, we ignore the effect of changes in the t-ratio on the r-ratio for purposes of simplifying our exposition.

The t-ratio appears in both the numerator and the denominator of the M^2 and bank credit multipliers. For m^2, if we disregard the effect of a change in the t-ratio on the r-ratio, the change in m^2 resulting from a change in the t-ratio is as follows:

$$\frac{\partial m^2}{\partial t} = \frac{(r-b)(1+t+d)+k-(r-b)(1+k+t)}{[(r-b)(1+t+d)+k]^2},$$

Simplifying the numerator we have

$$(r-b)\cdot d + k - (r-b)\cdot k.$$

Since

$$(r-b)\cdot d > 0,$$
$$k > (r-b)\cdot k,$$

and we conclude that

$$\frac{\partial m^2}{\partial t} > 0.$$

For the m^2 and $m^2 - 1$ multipliers, although an increase (decrease) in the t-ratio increases (decreases) the numerical value of the denominator, the corresponding change in the t-ratio in the numerator of these expressions offsets the effects of the changes in the denominator of the multipliers. Consequently, a rise (fall) in the t-ratio results in a rise (fall) in the M^2 and bank credit multipliers; and we conclude that

$$\varepsilon\,(m^2, t) > 0,$$
$$\varepsilon\,(m^2 - 1, t) > 0.$$

The response of the M^2 and bank credit multipliers to changes in the value of the t-ratio are opposite in sign to the response of the money multiplier (m^1) to changes in the t-ratio. Also, as the reader may confirm,

$$\frac{\partial m^2}{\partial t} = \frac{\partial(m^2-1)}{\partial t}, \quad \text{and} \quad \frac{t}{m^2-1} > \frac{t}{m^2}$$

therefore,

$$\varepsilon\,(m^2 - 1, t) > \varepsilon\,(m^2, t).$$

Appendix I: Reconciliation of Different Forms of the Base Concept

Table I.1 gives the relation between the three major base concepts. As discussed in Chapter 3, the difference between the net source base (B^a) and total source base (B) is Federal Reserve discounts and advances.

TABLE I.1

SOURCES AND USES OF THE NET SOURCE BASE, THE SOURCE BASE, AND THE MONETARY BASE, JANUARY 1970 (MILLIONS OF DOLLARS)*

Sources		Uses	
Federal Reserve holdings of Government securities	$56,346	Member bank deposits at Federal Reserve Banks less discounts and advances	$22,615
Federal Reserve float	3,442	Currency held by banks	6,622
Gold stock plus special drawing rights	11,296	Currency held by the public	46,100
Treasury currency outstanding			6,856
Other Federal Reserve assets	2,114		
Less:			
Treasury cash holdings	655		
Treasury deposits at Federal Reserve Banks	1,206		
Foreign deposits at Federal Reserve Banks	170		
Other deposits at F.R. plus F.R. liabilities and capital	2,686		
Equals:		Equals:	
Net source base	$75,337	Net source base	$75,337
Plus:		Plus:	
Federal Reserve discounts and advances	965	Federal Reserve discounts and advances	965
Equals:		Equals:	
Source base	$76,302	Source base	$76,302
Plus:		Plus:	
Reserve adjustment	3,172	Reserve adjustment	3,172
Equals:		Equals:	
Monetary base	$79,474	Monetary base	$79,474

* Data not seasonally adjusted.

The greatest difference among the three base concepts is the difference between the source base concepts (B^a and B) and the monetary base. As can be seen in Table I.1, the monetary base is arrived at by adding an item called "reserve adjustment" to the total source base.

The "reserve adjustment" adjusts the source base primarily for the effects of changes in reserve requirements on member bank deposits and also makes minor adjustments for shifts in the distribution of deposits subject to different reserve requirements as they affect the weighted average legal reserve ratios. Reserve adjustments are expressed in dollar amounts which are positive when the average reserve requirements fall and negative when they rise.

The monetary base is the same quantity which Brunner and Meltzer call the "extended base." The monetary base concept is explained by Leonall Andersen and Jerry Jordan in an article in the Federal Reserve Bank of St. Louis *Review*.[13] In addition, monetary base data are published regularly by the Federal Reserve Bank of St. Louis.

The most important difference between the source base concepts and the monetary base is in the effects of changes in reserve requirements on the base data. A change in reserve requirements on member bank demand or time deposits, or a shift of deposits between classes of bank or deposits *does not change* the amount of source base held by the banks. Base money is neither created nor destroyed by these actions. In the money supply hypothesis formulation used in this book, such changes would appear as changes in the r-ratio.

However, reserve adjustment changes do affect the magnitude of the monetary base. For example, in January 1968, reserve requirements on member bank demand deposits of $5 million and over were raised by 1/2 of one per cent. This lowered the reserve adjustment figure for the monetary base by $500 million in February 1968,[14] but had no effect on the total amount of source base. The effects on the source base and monetary base can be seen in Table I.2.

TABLE I.2

COMPARISON OF CHANGES IN THE SOURCE BASE AND MONETARY BASE RESULTING FROM RESERVE REQUIREMENT CHANGES (BILLIONS OF DOLLARS)

	Dec. 1967	Feb. 1968	Changes Due to Reserve Requirement Changes (Dec.–Feb.)	Changes Due to Other Factors (Dec.–Feb.)	Total Changes (Dec.–Feb.)
Source base*	$67.8	$67.1	$ 0	$−.7	$−.7
Reserve adjustments	5.0	4.5			
Monetary base	72.8	71.6	−.5	−.7	−1.2

* All data are not adjusted for seasonal variation.

[13] Leonall C. Andersen and Jerry L. Jordan, "The Monetary Base—Explanation and Analytical Use," Federal Reserve Bank of St. Louis *Review*, August 1968, pp. 7–11.

[14] The full effect of the reserve adjustment did not occur until February because the changes in reserve requirements came in mid-January.

Appendix II: Derivation of the Relationship $(m^2 - 1) B^a = E$ from the Consolidated Balance Sheet of the Banks and Monetary Authorities

TABLE II.1

CONSOLIDATED BALANCE SHEET OF COMMERCIAL BANKS, TREASURY, AND FEDERAL RESERVE

Assets	Liabilities
(1) Monetary gold stock	(6) Money stock
(2) United States securities	Nonmonetary liabilities
(2a) Held by Federal Reserve	(7) Time deposits
(2b) Held by commercial banks	(8) Treasury deposits
	(8a) at Federal Reserve Banks
(3) Commercial bank loans	(8b) at commercial banks
(4) Commercial bank holdings of other securities	(9) Treasury cash holdings
	(10) Foreign deposits
(5) Treasury currency	(11) Capital accounts—float*

* Federal Reserve float is entered as a negative item in "Capital and miscellaneous accounts net" in the consolidated balance sheet, see Federal Reserve *Bulletin*, October 1960, p. 1114.

Let

$$N = \text{capital accounts}$$

$$BC = \text{total bank credit}$$

$$C^p + D^p = \text{money supply}$$

$$(1) + (2a) + (5) - [8(a) + (9) + (10) + (11)] = B^a - N$$

$$2(b) + (3) + (4) = BC$$

$$\therefore \quad B^a - N + BC = D^p + C^p + T + D^t$$

since

$$m^2 B^a = D^p + C^p + T$$

$$B^a - N + BC = m^2 B^a + D^t$$

$$\therefore \quad BC - N - D^t = (m^2 - 1)B^a$$

$$\therefore \quad E = (m^2 - 1)B^a$$

Appendix III: Derivation of the Total Asset Multiplier

In Appendix II we derived from the consolidated balance sheet of the banks and monetary authorities the relationship

$$B^a + BC = D^p + C^p + T^d + D^t + N,$$
$$BC = (m^2 - 1)B^a + D^t + N.$$

From the Treasury deposit ratio

$$d = \frac{D^t}{D^p},$$

one can derive

$$D^t = dD^p.$$

To simplify our notation, let

$$Z = (r - b)\,(1 + t + d) + k$$

(i.e., the denominators of the multipliers). By definition of the multiplier,

$$\frac{(1 + k)B^a}{Z} = M^1 = D^p + C^p;$$

hence

$$\frac{1}{Z} = \frac{D^p + C^p}{(1 + k)B^a}.$$

Multiply both sides by dB^a:

$$\frac{d}{Z}B^a = \frac{d(D^p + C^p)}{1 + k}.$$

Using the definition

$$k = \frac{C^p}{D^p},$$

$$1 + k = \frac{D^p + C^p}{D^p}.$$

Hence

$$\frac{d}{Z}B^a = \frac{d(D^p + C^p)}{1} \cdot \frac{D^p}{D^p + C^p};$$

$$\therefore \qquad \frac{d}{Z}B^a = dD^p.$$

Substituting this result in our original equation, we have

$$BC = (m^2 - 1)B^a + \frac{d}{Z} B^a + N.$$

By definition

$$n = \frac{N}{D^p + D^t + T}.$$

Rewriting the above expression gives

$$N = n(D^p + D^t + T).$$

Dividing by D^p,

$$\frac{N}{D^p} = n(1 + t + d).$$

Using the above relation

$$\frac{1}{Z} B^a = D^p.$$

Substituting in the above relation yields

$$N = \frac{n(1 + t + d)B^a}{Z}.$$

Substituting in our original equation, we now have

$$BC = \left[m^2 - 1 + \frac{d}{Z} + \frac{n(1 + t + d)}{Z}\right] B^a.$$

Since

$$m^2 - 1 = \frac{(1 + t) - (r - b)(1 + t + d)}{Z},$$

we have

$$BC = \left[\frac{1 + t + d - (r - b)(1 + t + d) + n(1 + t + d)}{Z}\right] B^a.$$

Rearranging terms,

$$BC = \frac{(1 + t + d)[1 + n - (r - b)]}{(r - b)(1 + t + d) + k} B^a.$$

Hence the total asset multiplier is

$$a = \frac{(1 + t + d)[1 + n - (r - b)]}{(r - b)(1 + t + d) + k}.$$

The relation between the total bank credit multiplier (a) and the bank credit multiplier ($m^2 - 1$) may be expressed as follows:

$$a = (m^2 - 1) + \frac{d + n(1 + t + d)}{(r - b)(1 + t + d) + k}.$$

Using this expression, the reader can verify

$$\left|\frac{\partial a}{\partial r}\right| > \left|\frac{\partial (m^2 - 1)}{\partial r}\right|,$$

$$\frac{\partial a}{\partial b} > \frac{\partial (m^2 - 1)}{\partial b},$$

$$\left|\frac{\partial a}{\partial k}\right| > \left|\frac{\partial (m^2 - 1)}{\partial k}\right|,$$

$$\frac{\partial a}{\partial t} > \frac{\partial (m^2 - 1)}{\partial t}.$$

Also, it can be shown that

$$\varepsilon(a, i) > \varepsilon(m^2 - 1, i).$$

Chapter Four

Dependence of the Parameters of the Multipliers

In Chapter 3 definite relationships between the net source base and the monetary aggregates and bank credit were derived from the consolidated balance sheets of the commercial banks and the monetary authorities. These connecting links were called multipliers. The parameters of the multipliers were expressed as ratios. Each of these ratios was defined and the method of measuring the components of each of the ratios was discussed.

By definition, at any point in time, the magnitudes assumed by the stocks of money, M^2, and bank credit are equal to the magnitude of B^a at that point of time multiplied by the value of the appropriate multiplier. However, for policy purposes the major concern is with the equilibrium values of the monetary aggregates and bank credit, and with questions about how changes in policy instruments, institutional factors, and market interest rates will alter M^1, M^2, and E.

In this chapter the parameters of the multipliers are developed as being dependent upon the values assumed by other economic and institutional variables. Each ratio is considered individually. The factors upon which the ratio is hypothesized to depend are clearly stated and constraints are placed on the signs of the elasticities of each parameter with respect to these factors.

Reserve Ratio

The first parameter appearing in the denominator of each of the multipliers is the reserve ratio. In the previous chapter the reserve ratio was defined in (3.19) as follows:

$$r\text{-ratio} = r^d \delta u + r^t \tau (1 - u) + e + v.$$

To begin a detailed analysis of the reserve ratio, let us start by analyzing the first set of terms in the reserve ratio:

$$r^d \delta u + r^t \tau (1 - u).$$

The introduction of the term

$$u = \frac{1+d}{1+t+d}$$

permits an analysis of the effect of shifts between demand and time deposits. For example, suppose that the public decides to hold more time deposits relative to their holdings of demand deposits; then the t-ratio rises, and u decreases. Since r^d is set higher than r^t, this shift of deposits from demand to time deposits lowers required reserves of member banks and hence lowers the reserve ratio.

Weighted Average Reserve Requirements

The reserve requirement ratios r^d and r^t are weighted average reserve requirements, and hence they differ from actual (effective) reserve requirements. The weighting procedure is introduced to take into account the fact that reserve requirements differ by classes of member banks and size of deposit.

This method of expressing r^d and r^t permits the hypothesis to take into account and yield implications about institutional changes in the rules regarding member banks' required reserves. For example, changes such as the splintering of reserve requirements, the change from bi-weekly to weekly reserve settlement periods for the class of country member banks, and lagged reserve requirements can be analyzed within the contest of the fully developed hypothesis.

As an illustration, in January 1968, the Federal Reserve, along with raising reserve requirements on member bank demand deposits, changed the basis on which member banks were required to calculate their required reserves on demand deposits. Prior to January 11, 1968, reserve requirements by member banks were calculated on the basis of total net demand deposits. After January 11 and 18, member bank reserve requirements on demand deposits were differentiated, not only by reserve city versus country banks, but also by amount of deposits. Effective reserve requirements on the first \$5 million of net demand deposits were now different from effective reserve requirements on net demand deposits over \$5 million. Table 4.1 shows the effects of the change in effective reserve requirements and the effect of the splintering of requirements by size of deposits.

The increase in reserve requirements raised banks' required reserves. Since almost all reserve city banks' demand deposits were in the over \$5 million category, the change in requirements by size of deposits had little effect on offsetting the rise in reserve requirements on these banks. However, about two-fifths of country bank demand deposits were under \$5 million. Hence the change in requirements by size of deposits offset part of the effect of higher reserve requirements on country banks. The splintering of reserve requirements meant that required reserves of country banks on January 24, 1968, were about \$97.5 million less than if there had been no change in effective reserves by size of deposit accompanying the incease in reserve requirements.

Table 4.2 shows the computation of weighted average reserve requirements on time deposits (r^t) on September 7, 1966, and the computation of r^t

TABLE 4.1

COMPUTATION OF THE WEIGHTED AVERAGE RESERVE REQUIREMENT ON NET DEMAND DEPOSITS (DOLLAR AMOUNTS IN MILLIONS)

	January 10, 1968		January 24, 1968	
	Reserve City Banks	Country Banks	Reserve City Banks	Country Banks
Effective reserve requirement				
Over $5 million	16.5%	12.0%	17.0%	12.5%
Under $5 million			16.5%	12.0%
Total net demand deposits	$76,747	$53,772		
Over $5 million			$74,309	$33,325
Under $5 million			921	19,494
Total net demand deposits multiplied by the effective reserve requirement =	76,747 (.165)	53,772 (.12)	74,309 (.17) 921 (.165)	33,325 (.125) 19,494 (.12)
Total required reserves	$19,116		$19,289	
Total required reserves as a percentage of total net demand deposits =	$\frac{19,116}{130,519} = .1465$		$\frac{19,289}{128,049} = .1506$	
Weighted average reserve requirement	.1465		.1506	

TABLE 4.2

COMPUTATION OF THE WEIGHTED AVERAGE RESERVE REQUIREMENT ON TIME DEPOSITS (DOLLAR AMOUNTS IN MILLIONS)

	September 7, 1966		September 21, 1966	
	Reserve City Banks	Country Banks	Reserve City Banks	Country Banks
Effective reserve requirement				
Over $5 million	5%	5%	6%	6%
Under $5 million	4%	4%	4%	4%
Total time deposits				
Over $5 million	$37,217	7,594	36,578	7,624
Under $5 million	36,327	48,045	36,315	48,106
Total time deposits multiplied	37,217 (.05)	$7,594 (.05)	36,578 (.06)	7,624 (.06)
by the effective reserve requirement =	36,327 (.04)	48,045 (.04)	36,315 (.04)	48,106 (.04)
Total required reserves	$5,615		$6,029	
Total required reserves as a percentage of total time deposits =	$\frac{5,615}{129,183} = .0435$		$\frac{6,029}{128,623} = .0469$	
Weighted average reserve requirement	.0435		.0469	

TABLE 4.3

ANNUAL WEIGHTED AVERAGE RESERVE REQUIREMENTS ON DEMAND AND TIME DEPOSITS: 1929–1970

Year	Weighted Average Reserve Requirements on Demand Deposits	Weighted Average Reserve Requirements on Time Deposits
1929	.1015	.0300
1930	.1025	.0300
1931	.1038	.0300
1932	.1049	.0300
1933	.1071	.0300
1934	.1065	.0300
1935	.1076	.0300
1936	.1296	.0356
1937	.2019	.0575
1938	.1975	.0529
1939	.1917	.0500
1940	.1938	.0500
1941	.1970	.0517
1942	.2077	.0600
1943	.1861	.0600
1944	.1845	.0600
1945	.1835	.0600
1946	.1820	.0600
1947	.1815	.0600
1948	.1951	.0642
1949	.1935	.0629
1950	.1724	.0500
1951	.1910	.0597
1952	.1916	.0600
1953	.1845	.0600
1954	.1722	.0547
1955	.1646	.0500
1956	.1640	.0500
1957	.1637	.0500
1958	.1528	.0500
1959	.1487	.0500
1960	.1481	.0500
1961	.1484	.0500
1962	.1480	.0482
1963	.1475	.0400
1964	.1472	.0400
1965	.1468	.0400
1966	.1464	.0426
1967	.1465	.0426
1968	.1503	.0423
1969	.1538	.0423
1970	.1555	.0416

following the increase in reserve requirements effective September 8 and 15, 1966.

Table 4.3 presents the annual averages of monthly data for weighted average reserve requirements from 1929 through 1970. Examining this table, the reader can see several major changes in r^d and r^t. For example, weighted average reserve requirements on demand deposits and time deposits doubled between 1935 and 1937. In the postwar period from about 1952 to 1966, both average reserve requirements decreased; r^d by about one-fourth and r^t by about one-third. Then, beginning in July 1966, average reserve requirements on time deposits began to increase, and in January 1968 average reserve requirements on demand deposits began to increase.

Fully Developed Expression for the Reserve Ratio—A First Approximation

In this section a more complete expression for the reserve ratio is developed. To illustrate the process, the expression for the reserve ratio on January 10, 1968, is used. This will permit us to illustrate more closely the way in which shifts in deposits between classes of banks affect the *r*-ratio. For our example the reserve requirement on demand deposits is used. It is assumed the reader can then carry through the analysis for time deposits.

Referring to Table 4.1, on January 10 there were two different reserve classifications for member banks. To take these factors into consideration some notation is introduced.

$D_1{}^m$ = demand deposit liabilities subject to reserve requirements of member banks in the reserve city classification,

$r_1{}^d$ = reserve requirement on demand deposit liabilities applicable to reserve city banks,

$D_2{}^m$ = demand deposit liabilities subject to reserve requirements of member banks in the country bank reserve classification,

$r_2{}^d$ = reserve requirement on demand deposit liabilities applicable to country banks,

$D^p + D^t$ = total net demand deposit liabilities of commercial banks.

In the example from Table 4.1 the following values apply:

$$r_1{}^d = .165 \qquad D_1{}^m = \$76{,}747$$
$$r_2{}^d = .120 \qquad D_2{}^m = \$53{,}772.$$

Using our previous definition of r^d the following results apply:

$$r^d = r_1{}^d\left(\frac{D_1{}^m}{D^m}\right) + r_2{}^d\left(\frac{D_2{}^m}{D^m}\right),$$

where

$$D^m = D_1{}^m + D_2{}^m.$$

Checking with our example,

$$r^d = \frac{.165\,(76{,}747) + .12\,(53{,}772)}{130{,}519} = .1465.$$

Using the previous definition of δ, the following results:

$$\delta = \frac{D_1{}^m}{D^p + D^t} + \frac{D_2 m}{D^p + D^t}.$$

The expression for $r^d\delta$ may be written by using the above results in the following manner:

$$r^d\delta = \left[r_1{}^d\left(\frac{D_1{}^m}{D^m}\right) + r_2{}^d\left(\frac{D_2{}^m}{D^m}\right)\right]\left[\frac{D_1{}^m}{D^p + D^t} + \frac{D_2^m}{D^p + D^t}\right].$$

With this more fully developed expression, the result of shifts of deposits may be analyzed. For example, a shift of demand deposits from country banks to reserve city banks increases $D_1{}^m$, reduces $D_2{}^m$, and leaves total member bank deposits subject to reserve requirements (D^m) unchanged. Since $r_1{}^d$ is set higher than $r_2 d$, this shift of deposits between member banks raises $r^d\delta$ and hence raises the reserve ratio.

As a second example, suppose there is a shift of deposits from non-member banks to reserve city banks. Using the above expression we see that this raises the reserve ratio more than if the deposits flow into member banks in the country bank reserve classification.

Lagged Reserve Requirements

In September 1968, lagged reserve requirements were introduced. Under the lagged reserve requirement procedure member banks' required reserves are computed on the basis of deposit levels two weeks earlier. For example, member banks' required reserve for the statement week ending Wednesday, July 22, 1970 are computed on deposits subject to reserve requirements these banks held during the statement week of July 2 through July 8, 1970.

Since September 1968, under the lagged reserve requirement procedure, all member banks are on a one-week settlement period. However, the one-week settlement period is somewhat misleading. Through mid-August 1970, the following rules applied in determining whether a member bank has maintained a reserve balance in excess of or less than its required reserve balance for any computation period.

1. The required reserve balance of a bank shall be based upon the average daily net deposit balance held by the member bank at the close of business each day during the second computation period prior to the computation period for which the computation is made.

2. The reserve balance of a bank shall consist of the average daily balance with the Federal Reserve Banks held by the member bank at the close of business each day during the computation period for which the computation is made and the average daily currency and coin held by the member bank at the close of business each day during the second computation period prior to the computation perod for which the computation is made.

3. Any excess or deficiency in a member bank's required reserve balance will be carried forward to the next following computation period to the extent of 2 per cent of such required reserves, except that any portion of such excess or deficiency not offset in the next period may not be carried forward to additional computation periods.

4. Penalties on deficiencies in reserve balances remaining after the applications of the above will be assessed monthly on the basis of average daily deficiencies during each of the computation periods ending in the preceding calendar month.

5. Any such penalty will be assessed at a rate of 2 per cent per annum above the lowest rate applicable to borrowings by member banks from the Federal Reserve Bank.

To investigate the influence of lagged reserve requirements we shall first explain the modification it introduces into the previous derivation of the reserve ratio. Second, a few of its implications for the money supply process are discussed.

Derivation of the Reserve Ratio Using Lagged Deposits

On pages 24–27 we derived an explicit form for the reserve ratio, assuming required reserves were based on deposits in the current week. The derivation began in the following manner:

$$r = r^d\left(\frac{D^m}{D^p + D^t + T}\right) + r^t\left(\frac{T^m}{D^p + D^t + T}\right) + e + v\,.$$

The introduction of lagged reserve requirements requires the following modification:

$$r = r^d\left(\frac{D^m_{-2}}{D^p + D^t + T}\right) + r^t\left(\frac{T^m_{t-2}}{D^p + D^t + T}\right) + e + v\,.$$

The subscripts on member bank demand (D^m) and time deposits (T^m) signify that legal reserves (R_L) are dependent upon deposits held two weeks earlier (t − 2).

These expressions are manipulated as follows:

$$\left(\frac{D^m_{t-2}}{D^p + D^t + T}\right)\left(\frac{D^p + D^t}{D^p + D^t}\right) = \left(\frac{D^m_{t-2}}{D^p + D^t}\right)\left(\frac{D^p + D^t}{D^p + D^t + T}\right),$$

then a further multiplication:

$$\left(\frac{D^m_{t-2}D^m_t}{D^m_{t-2}D^m_t}\right)\left(\frac{D_{t-2}}{D^p + D^t}\right)\left(\frac{D^p + D^t}{D^p + D^t + T}\right) = \left(\frac{D^m_{t-2}}{D^m_t}\right)\left(\frac{D^m_t}{D^p + D^t}\right)\left(\frac{D^p + D^t}{D^p + D^t + T}\right).$$

Substituting δ and u in the above expression yields the following expression:

$$\left(\frac{D^m_{t-2}}{D_t^m}\right) \delta\, u.$$

A similar procedure applied to the reserve ratio for time deposits yields:

$$\left(\frac{T^m_{t-2}}{T_t^m}\right) \tau(1 - u).$$

If we now let:

$$w_1 = \left(\frac{D^m_{t-2}}{D_t^m}\right),$$

$$w_2 = \left(\frac{T^m_{t-2}}{T_t^m}\right),$$

then the reserve ratio may be rewritten, taking into account lagged reserve requirements as follows:

$$r = w_1 r^d \delta u + w_2\, r^t \tau(1 - u) + e + v.$$

Influence of Lagged Reserve Requirements on the Money Supply Process

Two more parameters (w_1 and w_2) are brought into the explicit form of the reserve ratio by lagging deposits subject to reserve requirements. Before the introduction of lagging w_1 and w_2 were equal to one, and hence did not directly affect the variability of the reserve ratio. However, any variability in the ratio of demand (time) deposits held two weeks earlier to demand (time) deposits in the current week is now impounded in the reserve ratio. Because w_1 and w_2 do not remain constant, but exhibit considerable variability, an additional unpredictable source of variation is now included in the reserve ratio. Therefore to this extent the Federal Reserve, by introducing lagged reserve requirements, made the prediction of changes in the money stock more difficult.

Lagged reserve requirement procedures have also raised some very complex questions about (1) the comparability of published data on bank reserves prior to lagging with bank reserve data after lagging, (2) their influence on bank behavior, and (3) their influence on day-to-day Federal Reserve open market operations. For example, a careful reading of (3) on page 52 reveals the introduction of an item called a reserve carryover. To the extent that the reserve carryover is positive, member banks may use this amount in the following week to meet legal reserve requirements. However, as currently reported, member bank reserves do not include this item. An examination of the 98-week period from late September 1968 through July 29, 1970, shows that the weekly reserve carryover for member banks averaged $120 million. In 60 per cent of the weeks, the reserve carryover exceeded $100 million, and in 10 weeks the reserve carryover was $200 million or more.

Since member banks may now use vault cash holdings of two settlement weeks earlier and a reserve carryover to meet legal reserve requirements, one would expect the behavior of the excess reserve ratio might be affected by these changes. To investigate these influences, weekly data on excess reserves were studied. The samples consisted of the 98-week period before and the 98-week period after and including September 18, 1968. Changes in the level of interest rates cause changes in the average level of the excess reserve ratio. Of more importance than the value of the standard deviation is the size of the standard deviation relative to the mean. Hence, the coefficient of variation (standard deviation/mean) is used as the measure of relative variability between the sample periods. These results are presented in Table 4.3.

TABLE 4.3

EXCESS RESERVES, EXCESS RESERVE RATIO AND TREASURY BILL RATE, 98 WEEKS BEFORE AND AFTER LAGGED RESERVE REQUIREMENTS*

	Mean	Standard Deviation	Coefficient of Variation
	98 Weeks before September 18, 1968		
Excess reserves	363.7	120.94	0.3325
e-ratio	0.001132	0.000374	0.3305
Treasury bill rate	4.738	0.59340	0.1252
	98 Weeks beginning September 18, 1968		
Excess reserves	231.0	136.64	0.5915
e-ratio	0.000645	0.000374	0.5797
Treasury bill rate	6.545	0.68879	0.1052

* Treasury bill rate is the market yield on 3-month Treasury bills.

In the sample period following the introduction of lagged reserve requirements there was considerably greater variability in the excess reserve ratio, which introduced an additional element of variability into the money supply process. It appears that as the positive reserve carryover for member banks increases, the banks react by reducing their excess reserves as currently reported. A week-by-week examination of movements in the *e*-ratio and reserve carryover shows that, in 73 of the 98 weeks, changes in the *e*-ratio and reserve carryover were in opposite directions.

With regard to the third question, the influence of lagging on Federal Reserve day-to-day open market operations, let us look at the stated purpose for lagged reserve requirements.

> The amendments were designed to facilitate more efficient functioning of the reserve mechanism. They did not represent any change in Federal Reserve monetary policy, but were expected to reduce uncertainties, for both member banks and the Federal Reserve, as to the amount of reserves required to be maintained during the course of any reserve computation period. Adoption of the amendments was therefore expected to moderate some of the pressures for reserve adjustments within the banking system that occasionally develop near the close of a reserve period and produce sharp fluctuations in the availability of day-to-day funds.[1]

The purpose of this procedure appears to have been to provide the Federal Reserve and member banks with better information and hence, reduce reserve adjustment pressures at the close of the weekly reserve period. An examination of three measures of "reserve adjustment pressures" for sample periods before and after lagging indicate that there were considerably greater reserve adjustment pressures at the end of reserve periods after lagging than before the change.[2] Also, the evidence shows that the absolute mean change in Federal Reserve holdings of government securities from Tuesday to Wednesday (the end of the reserve settlement period) was almost twice as great after lagging as before. Also it was much more variable, having a standard deviation of $306.8 million after lagging compared to $190 million before lagging.

In 33 of the 101 weeks before lagging there was no change from Tuesday to Wednesday in System holdings of securities. After lagging there were only 17 Tuesday to Wednesday periods when the Federal Reserve did not purchase or sell government securities. In 32 Tuesday/Wednesday periods after lagging, the Federal Reserve bought or sold approximately $400 million or more in government securities, compared to only 11 weeks in the preceding 101 weeks.

Another point concerning Federal Reserve behavior is whether lagging actually resulted in more accurate information for the Federal Reserve. At first glance the answer to this question might appear to be obvious. Before lagging, the amount of reserves member banks were required to hold in a given reserve settlement period depended upon the deposits held during that same period. Therefore, at the end of any settlement period when deciding the extent of reserve adjustment pressures building up in the banking system, the Federal Reserve had to estimate required reserves of member banks for that period. After the introduction of lagged reserve requirements, since the amount of required reserves was now based on deposits two weeks earlier, the Federal Reserve now should know exactly the amount of required reserves member banks must hold in any settlement week. Hence, with regard to one aspect of the member banks' reserve position, the Federal Reserve has better information.

Knowledge about the volume of banks' required reserves is only one part of the information that the Federal Reserve must have to gauge developing

---

[1] *Fifty-fifth Annual Report of the Board of Governors of the Federal Reserve System* (Washington, D.C.: Board of Governors, 1968), p. 82.

[2] The three measures of reserve adjustment pressure were (1) Federal funds rate, (2) member bank borrowings, and (3) open market operations. The sample periods were 101 weeks before lagging compared to 101 weeks after lagging, excluding the three weeks at the time of the introduction of lagged reserves.

reserve adjustment pressures. The Federal Reserve must also have accurate information on the total reserves member banks hold. Reserve adjustment pressures develop at the margin between total reserves and required reserves. If the volume of reserves member banks hold relative to required reserves exceeds or falls short of what they desire to hold, then at the end of the reserve settlement period there may occur sharp day-to-day fluctuations in the demand and supply of reserve funds.

A comparison of a measure of the best information the Federal Reserve had on member bank reserves with the final figures on member bank reserves gives a very interesting result. On average, in the period after the introduction of lagged reserve requirements, the Federal Reserve's weekly errors in predicting total member bank reserves were twice as great as before the introduction of lagging. Further, an examination of the sign pattern and magnitude of these errors is interesting. In 21 of the 101 weeks after lagging, the Federal Reserve missed total reserves by $75 million or more, compared to only 4 weeks in the 101 week period before lagging. Also, in the period before lagging, the direction of error was fairly evenly divided between overestimates and underestimates.[3] However, after lagging, in 96 of the 101 weeks the Federal Reserve underestimated the amount of total member bank reserves.

Therefore, an examination of the data does not lend any support to the conjecture that the introduction of lagged reserve requirements permitted the Federal Reserve to better gauge the extent of reserve adjustment pressures at the end of reserve settlement periods. Indeed, the evidence indicates that after lagging the Federal Reserve has been less able to accurately determine the extent to which it should intervene in the money market to prevent short-term pressures.

Other Developments

During 1969, the Federal Reserve System made certain amendments to Regulations *D* and *M*.[4] The amendment to Regulation *D*, which was effective July 31, 1969, restated the definition of gross demand deposits to include outstanding checks or drafts arising out of Eurodollar transactions. This change in Regulation *D* increased the volume of demand deposits subject to reserve requirements by roughly $3.3 billion at the time it was imposed and, in turn, increased required reserves by roughly $600 million.[5]

During 1969, to avoid the restraint of Regulation *Q* ceiling rates, banks attempted to secure nondeposit funds by sale of loans to affiliates and to non-

---

[3] 59 underestimates and 42 overestimates.

[4] Federal Reserve *Bulletin*, August 1969, pp. 655–657.

[5] The change in the definition of gross demand deposits also necessitated an upward revision of the money supply series. Prior to this change the "bills payable" and so-called "London checks" were carried on the books of the payee bank as cash items in process of collection until the reserves associated with the transfer became available. Such cash items are deducted from demand deposits to compute the deposit component of M^1, therefore understating the volume by roughly $3.3 billion in July 1969. See Federal Reserve *Bulletin*, October 1969, pp. 787–803 and Albert E. Burger, "Revision of the Money Supply Series," Federal Reserve Bank of St. Louis *Review*, October 1969, pp. 6–9.

bank investors under repurchase agreements. By mid-July 1969, this type of outstanding liability amounted to \$1.7 billion. On July 25, 1969, the Board of Governors put into effect changes in Regulations *D* and *Q* which stated that all such liabilities arising out of transactions with nonbank institutions or from the sale of assets, other than federal government securities, would be considered deposit liabilities subject to reserve requirements and interest ceilings.

Effective October 16, 1969, member banks with one or more foreign branches were required to maintain reserves against their foreign branch deposits. Essentially, these amendments placed a 10 per cent marginal reserve requirement on net borrowings of banks from their own foreign branches to the extent that such borrowings exceed the amount outstanding in a base period. Reserve requirements were also placed on direct bank borrowings from foreign sources, other than their own foreign branches. The additional required reserves from these sources amounted to roughly \$400 million in late October.

Effective October 1, 1970, the Board of Governors of the Federal Reserve System applied a 5 per cent reserve requirement on funds obtained by member banks through the issuance of commercial paper by their affiliates, and at the same time reduced from 6 to 5 per cent the reserves that member banks must hold against time deposits in excess of \$5 million. This dual action resulted in a \$350 million reduction of required reserves. This apparently was another attempt to use reserve requirements to selectively control bank credit. In the press release at that time, the Board stated, "The greater portion of the net reserves thus released will become available to banks that in the present circumstances might be expected to use a sizeable share of the available funds in financing housing and state and local governments."

Increased Variability of the Reserve Ratio

In the period 1950 through mid-1962 member bank deposits were divided into four categories for reserve requirement purposes. In mid-1962 the central reserve city classification was dropped, and until mid-1966 there were only three such categories. Beginning in mid-1966 the number of reserve categories was increased to five, in 1968 to seven, in 1969 to nine, and by the end of 1970 there were eleven categories for reserve requirement purposes, or four times as many categories as in the early 1960's! Increased splintering of reserve requirements and the introduction of lagged reserve requirements both have tended to introduce greater variability in the reserve ratio, therefore making it more difficult for the Federal Reserve to predict the results of any policy action.

Having followed the analysis to this point, the reader can see the meaning of this statement by reflecting on what such splintering implies for the components $r^d\delta$ and $r^t\tau$ of the reserve ratio. Carrying the analysis forward to January 24, 1968, in Table 4.1, it can be seen we must use four legal reserve requirements, each weighted by the proportion of member bank demand deposits subject to that reserve requirement. For example, we now have

r_{11}^d = reserve requirement on net demand deposit over \$5 million held by reserve city banks.

r_{12}^d = reserve requirements on net demand deposits under \$5 million held by reserve city banks.

r_{21}^d = reserve requirements on demand deposits over \$5 million held by country banks.

r_{22}^d = reserve requirements on demand deposits under \$5 million held by country banks.

Therefore r^d now becomes

$$r^d = \left[r_{11}^d \left(\frac{D_{11}^m}{D^m} \right) + r_{12}^d \left(\frac{D_{12}^m}{D^m} \right) + r_{21}^d \left(\frac{D_{21}^m}{D^m} \right) + r_{22}^d \left(\frac{D_{22}^m}{D^m} \right) \right],$$

where

D_{11}^m = net demand deposits over \$5 million held by reserve city banks.

In the example from Table 4.1 for January 24, 1968,

$$D_{11}^m = \$74{,}309 \qquad D_{21}^m = \$33{,}325,$$
$$D_{12}^m = \$921, \qquad D_{22}^m = \$19{,}494.$$

Likewise, a further specification of δ must be introduced to complete the formulation of $r^d\delta$. For example,

$$\delta = \delta_{11} + \delta_{12} + \delta_{21} + \delta_{22},$$

where

$$\delta_{ij} = \frac{D_{ij}^m}{D^p + D^t},$$

$$i = 1, 2, 3, 4,$$

$$j = 1, 2, 3, 4.$$

Now, a shift of deposits between member banks in the same general reserve classification can affect the reserve ratio. For example, if demand deposits flow out of country banks with deposits under \$5 million to country banks with deposits over \$5 million, the result is to raise $r^d\delta$ since r_{21}^d is greater than r_{22}^d.

Given the recent developments in reserve regulation by the Federal Reserve, a complete specification of $r^d\delta$ and $r^t\tau$ assumes even more complicated forms. The important point is not that it takes more space to completely specify the r-ratio but that as the Federal Reserve has tried to plug imagined loopholes in their policy control, they have by these actions introduced increased variability in the reserve ratio.

Excess Reserve Ratio

Relation (4.1) specifies the determination of the excess reserve ratio. The excess reserve ratio (e-ratio) depends on the interest rate (i), the discount rate (ρ), and an index of other factors (π_1) influencing the demand for excess reserves. Factors included in π_1 are the variance of interest rates, variance of currency flows between the banks and the public, and banks' anticipations about the variance of deposit flows.

$$e = f(i,\rho,\pi_1) \qquad \text{excess reserve ratio} \tag{4.1}$$

The primary reason why member banks hold excess reserves is that they want to be able to meet the cash demands of their depositors without drawing down their legal reserves and hence incurring a penalty cost on reserve deficiencies. However, excess reserves are nonearning assets. The opportunity cost to the banks is the yield they must give up by not acquiring an earning asset such as Treasury bills.[6]

Another way to view banks' demand for excess reserves is to consider the possible costs of short-term reserve adjustments that banks might face given that they decide to reduce excess reserves and acquire Treasury bills. For member banks, one source of funds to meet short-term reserve adjustments is the discount window of the Federal Reserve Banks. The cost of short-term reserve adjustments, by this method, is the discount rate.

Let us consider a simple example. As a bank draws down its excess reserves and acquires Treasury bills, the probability that it may not be able to meet the short-run cash demands of its depositors increases. This increases the probability that a bank may have to borrow at the discount window to make short-term reserve adjustments. The member bank must balance the yield available on Treasury bills against the cost of borrowing from the Federal Reserve Banks.

The e-ratio is therefore postulated to be negatively related to changes in the interest rate (i) and positively related to the discount rate (ρ) and π_1.

$$\frac{\partial e}{\partial i} < 0 \qquad \frac{\partial e}{\partial \rho}, \frac{\partial e}{\partial \pi_1} > 0.$$

The numerical value of the excess reserve ratio depends upon the level of interest rates. When interest rates, relative to their past historical average are at low levels, the quantity of excess reserves relative to deposit liabilities demanded by banks increases. When short-term interest rates rise, the banks' desired e-ratio decreases.[7]

---

[6] The concept of an "opportunity cost" is one of the most important basic concepts in economics. Since all economic units have limited wealth, they must choose how to allocate their given wealth among available real and financial assets. The items that an economic unit must forego in order to acquire a specific item *a* represent the "opportunity cost of *a*." Every real and financial asset has an opportunity cost.

[7] See the historical analysis of movements in the e-ratio at the end of this section.

To carry the analysis a step forward, the elasticity of the r-ratio with respect to the e-ratio is written as

$$\varepsilon(r, e) = \left(\frac{\partial r}{\partial e} \cdot \frac{e}{r}\right).$$

Since:

$$\frac{\partial r}{\partial e} = 1,$$

then:

$$\varepsilon(r, e) = \frac{e}{r};$$

therefore:

$$\varepsilon(r, e) \to 0 \quad \text{as} \quad e \to 0,$$

$$\varepsilon(r, e) \to 1 \quad \text{as} \quad e \to r.$$

As interest rates rise (fall) to higher (lower) levels, the percentage response of the r-ratio to changes in the e-ratio decreases (increases).

We notice an important point. The elasticity of the r-ratio with respect to interest rates may be written as

$$\varepsilon(r, i) = \varepsilon(r, e) \cdot \varepsilon(e, i).$$

Hence, since the numerical value of the $\varepsilon(r, e)$ decreases as the excess reserve ratio approaches zero, the $\varepsilon(e, i)$ can remain the same or rise; and the effect of interest-rate-induced changes in the e-ratio on the multipliers is reduced as interest rates rise to higher levels. A one per cent change in the interest rate could lead to the same percentage change in the banks' e-ratio in two separate periods, and the magnitude of this effect on the money and bank credit processes could be quite different.

The response of the multipliers to changes in the banks' desired holdings of excess reserves relative to deposits decreases (increases) as interest rates vary from the lower range of their historical averages to the upper range, and vice versa. This is summarized as

$\varepsilon(m, e)$ decreases as interest rates rise,

$\varepsilon(m, e)$ increases as interest rates fall.

Therefore, during periods of extremely low levels of short-term interest rates, the multipliers tend to be quite sensitive to changes in the banks' desired e-ratio. When interest rates have risen to high levels, and banks have reduced their e-ratio, the multipliers are much less sensitive to such changes.

Historical Background on Excess Reserve Ratio[8]

Figure 4.1 depicts yearly averages for the banks' excess reserve ratio (e = member bank excess reserves/$D^p + D^t + T$) and the yields on 3-month Treasury bills during the period 1929–1941.[9] Figure 4.2 gives a graph of the e-ratio and yields on Treasury bills 1947–1969. The war years, 1942–1946, are excluded. We shall now proceed to examine the excess reserve behavior of commercial banks over these 36 years.

1929 through 1941. During this thirteen-year period, short-term interest rates fell from an average of 4.19 per cent in the last three years of the 1920's to an average of .027 per cent in 1938–1940, reaching an average of .01 per cent in 1940. As banks' holdings of excess reserves rose from about $50 million in 1929–1930 to $6,326 million in 1940, the commercial banks' excess reserve ratio rose from .0009 in 1929 to .1213 in 1940. In other words, in 1929, the banks held about 9 cents of excess reserves for each $100 of nonbank deposit liabilities (total deposit liabilities less interbank deposits); in 1940 they held $12.13 of excess reserves for each $100 of nonbank deposit liabilities.

A very prominent feature of the excess reserve ratio during this period is the wide fluctuations occurring in the ratio. Referring to Table 4.4 and Figure 4.1, the e-ratio rose from .0009 in 1929 to .0663 in 1935, then fell to .0288 by 1937, rose to .1213 in 1940, and then fell to .0912 in 1941. The sharp fluctuations in the e-ratio are closely associated with changes in short-term interest rates. In 1937 the Treasury bill yield rose to an average of .45 per cent, about three times higher than its average in the preceding two years. After 1937, until 1941, the price of Treasury bills rose to record highs; while yields fell to record lows. In 1941 the Treasury bill yield rose from .01 per cent in 1940 to .13 per cent. The banks reduced their average holdings of excess reserves per $100 deposits by $3, a 25 per cent decrease.

As shown in Table 4.5, the spread between the Treasury bill rate and the discount rate widened in the 1930's. Although the discount rate was adjusted downward from 5.2 per cent in 1929 to $2\frac{1}{2}$ per cent in 1933, and then to 1 per cent in the late 1930's, the yields on short-term securities fell even more rapidly. In 1929 the yield on short-term securities averaged 17 basis points below the discount rate. By 1933, however, this spread had widened to 198 basis points. If a bank reduced its excess reserves and bought short-term securities, and

---

[8] For a more complete discussion on banks' demand for excess reserves, see Peter Frost, "Banks' Demand for Excess Reserves" unpublished dissertation, University of California at Los Angeles, 1966, available from University Microfilms, Inc., Ann Arbor, Michigan.

[9] The yield on 90-day bankers' acceptances 1929–1931 is used as a proxy for the short-term interest rate because the total volume of Treasury bills outstanding during this period was so small that the Treasury bill yield is not as representative of market yields. The average volume outstanding of Treasury bills and bankers' acceptances during this period is as follows:

	Treasury Bills	*Bankers' Acceptances*
1929	$100 million	$1,298 million
1930	142	1,471
1931	511	1,253
1932	629	784

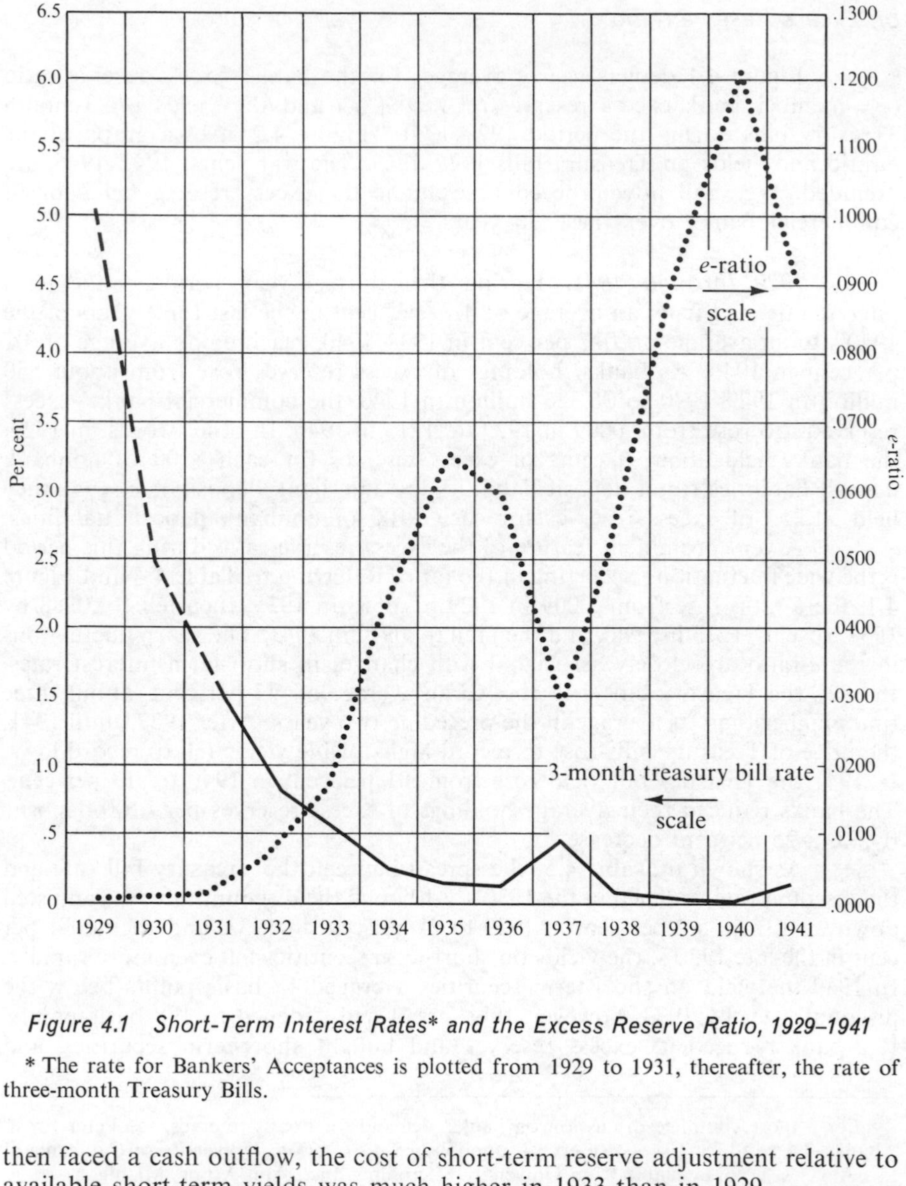

Figure 4.1 Short-Term Interest Rates and the Excess Reserve Ratio, 1929–1941*

* The rate for Bankers' Acceptances is plotted from 1929 to 1931, thereafter, the rate of three-month Treasury Bills.

then faced a cash outflow, the cost of short-term reserve adjustment relative to available short-term yields was much higher in 1933 than in 1929.

1947 through 1969. The dominant general features of the postwar period are the long-run downward trend in the excess reserve ratio and the general long-run upward trend in short-term interest rates. A significant part of the long-run downward trend in the *e*-ratio probably reflects institutional factors such as the elimination of the risk of bank-runs and the more efficient use of the reserve base by banks through the development of the Federal funds market. As shown by Figure 4.2 and Table 4.4, these long-run trends in the

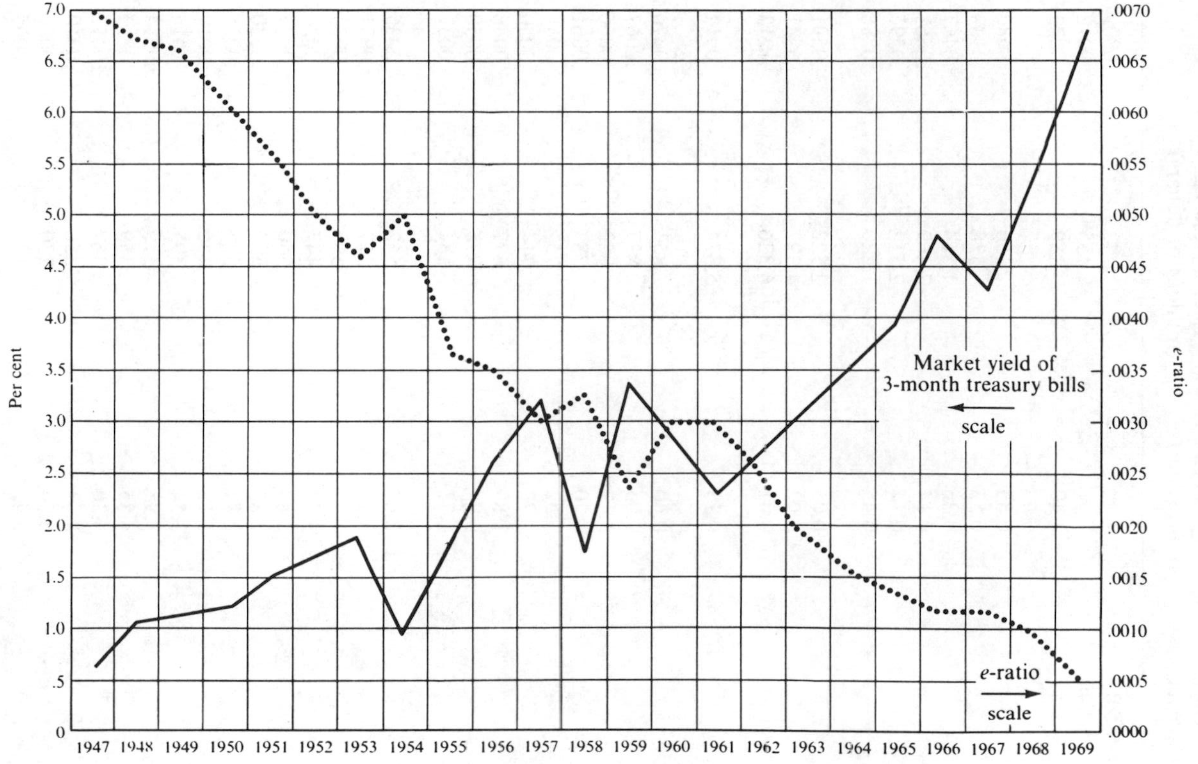

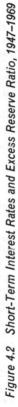

* Yearly rates are averages of monthly rates.

Figure 4.2 Short-Term Interest Rates and Excess Reserve Ratio, 1947–1969

TABLE 4.4

SHORT-TERM INTEREST RATES, EXCESS RESERVES, AND THE EXCESS RESERVE RATIO

Year	Short-Term Interest Rates: Bankers' Acceptances	Short-Term Interest Rates: Treasury* Bills (3 mo.)	Excess Reserves (millions of dollars)	*e*-Ratio
1929	5.03		43	.0009
1930	2.48		55	.0012
1931	1.57	1.40	89	.0023
1932		0.88	256	.0080
1933		0.52	528	.0183
1934		0.26	1,564	.0467
1935		0.14	2,469	.0663
1936		0.14	2,512	.0596
1937		0.45	1,220	.0288
1938		0.05	2,522	.0591
1939		0.02	4,392	.0941
1940		0.01	6,326	.1213
1941		0.13	5,324	.0912
1947		0.60	853	.0070
1948		1.05	837	.0067
1949		1.12	822	.0066
1950		1.20	783	.0061
1951		1.52	757	.0056
1952		1.72	714	.0050
1953		1.89	677	.0046
1954		0.94	775	.0050
1955		1.73	586	.0037
1956		2.63	562	.0035
1957		3.22	517	.0031
1958		1.77	590	.0033
1959		3.39	447	.0024
1960		2.88	550	.0029
1961		2.35	599	.0030
1962		2.77	525	.0025
1963		3.16	446	.0019
1964		3.54	395	.0016
1965		3.95	379	.0014
1966		4.85	359	.0012
1967		4.30	367	.0012
1968		5.33	356	.0010
1969		6.64	230	.0006
1970		6.42	185	.0005

* Rates for 1931–1940 are average rates on new issues offered; thereafter, they are averages of monthly rates on market yield.

TABLE 4.5

BASIS POINT DIFFERENCES BETWEEN THE THREE-MONTH TREASURY BILL RATE AND THE DISCOUNT RATE

Year	Discount Rate (per cent)*	Difference between the Treasury Bill Rate and the Discount Rate (basis points)†
1929	5.2	−17
1930	3.0	−52
1931	2.1	−70
1932	2.8	−192
1933	2.5	−198
1934	1.5	−124
1935	1.5	−136
1936	1.5	−136
1937	1.3	−85
1938	1.0	−95
1939	1.0	−98
1940	1.0	−99
1941	1.0	−87
1947	1.00	−40
1948	1.35	−30
1949	1.50	−38
1950	1.58	−38
1951	1.75	−23
1952	1.75	−3
1953	2.00	−11
1954	1.60	−66
1955	2.00	−27
1956	2.77	−14
1957	3.08	14
1958	2.14	−37
1959	3.38	1
1960	3.50	−62
1961	3.00	−65
1962	3.00	−23
1963	3.21	−5
1964	3.54	0
1965	4.04	−9
1966	4.50	35
1967	4.17	13
1968	5.13	20
1969	5.88	76

* Yearly rates are weighted averages of monthly rates at the Federal Reserve Bank of New York. In the 1929–1941 period, especially in the early years of the 1930's, there was often a considerable divergence between the discount rates of the individual Reserve Banks. The Federal Reserve Bank of New York's discount rate was consistently the lowest rate of the twelve banks, and the New York Bank accounted for the largest amount of lending to member banks of any of the twelve banks. *See Banking and Monetary Statistics*, Table 115, pp. 439–442.

† For 1929–1930 the yields on bankers' acceptances are used.

e-ratio and short-term interest rates, however, were not uninterrupted and did not proceed at the same pace over the entire period.

During this period, as in the prewar period, a close relationship between short-term interest rates and the banks' excess reserve ratio can be observed. As an illustration, from 1947 through 1953, with the average yearly yield on Treasury bills rising steadily from .60 per cent to 1.89 per cent, the *e*-ratio fell steadily from an average of .0070 in 1947 to .0046 for 1953. In 1954, short-term rates fell and the *e*-ratio rose. After 1954, Treasury bill yields rose over the next three years and the *e*-ratio resumed its downward trend. In 1958, short-term rates declined and the *e*-ratio rose. During 1959 bill yields, on average, rose sharply and the *e*-ratio fell from .0033 to .0024. In 1960, the *e*-ratio increased, again associated with a marked dip in the short-term yields. After 1961, short-term market interest increased very rapidly; in 1969 average yields were about three times as high as in 1960–1961. As market interest rates rose sharply, banks reduced their holdings of excess reserves from $550–600 million in 1960–1961 to $230 million in 1969. The *e*-ratio declined to .0006 in 1969, compared to .0030 in 1960–1961.

Vault Cash Ratio

The last term in the reserve ratio is the nonmember bank vault cash ratio (*v*-ratio). It is consistently small and may be approximated over recent years by a constant with the value of .004. As an illustration, the yearly average for the *v*-ratio for the six years 1964 through 1970 was as follows:

Year	*v-ratio*
1964	.0037
1965	.0038
1966	.0038
1967	.0039
1968	.0036
1969	.0039
1970	.0040

Summary of Factors Influencing the Reserve Ratio

The reserve ratio depends upon

1. Effective legal reserve requirements set by the Board of Governors.
2. Distribution of bank deposits between member and nonmember banks.
3. Distribution of deposits among member banks by deposit size.
4. Distribution of member banks by reserve classification.
5. Distribution of member bank deposits between demand deposits and time deposits.
6. Member bank excess reserve behavior which is dependent upon market interest rates, the Federal Reserve Banks' discount rate, and expected variance of deposit and reserve flows.
7. Nonmember bank vault cash behavior.

Borrowing Ratio

The effect of changes in the amount of member bank borrowings on the money supply and bank credit processes is summarized in the b-ratio. The borrowing ratio is postulated to depend upon the bank credit market interest rate (i), the Federal Reserve Banks' discount rate (ρ) and an index of other factors (π_2) affecting member bank borrowing from the Federal Reserve Banks. The major influence determining π_2 is the restrictions placed on member bank borrowing as a part of the Federal Reserve Banks' administration of the discount window:

$$b = f(i, \rho, \pi_2). \tag{4.2}$$

The b-ratio is postulated to be positively related to the bank credit market interest rate (i) and negatively related to the discount rate (ρ) and other borrowing costs (π_2). Therefore:

$$\frac{\partial b}{\partial i} > 0 \qquad \frac{\partial b}{\partial \rho}, \frac{\partial b}{\partial \pi_2} < 0.$$

Borrowing at the discount window by member banks of the Federal Reserve System results in an increase in the amount of base money held by the *whole* banking system. Instead of base money being transferred from the public to banks, as in the case of a change in the currency ratio, or base money being transferred among the banks, as in the case of Federal funds borrowings, lending through the discount window increases the total stock of base money. The total potential volume of bank deposits is greater, the larger the volume of member bank borrowing from the Federal Reserve Banks.

Base money obtained through the discount window is not without cost to the banks. The explicit cost is the discount rate. The total cost includes the discount rate and any "administrative requirements" imposed as a condition of borrowing by the Federal Reserve Banks. When considering whether to expand or contract borrowings, banks must weigh these costs against the available yields on earning assets and the costs of alternative funds to meet reserve demands such as holding more excess reserves or borrowing Federal funds. As the available yields on earning assets rise (fall), for any given total cost of borrowing, member banks' demand for base money via the discount window increases (decreases).

The response of the b-ratio to changes in the interest rate also depends upon the willingness of the Federal Reserve to permit the aggregate level of member bank borrowings to rise. The addition to the total cost for member banks of borrowing from the Federal Reserve Banks' discount window resulting from tighter administration of the discount window is denoted by π_2. This is represented in the following manner:

$$\begin{aligned} &\varepsilon(b, i) > 0, && \pi_2 = 0, \\ &\varepsilon(b, i) \to 0, && \text{as } \pi_2 \text{ increases.} \end{aligned}$$

The effect of changes in member bank borrowings relative to total deposit liabilities (excluding interbank deposits) on the money supply and bank credit processes also depends upon the size of the borrowing ratio. When short-term interest rates are at very low levels and the discount rate is above short-term interest rates, member banks' demands for borrowings from the Federal Reserve approach zero and the *b*-ratio becomes very small. As the *b*-ratio approaches zero, the effect of percentage changes in the *b*-ratio on the multipliers is reduced.[10] As short-term interest rates rise, and if the discount rate is not adjusted upward, the quantity of borrowings demanded by member banks rises. The numerical value of the *b*-ratio increases, and hence it begins to exercise a greater influence on the money supply and bank credit process.

At the upper end of the range of interest rates, perhaps with the discount rate considerably below short-term market rates, the quantity of borrowings demanded is large. However, as member bank borrowings rise to high levels, the Federal Reserve Banks may become less willing to accommodate the borrowing demands of member banks. A tighter administration of the discount window is instituted. This result can be illustrated with the graph shown in Figure 4.3. As market rates rise from i_1 to i_2 the quantity of borrowings

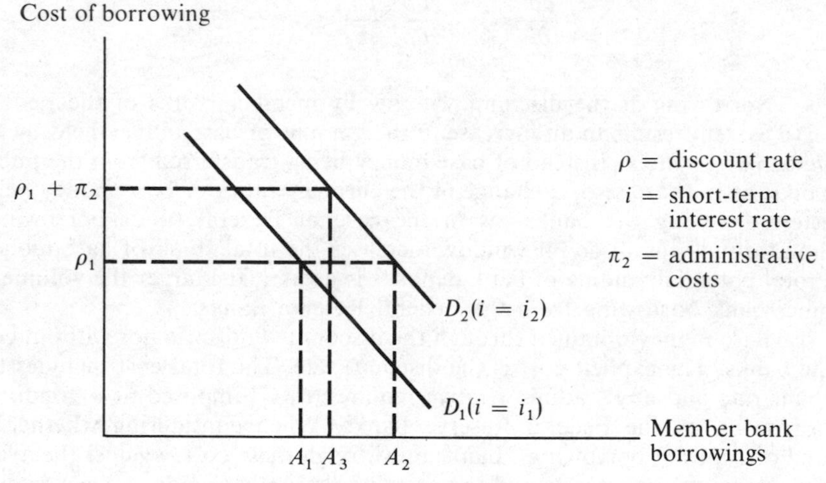

Figure 4.3

demanded by banks rises from A_1 to A_2 for the given discount rate ρ_1. However, if as the level of member bank borrowings rises, by administrating the discount window the Federal Reserve adds an amount π_2 to the banks' borrowing costs, then borrowings rise only to A_3. These results can be expressed in elasticity terms as follows:

$\varepsilon(m, b)$ small when interest rates are at low levels,

$\varepsilon(m, b)$ rises as interest rates rise to medium levels,

---

[10] $\varepsilon(m^1, b) = b(1 + t + d)/(r - b)(1 + t + d)$, therefore as $b \to 0$ the numerical value of the elasticity of m^1 with respect to the borrowing ratio approaches zero.

$\varepsilon(m, b)$ decreases as interest rates reach high levels and the Federal Reserve institutes administration of the discount window.

Historical Background on the Borrowing Ratio

Table 4.6 presents the level of member bank borrowings and the b-ratio for the periods 1929–1941 and 1947–1970. Through the 1930's, as short-term interest rates fell to very low levels, the level of member bank borrowings fell virtually to zero. With the cost of borrowing from the Federal Reserve Banks approximately 100 basis points above available short-term rates (see Table 4.5), the banks reduced their borrowings from $943 million in 1929 to below $10 million in the last half of the 1930's.

In the postwar period, 1947–1959, the average level of member bank borrowings rose from around $100–$150 million during 1947–1950 to levels of $700–$830 million during five of the eleven years from 1950 through 1961. One noticeable feature of this period is the increased size of the fluctuations in the b-ratio. For 1951–1961 the average change in the b-ratio was .0021, about 10 times as large as the average change of .0002 in the 1947–1950 period, compared to almost no change in the average level during the 1935–1941 period.

An examination of 1951 through 1961 illustrates the close relationship between the b-ratio and short-term interest rates. In 1954, 1958, and 1960–1961 the average level of Treasury bill yields declined. Table 4.6 shows a sharp decline in the level of member bank borrowings and the b-ratio in these years. In the following years, as short-term interest rates resumed their long-run upward trend, member bank borrowing and the b-ratio responded by increasing.

From 1953 to 1954 the b-ratio declined from .0052 to .0010. Then the b-ratio rose to .0038 in 1955 and .0051 in 1956. In the 1957–1961 period we observe a similar result. In 1958, with the average level of Treasury bill rates about one-half the 1957 level, the b-ratio fell to .0017 from .0050 in 1957. As short-term yields rose markedly in 1959, the average level of member bank borrowings increased $2\frac{1}{2}$ times the 1958 level and the b-ratio rose to .0043.

In 1960 short-term interest rates fell, and it was not until 1964 that they rose to their 1959 levels. The average borrowing ratio declined over this period. During the 1964–1966 period interest rates began to accelerate and banks increased their average borrowings to $635 million compared to $248 million in 1963. Interest rates then dropped sharply during the first half of 1967 and the borrowing ratio declined.

Interest rates increased to record levels from mid-1967 through 1969. By 1969 the average level of Treasury bill rates had risen to 6.64 per cent, more than double its average in the early part of the 1960's. The borrowing ratio rose to .0030, about three times its average level over the earlier part of the 1960's.

In both 1966 and 1969 there are strong indications that the total cost for member banks borrowing at the Federal Reserve exceeded the discount rate. From January to May 1966, member bank borrowing rose from $406 million to $722 million. After May, the discount rate remained at 4.5 per cent, but market interest rates continued to rise, and the alternative costs of borrowing such as Federal funds and Eurodollars rose sharply. However, member bank

TABLE 4.6

MEMBER BANK BORROWINGS AT FEDERAL RESERVE BANKS AND THE b-RATIO

Year	Member Bank Borrowings (millions of dollars)	b-ratio $\left(\frac{\text{Member Bank Borrowing}}{D^p + D^t + T}\right)$
1929	$943	.0206
1930	271	.0061
1931	323	.0082
1932	518	.0162
1933	234	.0018
1934	29	.0009
1935	7	.0002
1936	6	.0001
1937	14	.0003
1938	9	.0002
1939	4	.0001
1940	3	.0001
1941	5	.0001
1947	156	.0013
1948	140	.0011
1949	115	.0009
1950	106	.0008
1951	289	.0021
1952	780	.0055
1953	768	.0052
1954	147	.0010
1955	606	.0038
1956	831	.0051
1957	837	.0050
1958	294	.0017
1959	799	.0043
1960	431	.0023
1961	79	.0004
1962	104	.0005
1963	248	.0011
1964	289	.0012
1965	470	.0017
1966	635	.0022
1967	173	.0005
1968	563	.0016
1969	1101	.0030
1970	803	.0021

borrowings did not show a noticeable increase. Likewise, in 1969, after peaking at about $1,600 million in early May, member bank borrowings declined over most of the remainder of the year. As in 1966, this decline in borrowings occurred even though short-term interest rates continued to rise very sharply and the cost of Federal funds and Eurodollars rose to record peaks while the discount rate remained fixed.

Some economists claim this is due to the "reluctance of member banks to be indebted to the Federal Reserve," yet member banks were not "reluctant" to increase borrowings in previous periods when interest rates rose relative to the discount rate. The contention that the quantity of borrowings demanded by banks depends upon the total cost of borrowing at the discount window seems to square better with the empirical evidence. Banks became "reluctant to borrow from the Federal Reserve" simply because the total cost of borrowings was raised by a tighter administration of member bank borrowings by the Federal Reserve Banks.

Free Reserve Ratio

Instead of considering excess reserves and member bank borrowing separately, these two items are sometimes combined into what is called *free reserves* (R^f), where free reserves are defined as[11]

$$R^f = R^e - A.$$

The free reserve ratio (f) is the difference between the excess reserve ratio and the borrowing ratio:

$$f = e - b \qquad \text{free reserve ratio.}$$

Since the e-ratio and b-ratio are dependent upon the interest rate, this means the free reserve ratio is dependent on interest rates. Likewise, the f-ratio is dependent upon the discount rate and π_1 and π_2. Since

$$\varepsilon(e, i) < 0,$$

$$\varepsilon(b, i) > 0,$$

the elasticity of the free reserve ratio with respect to the interest rate becomes

$$\varepsilon(f, i) < 0.$$

Calculating the free reserve ratio using the data previously given on the e-ratio and the b-ratio, the reader can see that in periods when interest rates fall (rise) the f-ratio rises (falls). For example, the f-ratio rose from $-.0049$ in 1930 to .1212 in 1940 as interest rates declined to record low levels. In the postwar period, 1947–1953, as short-term interest rates rose, the f-ratio declined from .0057 to $-.0006$.

---

[11] When member bank borrowings exceed excess reserves, this item is frequently referred to as *net borrowed reserves*.

Combining the *e*-ratio and *b*-ratio into one conglomerate expression called the *free reserve ratio* tends to obscure much of the important behavioral response of the banks' underlying changes in the *f*-ratio. An important distinction must be made between changes in the actual free reserve ratio and changes in the banks' desired *f*-ratio. Changes in the actual *f*-ratio may be induced by changes in the stock of base money. Changes in banks' desired *f*-ratio result from variation in one of those factors on which the *e*-ratio and *b*-ratio are dependent (interest rates, discount rates, and such factors as administration of the discount window and expected deposit variability summarized in π_2 and π_1).

Suppose that an observed increase in the free reserve ratio results from an increase in the base. Banks then adjust their actual free reserve ratio to their desired *f*-ratio. Money and bank credit expand and short-term interest rates fall. The expansion of *M* and *E* and the extent of the decline in interest rates depends upon the sensitivity of the *e*-ratio and *b*-ratio to interest rates.

On the other hand, let us suppose that the discount rate is increased or alternatively that banks believe that the probability of large deposit outflows is increasing. These factors result in a rise in banks' desired free reserve ratio. As banks adjust their actual *f*-ratio to the new higher desired level, money and bank credit decline and interest rates rise.

An observed rise (fall) in the free reserve ratio can have completely opposite implications for the future growth of money, bank credit, and the level of credit market interest rates. For any given value of the *f*-ratio there are an infinite number of different combinations of the *e* and *b*-ratios. It is not likely that banks are indifferent with respect to these different combinations. To decide what an observed change in the free reserve ratio implies for *M*, *E*, and interest rates requires that the conglomerate *f*-ratio be broken down and that the underlying behavior of the banks be analyzed.

The longest prolonged rise in the *f*-ratio, in the period we have examined, occurred in the 1930's. The change in the *f*-ratio in this period was dominated by the rising *e*-ratio. As interest rates declined to very low levels and the spread between the discount rate and short-term interest rates widened, banks' demand for excess reserves rose and their demand for borrowings fell almost to zero. Also, as discussed in previous sections, the reserve ratio became very sensitive to changes in the *e*-ratio. Hence a decline in interest rates, raising the desired *e*-ratio and hence the *f*-ratio, exerted an important downward influence on the multiplier. The rise in the *f*-ratio appears to represent a rise in banks' desired *f*-ratio. Under these conditions the rising *f*-ratio signaled that any given open market operation would have less of an expansionary effect on the money supply process and bank credit than before.

In the postwar period changes in the *f*-ratio were dominated by changes in the *b*-ratio. When the yields available on earning assets increased, banks expanded their ratio of borrowings to deposits and the *f*-ratio fell. However, the fall in the *f*-ratio was accompanied by an expansion of money and bank credit. The fall in the free reserve ratio meant that any size of open market operation had a greater expansionary effect on money and bank credit than previously.

Administration of the discount window, under these conditions, would further obscure the implications of a given level of free reserves. If banks' borrowings are held below the level desired by banks, then the level of free reserves would be higher than that desired by banks. Although the level of free reserves might be unchanged, an increase in the base would be expected to have an even more expansionary effect than before. To adjust the actual f-ratio to the desired level, banks would expand their deposits. Free reserves, after the adjustment, remain at the previous level, but the actual f-ratio falls to the desired level and money and bank credit expand.

Time Deposit Ratio

The third ratio which enters the multipliers is the time deposit ratio. The dependence of the t-ratio is expressed in relation (4.3):

$$t = f\left(i^f, i^t, \frac{W}{P_a}, \frac{Y}{Y_p}\right), \tag{4.3}$$

where

i^f = index of yields on financial assets, other than time deposits, traded on the credit market,

i^t = index of banks offering yields on time deposits,

$\frac{W}{P_a}$ = real value of the stock of nonhuman wealth held by the public,

$\frac{Y}{Y_p}$ = ratio of current income to permanent income.

As the banks raise their offering yields on time deposits, other factors constant, wealthholders are postulated to increase the portion of bank deposits they hold in time deposits. As yields on other assets rise, wealthholders restructure their portfolios of assets and the t-ratio falls. Other factors constant, as wealthholders' real wealth rises or their ratio of transitory income (Y) to permanent income (Y_p) increases, they are postulated to increase the portion of bank deposits that they hold as time deposits:

$$\frac{\partial t}{\partial i^t}, \frac{\partial t}{\partial (W/P_a)}, \frac{\partial t}{\partial (Y/Y_p)} > 0 \qquad \frac{\partial t}{\partial i^f} < 0.$$

The t-ratio is viewed as being determined by the portfolio decisions of the public and interest rate actions of the commercial banks that influence such decisions. The competitive response of banks to the influence of rising yields on other assets on the public's demand for time deposits is expressed in relation (4.4):

$$i^t = f(i^f, Q^*), \tag{4.4}$$

where

Q^* = Regulation Q ceiling rates on time deposit interest rates.

The time deposit interest rate (i^t) is postulated to be positively related to the index of interest rates on financial assets (i^f) subject to conditions involving Regulation *Q* ceiling rates:

$$\frac{\partial i^t}{\partial i^f} > 0 \qquad \text{subject to } Q^*.$$

The relationship between i^t and i^f represents the response of banks to changes in market interest rates. As yields on other market assets rise, banks experience increasing difficulty in attracting and holding time deposits. Banks are postulated to react to this by raising the rate i^t which they offer on time deposits. The ability of banks to respond to changes in i^f by raising i^t is constrained by ceiling rates set by the Board of Governors.

Elasticity of the t-ratio with Respect to the Index of Interest Rates (i)

The elasticity of the *t*-ratio with respect to the index of interest rates (i) on assets traded by commercial banks depends upon three factors:

1. For a given percentage change in interest rates (i^f) on other assets, the response of the public with respect to their desired allocation of bank deposits between demand and time deposits. This is summarized as

$$\varepsilon(t, i^f).$$

2. For a given percentage change in i^t, the response of the public with respect to their desired allocation of bank deposits between demand and time deposits. This is summarized as

$$\varepsilon(t, i^t).$$

3. The competitive response of commercial banks to a percentage change in i^f. This is summarized as

$$\varepsilon(i^t, i^f).$$

These factors may be combined, and the total elasticity of the τ-ratio with respect to the interest rate may be expressed as follows:

$$\varepsilon(t, i) = [\varepsilon(t, i^f) + \varepsilon(t, i^t) \cdot \varepsilon(i^t, i^f)] \cdot \varepsilon(i^f, i).$$

where the elasticities in the brackets are partial elasticities and $\varepsilon(i^f, i)$ is a weighting factor. Referring to the basic definition of the *t*-ratio,

$$t = \frac{\text{Time deposits}}{\text{demand deposits held by the public.}}$$

It can be seen that the *t*-ratio depends on both the volume of time deposits and the volume of demand deposits.

The $\varepsilon(t, i^f)$ and $\varepsilon(t, i^t)$ can be expressed as

$$\varepsilon(t, i^f) = [\varepsilon(T, i^f) - \varepsilon(D^P, i^f)],$$
$$\varepsilon(t, i^t) = [\varepsilon(T, i^t) - \varepsilon(D^P, i^t)].$$

As the gap between the index of yields on other market assets (i^f) and the yields that banks offer on time deposits (i^t) widens, these other market assets become a more attractive means of holding wealth than time deposits. The public switches from time deposits to other assets, such as Treasury bills, commercial paper, savings and loan shares, and corporate bonds. Time deposits decline with a rise in the yield on alternative financial assets, and they increase with a rise in the yields that banks offer on time deposits:

$$\varepsilon(T, i^f) < 0,$$
$$\varepsilon(T, i^t) > 0.$$

With respect to demand deposits held by the public, as yields on time deposits and other market assets rise (fall), the opportunity cost to the public of holding demand deposits increases (decreases). The public responds by switching from (to) demand deposits to (from) other assets:

$$\varepsilon(D^P, i^f) < 0,$$
$$\varepsilon(D^P, i^t) < 0.$$

Referring to the expressions above, we see that since

$$\varepsilon(T, i^t) > 0, \qquad \varepsilon(D^P, i^t) < 0,$$

then

$$\varepsilon(t, i^t) > 0.$$

The numerical value, but not the sign, of $\varepsilon(t, i^t)$ depends upon the numerical values of the elasticities of time deposits and demand deposits with respect to yields offered by banks on time deposits. The larger (smaller) the $\varepsilon(T, i^t)$ and $\varepsilon(D^P, i^t)$, the larger (smaller) is the numerical value of the elasticity of the t-ratio with respect to i^t.

The sign and the numerical value of $\varepsilon(t, i^f)$ depend upon the numerical values of $\varepsilon(T, i^f)$ and $\varepsilon(D^P, i^f)$. It is postulated that the substitution between securities and time deposits dominates the substitution between demand deposits and securities resulting from a change in i^f:[12]

$$|\,\varepsilon(T, i^f)\,| > |\,\varepsilon(D^P, i^f)\,|,$$

[12] The symbols | | represent the absolute value, or the value of the term enclosed in the expression without regard to its sign. For example, in the real number system we would say +2 is greater than −3. However, |−3| is greater than |2|.

and we derive the conclusion that[13]

$$\varepsilon(t, i^f) < 0.$$

The banks' supply behavior with respect to time deposits is described as a price setting function of i^f and Regulation Q ceiling rates. The price (i^t) that banks are willing to pay to induce the public to alter their desired ratio of time to demand deposits depends upon (1) the yields which banks can earn on the increased volume of earning assets the banks can acquire, given an increase in time deposits. It also depends upon the maximum price that banks are able to pay to attract time deposits, which is determined by (2) the level of Regulation Q ceiling rates on time deposits.

The competitive response by banks to the effect on their time deposits of changes in the available yields on other assets is expressed by the elasticity of the banks' offering yields on time deposits with respect to the yields on other market assets:

$$\varepsilon(i^t, i^f) \qquad \text{competitive response of banks.}$$

When i^f rises relative to i^t, then the public switches from time deposits to other assets and, in the resulting portfolio adjustment process, the ratio of time deposits to demand deposits falls. If banks are to induce the public to maintain the same t-ratio as before the rise in i^f, the banks must raise their offering yields on time deposits.

Constraint on $\varepsilon(i^t, i^f)$

Banks operate under regulations imposed by the Federal Reserve System. These regulations impose constraints on the ability of banks to raise the yields they offer on time deposits (i^t). A major constraint which must be taken into consideration in the hypothesis is Regulation Q—which sets the ceiling rates on the yields banks can offer on time deposits. Once Regulation Q

---

[13] Jerry Jordan, in a study of deposit-type financial assets using cross-section data 1956–66, found that

1. The elasticity of demand for time deposits with respect to interest rates (own and cross yields) is greater than the interest elasticities of demand for demand deposits.
2. $\varepsilon(t, i^f)$ was estimated to be negative and statistically significant.
3. $\varepsilon(t, i^t)$ is positive and significant.

Jerry L. Jordan, *The Market for Deposit-Type Financial Assets*, unpublished Ph.D. dissertation, (University of California, Los Angeles, 1969); available as Working Paper No. 8, Federal Reserve Bank of St. Louis, pp. 159–166. For a discussion and summary of separate estimates of these elasticities by Goldfeld, deLeeuw, and Teigen, see Ronald Teigen, "An Aggregate Quarterly Model of the U.S. Monetary Sector, 1953–1964," *Targets and Indicators of Monetary Policy*, Karl Brunner, ed. (San Francisco: Chandler Publishing Company, 1969), pp. 212–213.

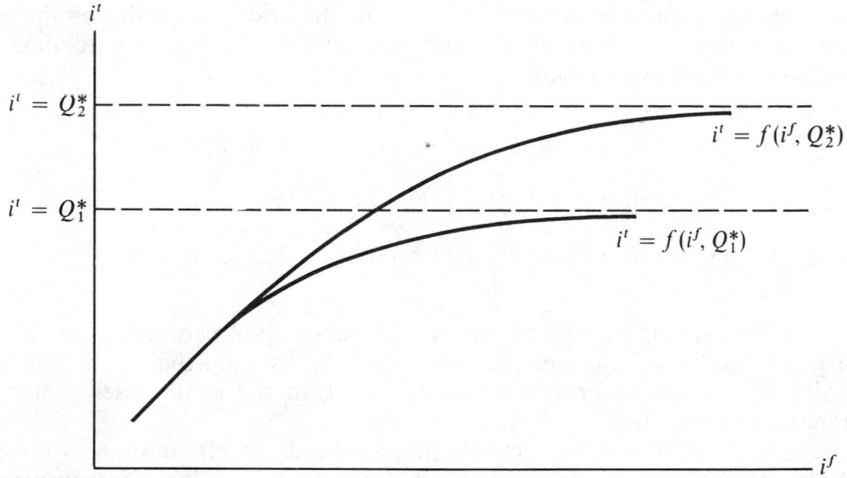

Figure 4.4

is introduced into the analysis, as the yields offered by banks on time deposits approach their Regulation Q ceilings, the ability of banks to respond to a rise in i^f by raising i^t approaches zero.

Graphically, i^t may be expressed as a function of i^f as shown in Figure 4.4. As $i^t \to Q^*$ we can see that the change in i^t resulting from a change in i^f becomes smaller:

$$\frac{\partial i^t}{\partial i^f} \to 0.$$

And, correspondingly, we have the result that as the yields which banks offer on time deposits approach Regulation Q limits:

$$\varepsilon(i^t, i^f) \to 0 \text{ as } i^t \to Q^*.$$

Total $\varepsilon(t, i)$

Having discussed each of the components of the elasticity of the t-ratio with respect to the bank credit market interest rate, the total expression for $\varepsilon(t, i)$ can be rewritten, and each of the components can be expressed with its expected sign:

$$\varepsilon(t, i) = [\varepsilon(t, i^f) + \varepsilon(t, i^t) \cdot \varepsilon(i^t, i^f)] \cdot \varepsilon(i^f, i),$$
$$\varepsilon(t, i^f) < 0$$
$$\varepsilon(t, i^t) > 0$$
$$\varepsilon(i^t, i^f) > 0 \qquad i^t \text{ sufficiently below } Q^*,$$
$$\varepsilon(i^t, i^f) \to 0 \qquad i^t \text{ approaches } Q^*.$$
$$\varepsilon(i^f, i) > 0$$

The sign of the total elasticity of the t-ratio with respect to interest rates depends upon whether the first term in the brackets dominates the expression or whether the product of the two terms in the brackets dominates. This may be expressed as follows:

$$(1) \quad \varepsilon(t, i^t) \cdot \varepsilon(i^t, i^f) > |\, \varepsilon(t, i^f) \,|, \qquad \text{then } \varepsilon(t, i) > 0,$$

$$(2) \quad \varepsilon(t, i^t) \cdot \varepsilon(i^t, i^f) = |\, \varepsilon(t, i^f) \,|, \qquad \text{then } \varepsilon(t, i) = 0,$$

$$(3) \quad \varepsilon(t, i^t) \cdot \varepsilon(i^t, i^f) < |\, \varepsilon(t, i^f) \,|, \qquad \text{then } \varepsilon(t, i) < 0.$$

We see that the sign of the $\varepsilon(t, i)$ depends upon bank behavior. If, as market interest rates change, the banks respond by adjusting i^t so that the $\varepsilon(t, i^t) \cdot \varepsilon(i^t, i^f)$ remains greater than $|\, \varepsilon(t, i^f) \,|$, then the t-ratio rises (falls) as interest rates rise (fall).[14]

If the $\varepsilon(t, i) = 0$, this implies that banks adjust offering rates on time deposits only enough to offset any change in the t-ratio resulting from increases or decreases in the yields on other market assets.

If the $\varepsilon(t, i) < 0$ this implies that banks do not adjust i^t by a large enough percentage to offset the influence of changing market interest rates on the t-ratio.

For a given stock of net source base, the three main ways in which the banking system can expand the amount of earning assets it holds are: (1) reduce excess reserves relative to deposits, (2) borrow base money from the Federal Reserve, and (3) induce the public to increase its t-ratio. At low levels of interest rates the banks' holdings of excess reserves tend to be large and the banks respond to an increase in market interest rates by reducing excess reserves. This method of expanding holdings of earning assets is cheaper for the banks than raising i^t to increase the t-ratio. Therefore, when interest rates are at low levels, banks would vary their offering yields only enough to maintain the existing ratio of time to demand deposits:

$$\varepsilon(t, i) \to 0.$$

At high levels of interest rates, the banks have reduced their holdings of excess reserves to low levels and they find that the total cost of borrowing base money from the Federal Reserve Banks is increasing. As market interest rates rise, assuming B^a is not increased, the lowest-cost way (of the three ways mentioned above) for banks to increase their holdings of earning assets is the third way. Therefore, under these conditions, as i^f rises

$$\varepsilon(t, i) > 0.$$

---

[14] The interest rate response of banks that is necessary to insure this result depends upon the partial elasticities of the t-ratio with respect to the interest rates i^t and i^f. If the own-price elasticities of the t-ratio exceeds the cross price elasticity of the t-ratio (i.e. $|\varepsilon(t, i^t)| > |\varepsilon(t, i^f)|$), then banks need not change i^t by as large a percentage as the rise in i^f to insure that $\varepsilon(t, i) > 0$.

Regulation Q Effects

We have seen that the rates banks offer on time deposits depend not only upon what banks are willing to pay, but also upon what they can pay. The upper limit on time deposit yields is set by the Federal Reserve Board under Regulation Q.

As market yields rise, and as the yields on time deposits approach Regulation Q ceiling rates, the numerical value of the elasticity of time deposit rates with respect to yields on other credit market assets becomes smaller. Consequently, the absolute value of the product of the last two terms in the total elasticity of the t-ratio with respect to interest rates decreases:

$$|\,\varepsilon(t, i^t) \cdot \varepsilon(i^t, i^f)\,| \to |\,\varepsilon(t, i^f)\,|,$$

and $\varepsilon(t, i)$ approaches zero.

When Regulation Q is effectively restraining banks from raising the yields they offer on time deposits, the $\varepsilon(i^t, i^f)$ becomes very small, and the first term of the expression for the total $\varepsilon(t, i)$ dominates:

$$i^t \to Q^* \quad \text{and} \quad \varepsilon(i^t, i^f) \to 0,$$
$$|\,\varepsilon(t, i^t) \cdot \varepsilon(i^t, i^f)\,| < |\,\varepsilon(t, i^f)\,|.$$

The sign of the elasticity of the t-ratio with respect to the bank credit market interest rate is reversed from the case in which the yields that banks offer on time deposits (i^t) are sufficiently below Regulation Q, and

$$\varepsilon(t, i) < 0.$$

Under these conditions, wealthholders switch from time deposits to other assets. This process has been labeled disintermediation. The result that $\varepsilon(t, i) \to 0$ and then becomes negative does not, under these conditions, imply that it is no longer profitable for banks to raise their offering rates on time deposits. Although they are willing to raise i^t, banks are unable to do so. As market interest rates begin to decline, it remains profitable for banks to increase time deposits. Hence, as interest rates fall, banks may reduce i^t, but not by a large enough amount to prevent the t-ratio from rising.

Response of Money and Bank Credit to the t-ratio

The response of the M^2 and bank credit multipliers to changes in the value of the t-ratio are opposite in sign to the response of the money multiplier (m^1) to changes in the t-ratio. From the difference between the signs of the elasticities of the multipliers, it follows that the elasticity of M^2, and E with respect to the t-ratio are opposite in sign to the elasticity of M^1.

$$\varepsilon(M^1, t) < 0,$$
$$\varepsilon(M^2, t) > 0,$$
$$\varepsilon(E, t) > 0.$$

Graphically the relation between money (M^1) and bank credit may be derived as shown in Figure 4.5. Graph II expresses the relation between M^1 and B^a given the m^1 multiplier. Graph IV gives the relation between E and B^a for a given value of the bank credit multiplier. For a stock of base, and given the values of the money and bank credit multipliers, a definite amount of M^1 and E will result.

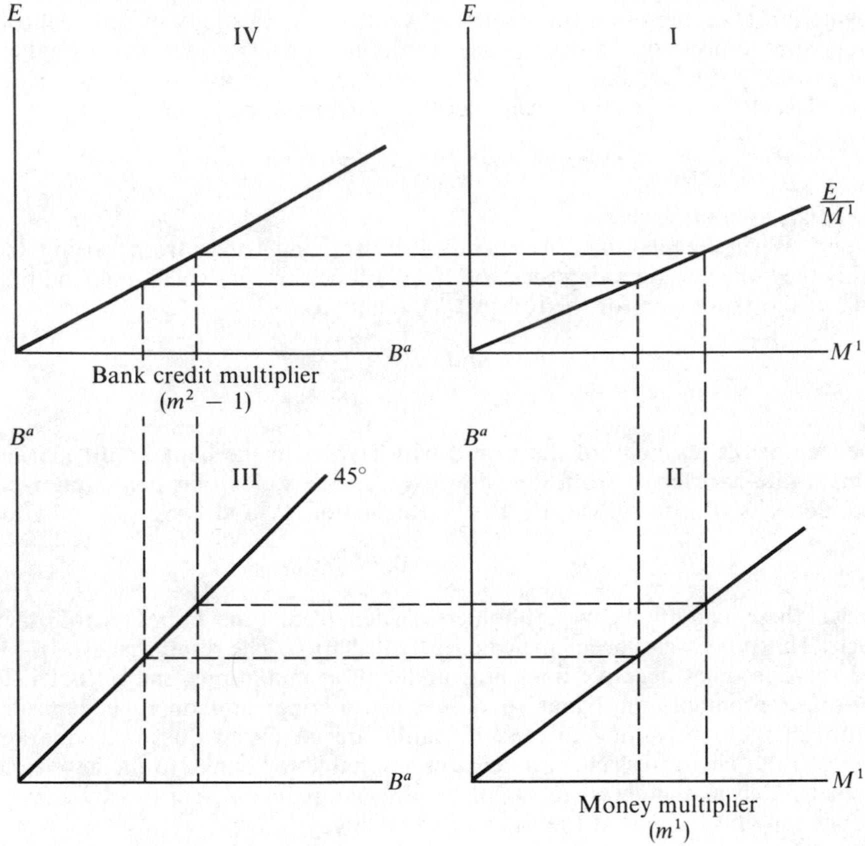

Figure 4.5 Relation between Money and Bank Credit

The effect of an increase in the t-ratio is shown in Figure 4.6. The rise in the t-ratio increases the amount of bank credit associated with any stock of base. Graphically, this appears as a rotation of the line expressing the bank credit multiplier to the left to $(m^2 - 1)_1$. The line $(m^2 - 1)_1$ associates a larger stock of E with every given stock of B^a than does the line labeled $m^2 - 1$. Correspondingly, in Graph II the fall in the money multiplier resulting from the rise in the t-ratio is shown by a rotation of the line expressing the relation between M^1 and B^a to $(m^1)_1$.

In Graph I the result of the rise in the t-ratio on the ratio of E/M^1 is shown. The amount of bank credit corresponding to any money stock is larger. Consequently we reach the important conclusion that a change in the

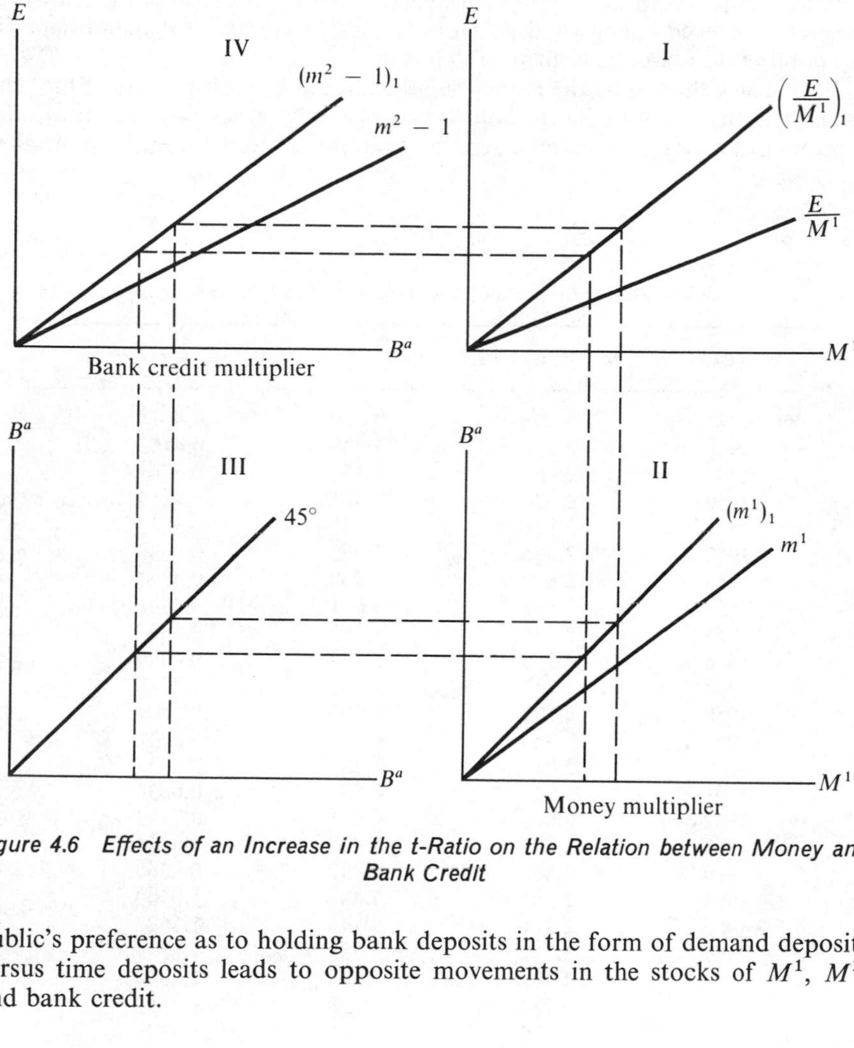

Figure 4.6 Effects of an Increase in the t-Ratio on the Relation between Money an Bank Credit

public's preference as to holding bank deposits in the form of demand deposits versus time deposits leads to opposite movements in the stocks of M^1, M^2, and bank credit.

Historical Background

In the post-World War II period, changes in the public's desired allocation of bank deposits between demand and time deposits came to exercise a progressively more important influence on the money and bank credit process. As shown in Table 4.7, over the first six years of the postwar period the t-ratio averaged .4088 on a yearly basis. Over the next five years, 1953 through 1957, the average value for the t-ratio rose to .4640. The t-ratio then increased to .5895 on a yearly average basis over the next three years, reaching .6137 in 1960.

From 1960 through 1968 the rate of increase of the t-ratio accelerated. In 1968 the yearly average t-ratio reached 1.2963, approximately double the 1960 level and more than three times its 1947–1952 average. In other words, over the first six years of the postwar period, the public desired to hold, on average, about $41 of time deposits for each $100 of demand deposits. However, by 1968 a marked change had developed; for every $100 of demand deposits, the public held about $130 of time deposits.

The influence on the money supply and bank credit process of the portfolio decision by the public to hold a progressively larger proportion of bank deposits in time deposits can be seen by examining the data on the multipliers in Table 4.7.

TABLE 4.7

YEARLY AVERAGE VALUES FOR THE M^1, M^2 MULTIPLIERS, AND t-RATIO

Year	$m^1 = M^1/B^a$	$m^2 = M^2/B^a$	$t = T/D^p$
1947	2.503	3.269	0.4014
1948	2.456	3.239	0.4153
1949	2.466	3.271	0.4241
1950	2.626	3.471	0.4119
1951	2.546	3.341	0.3970
1952	2.576	3.392	0.4030
1953	2.600	3.468	0.4254
1954	2.655	3.611	0.4562
1955	2.776	3.792	0.4607
1956	2.786	3.827	0.4699
1957	2.783	3.903	0.5078
1958	2.795	4.063	0.5709
1959	2.889	4.235	0.5839
1960	2.861	4.257	0.6137
1961	2.928	4.525	0.6838
1962	2.896	4.691	0.7793
1963	2.903	4.927	0.8814
1964	2.868	5.047	0.9660
1965	2.845	5.235	1.0700
1966	2.811	5.343	1.1527
1967	2.761	5.453	1.2529
1968	2.769	5.568	1.2963
1969	2.784	5.528	1.2662
1970	2.739	5.456	1.2840

The money multiplier (m^1) increased from a yearly average of 2.529 over the 1947–1952 period to a peak of 2.928 in 1961. However, after 1961 the yearly average of the money multiplier decreased steadily, reaching an average of 2.739 in 1970. The long-run downward trend in the money multiplier from 1961 primarily reflected the rising t-ratio.

The m^2 multiplier increased over the postwar period from an average of 3.331 in the first six years to 5.568 in 1968, a 67 per cent increase. The increase of the m^2 multiplier was closely associated with the rising t-ratio. Especially after 1960 we note that the rapid increases of m^2, and the bank credit multiplier ($m^2 - 1$), are associated with the sharply rising t-ratio.

The year 1969 presents an interesting contrast. In 1969, for the first time since 1951, the m^2 multiplier declined from its average in the previous year.

Checking the t-ratio, it can be seen that this decline in m^2 is associated with a decline in the yearly average ratio of time to demand deposits. Although during several previous periods the t-ratio declined, 1969 was the first time since 1951 that the yearly average for the t-ratio fell from the previous year's level. The 1969 reduction in the t-ratio was associated with the prolonged effective constraint of Regulation *Q*.

Regulation Q

The authority to regulate the maximum interest rates that member commercial banks can pay on time deposits was granted to the Federal Reserve Board in the Banking Act of 1933. To implement its authority over time deposit interest rates, the Board issued Regulation *Q*, which became effective November 1, 1933. Since February 1, 1936, the maximum interest rates payable by all commercial banks insured by the Federal Deposit Insurance Corporation have been the same as Regulation *Q* rates in effect for member banks of the Federal Reserve System.

Regulation *Q*, along with the other banking reforms of the mid-1930's, was formulated against the background of the severe banking crisis of the early 1930's. Between 1929 and 1933 the number of commercial banks in operation declined from 24,970 to 14,207, and total bank deposits fell from $49.4 billion to $32.1 billion. The theme of the banking reforms was the safety and stability of the commercial banking system. The main reason given for the enactment of Regulation *Q* was to prevent destructive interest rate competition among banks.[15]

The ceiling rate on time deposit interest rates was initially set at 3 per cent on November 1, 1933, but was lowered in 1935 to 2½ per cent.[16] In 1936 the Board introduced a policy of differential rates on different classes of time deposits. The ceiling rate on time deposits maturing in less than 90 days was set at 1 per cent, and on those of 90 days to 6 months maturity the rate was set at 2 per cent. After January 1, 1936, the Regulation *Q* ceiling rates remained unchanged for 21 years. In the 1950's, as market rates began to rise above *Q* ceiling rates, the Federal Reserve made a slight upward adjustment, effective January 1, 1957, in Regulation *Q* rates of ½ per cent on time deposits payable in 90 days or more. The new rates remained in effect for five years. In January 1962, Regulation *Q* rates were changed again, and a further splintering of ceiling rates was introduced. During the next four years Regulation *Q* ceilings were

---

[15] The hypothesis that interest rate competition among banks leads to a greater danger of bank failures has been refuted by studies of bank behavior. George Benston in a detailed study of bank investment behavior concluded that the results of his study "are consistent with the hypothesis that, rather than being an indication of imprudent banking practices, higher rates of interest payment on demand deposits may be indicative of flexibility and strength in meeting withdrawal demands without failing.... Thus I found that the profit target hypothesis, which was used to support the prohibition of interest payments on demand deposits, has no basis in fact," George J. Benston, "Interest Payments on Demand Deposits and Bank Investment Behavior," *Journal of Political Economy*, LXXII (October 1964), 431–449.

[16] For a more complete history of Regulation *Q* see Charlotte E. Ruebling, "The Administration of Regulation *Q*," Federal Reserve Bank of St. Louis *Review*, February 1970, pp. 29–40 (available as Reprint No. 53).

revised upward three more times—in July 1963, November 1964, and December 1965.

The main reason for the upward adjustment of Regulation *Q* ceilings during the first half of the 1960's was to permit banks to respond competitively to rising yields on other market assets. From 1961 through 1964 balance of payments considerations related to an outflow of funds to higher rates abroad were often cited as a supplementary reason. In December 1965, the increase in Regulation *Q* was to permit an orderly expansion in bank credit as other policy instruments exercised additional restraint.

Over the first half of 1966, in order to continue aquiring high-yielding business loans, banks bid aggressively for time deposits. Large commercial banks, restricted under Regulation *Q* to a maximum rate of 4 per cent on passbook savings, began in early 1966 to compete for household savings by offering small denomination, nonnegotiable certificates of deposit. On these types of time deposits banks could pay up to 5½ per cent on less than 90-day maturities. In this manner commercial banks were able to compete directly with assets offered small savers by other financial institutions, such as savings and loans and mutual savings banks.[17]

In July 1966, the Federal Reserve Board lowered Regulation *Q* ceiling rates, and splintered other time deposit rates according to size of deposit. Specifically, the rate that commercial banks could offer on small denomination multiple maturity certificates of deposit with less than 90 days maturity was lowered to 4 per cent from 5½ per cent.[18] The significance of this action was that it marked an attempt by the Federal Reserve Board to use Regulation *Q* as a policy instrument to direct the flows of credit in the economy. Banks were to be constrained from competing with savings and loans for household savings.

After mid-1966 the Federal Reserve Board came increasingly to view Regulation *Q* not simply as a safeguard against destructive rate competition among banks, but as a means of selectively controlling bank credit and regulating the distribution of funds between commercial banks and other nonbank financial intermediaries. Table 4.8 gives the structure of Regulation *Q* ceiling rates from late 1965 to early 1970. A careful examination of the progressive splintering of the rate structure reveals that its purpose was to permit a control on the type of funds for which banks could compete.

In the 1966 through 1969 period, as yields on loans and securities rose, banks responding to the profit motive became very inventive in finding ways around Regulation *Q* ceiling rates—through Eurodollar borrowings and the issuance of commercial paper by bank holding companies.[19] The Federal Reserve found itself in the position of the little Dutch boy who tried to hold back the sea by sticking his fingers into the hole in the dike. The Federal

---

[17] See Albert E. Burger, "An Historical Analysis of the Credit Crunch of 1966," Federal Reserve Bank of St. Louis *Review*, September 1969, pp. 13–30 (available as Reprint No. 45).

[18] Multiple maturity time deposits include time deposits that are automatically renewable at maturity without action by the depositor and deposits that are payable after written notice of withdrawal.

[19] For an example of a very imaginative move to avoid the constraint of Regulation *Q*, see how First Pennsylvania Banking and Trust raised $20 million in funds by selling 30-month capital notes at $100 each and yielding 7¼ per cent. "Fast on his Feet in Philadelphia," *Business Week*, February 14, 1970, p. 76.

TABLE 4.8

MAXIMUM INTEREST RATES PAYABLE ON TIME AND SAVINGS DEPOSITS
(PER CENT PER ANNUM)

Type of deposit	Effective Date				
	Dec. 6, 1965	July 20, 1966	Sept. 26, 1966	April 19, 1968	Jan. 21 1970
Savings deposits	4	4	4	4	4½
Other time deposits					
Multiple maturity					
90 days or more		5	5	5	5
Less than 90 days (30–89 days)		4	4	4	4½
Single maturity					
Less than $100,000					
30 days to 1 year					5
1 year	5½	5½	5	5	5½
2 year					5¾
$100,000 or more					
30–59 days				5½	6¼
60–89 days				5¾	6½
90–179 days		5½	5½	6	6¾
180 days to 1 year				6¼	7
1 year or more				6¼	7½

Source: Federal Reserve *Bulletin*; such a table appears in each issue.

Reserve was frequently forced to extend and stretch the definition and applicability of Regulation *Q* to cover the rapidly developing loopholes.[20]

History of the Constraint of Regulation Q

The existence of conditions in which the Regulation *Q* ceiling rates effectively constrained commercial banks from competing for time deposits is a fairly recent phenomenon. Prior to 1966, every time the yields which banks offered on time deposits approached Regulation *Q* ($i^t \rightarrow Q^*$) such that banks were effectively constrained from offering yields on time deposits that were competitive with yields on other market assets (i^f), the Federal Reserve authorities raised Regulation *Q* ceiling rates. During the period 1962–1965,

[20] See "Amendment to Regulation *Q*" and "Interpretation of Regulation *Q*," Federal Reserve *Bulletin*, January 1970, pp. 37–38; and "Increase in Interest Rates and Proposed Change in Federal Reserve Requirements," Federal Reserve *Bulletin*, January 1970, pp. 105–106.

the Regulation Q ceiling rates were raised four times. In December 1965, when the discount rate was raised from 4 to $4\frac{1}{2}$ per cent, the Regulation Q ceiling rate on time deposits other than passbook accounts was raised from 4–$4\frac{1}{2}$ per cent to $5\frac{1}{2}$ per cent on all maturities of other time deposits. Indeed, in the period 1962–1965, the banking community came to expect that the Federal Reserve would not permit Regulation Q to effectively constrain banks from raising the yields on time deposits in order to compete with yields on other market assets.

However, in the first half of 1966, market interest rates rose sharply. By the end of June, large commercial banks had increased the yields they were offering on other time deposits, even on shortest maturities, to the Regulation Q ceiling of $5\frac{1}{2}$ per cent. In the summer of 1966, as yields on commercial paper and Treasury bills continued to rise, the Federal Reserve held Regulation Q ceiling rates at $5\frac{1}{2}$ per cent on large denomination CD's (certificates of deposit) and in late July lowered the ceiling rates on multiple maturity time certificates. It was not until April 19, 1968, that ceiling rates on time deposits were raised, and this time only for large denomination single maturity CD's with maturities over 60 days.

Figure 4.7 depicts the relationship on a monthly basis from mid-1965

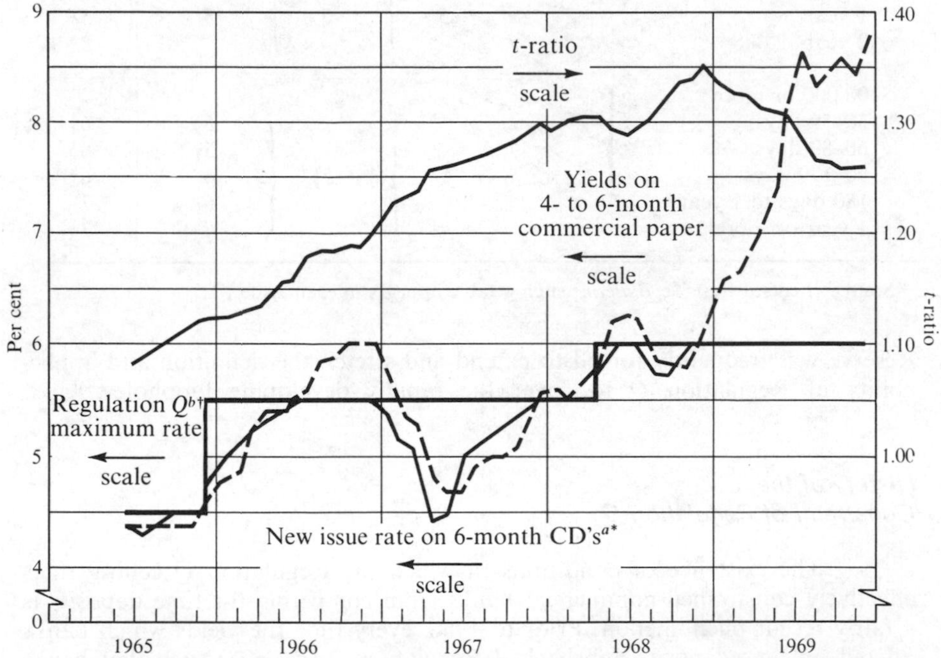

* Average new issue rates on six month certificates of deposit of $100,000 or more. Data are estimated by the Federal Reserve Bank of St. Louis from guide rates published in the Bond Buyer and are monthly averages of Wednesday figures.

† Rate on deposits in amounts of $100,000 or more maturing in 90–179 days.

Source: Federal Reserve Bank of St. Louis.

Figure 4.7 Relationship between the t-Ratio and Short-Term Interest Rates through 1969 among the t-ratio, credit market interest rates on assets competitive with time deposits (i^f), the yields offered by banks on time deposits (i^t), and Regulation Q. The interest rate on 4–6 month prime commercial paper is used as a proxy for the interest rate (i^f). The yield offered by banks on newly issued

TABLE 4.9

COMPARISON OF YIELD ON SHORT-TERM BUSINESS LOANS AND LARGE CD'S

Month	Short-Term Business Loans* (per cent per annum)	Difference between Yields On Short-term Business Loans and Large CD's (basis points)
1965		
Sept.	5.00	58
Dec.	5.27	52
1966		
Mar.	5.55	31
June	5.82	37
Sept.	6.30	80
Dec.	6.31	81
1967		
Feb.	6.13	100
May	5.95	148
Aug.	5.95	82
Nov.	5.96	52
1968		
Feb.	6.36	86
May	6.84	84
Aug.	6.89	114
Nov.	6.61	61
1969		
Feb.	7.32	132
May	7.86	186
Aug.	8.82	282
Nov.	8.83	283

* Weighted average rates.

Source: Federal Reserve *Bulletin*.

certificates of deposit in denominations of $100,000 and over with 6 months' maturity is used as a proxy for the rate (i^t). Table 4.9 gives the spread between the rate on large CD's and the average yield on bank business loans.

Over the last half of 1965 and first half of 1966, as market interest rates rose, the banks responded by raising the yields offered on time deposits. The average offering rate on large CD's rose from 4.38 per cent in June 1965, to

TABLE 4.10

MEMBER BANKS CHANGING THE MAXIMUM RATE PAID ON TIME AND SAVINGS DEPOSITS OF INDIVIDUALS, PARTNERSHIPS AND CORPORATIONS (IPC) SELECTED PERIODS

Periods	Percent of Banks Surveyed Raising or Lowering Rates	Consumer-Type Time*		Business-Type Time†		Savings Deposit
		Size of Bank		Size of Bank		Size of Bank
		All Sizes	Total Deposits of $100 Million and Over	All Sizes	Total Deposits of $100 Million and Over	All Sizes
May 11, 1966, to January 31, 1967	Raising rates	54.0		71.0		9.0
January 31, 1967, to April 28, 1967	Lowering rates	4.6	16.2	20.6	49.3	0.5
April 28, 1967, to July 31, 1967	Raising rates	5.4	15.1	14.1	34.5	0.8
July 31, 1967, to October 31, 1967	Raising rates	4.3	5.6	16.0	35.5	1.0

* Certificates of deposit less than $100,000.

† Certificates of deposit over $100,000.

Source: Federal Reserve *Bulletin*.

4.95 in January 1966; it then rose to 5.45 in June. In the notation employed in the previous sections,

$$\varepsilon(i^t, i^f) > 0.$$

Although the banks' marginal cost of time deposits rose sharply, the yield on short-term business loans also increased markedly. If the available yields on business loans had remained at the June 1965 levels, then it would not have been profitable for banks to pay 5.45 per cent for time deposits. However, since business loan rates rose to an average of 5.82 in June 1966, banks were willing to raise i^t to induce the public to increase its holdings of time deposits relative to demand deposits. During this period, as interest rates rose, the t-ratio increased. Hence,

$$\varepsilon(t, i) > 0.$$

By early July 1966, the yields banks were offering on time deposits were at Regulation Q ceiling levels. Market-determined interest rates continued to rise. The spread between the now fixed marginal cost of time deposits and yields on business loans widened. The spread increased from 37 basis points in June to 80 basis points in September. The banks were willing, but unable, to raise time deposit yields. In terms of elasticities,

$$\varepsilon(i^t, i^f) = 0;$$

and hence

$$\varepsilon(t, i) \rightarrow 0.$$

In mid-December 1966, market yields began to decline and the banks began to lower the rates offered on time deposits from the 5.5 per cent ceiling rate to 4.45 per cent in April 1967. The banks maintained i^t at a high enough level so that the t-ratio increased. Although banks reduced i^t, they did not lower their offering rates enough to cause the t-ratio to remain constant or decline. Examining Table 4.11, the explanation of the banks' behavior becomes apparent. By February 1967, the spread between i^t and the yield on short-term business loans had risen to 100 basis points, and in May it increased to 148 basis points.

In the April-May period of 1967 the downward trend of i^f was reversed. Banks responded by raising yields on time deposits. The competitive response by the banks offset the negative effect of the rise in yields of other financial assets on the t-ratio, and the t-ratio continued to increase. In mid-December 1967, $i^t = Q^*$ and the rise in the t-ratio came to a halt. In April 1968, Regulation Q ceilings were raised to 6 per cent. However, market rates (i^f) and yields offered by banks (i^t) rose rapidly, and by mid-May again $i^t = Q^*$. As i^f continued to rise, the t-ratio declined through mid-June 1968.

Credit market yields began to decline in the latter half of June 1968. The decline continued until early October. Again, concurrently with the fall in i^f, yields offered by banks on time deposits eased from the 6 per cent ceiling rate in June to an average of 5.73 per cent in September. In August 1968, the spread between the rate on bank business loans and the rate on large CD's had increased to 114 basis points compared to approximately 85 basis points

TABLE 4.11

AVERAGE OFFERING RATES AT MEMBER BANKS ON TIME AND SAVINGS DEPOSITS, IPC, SURVEY DATES, 1967

Type of Deposit	Most Common Rate, 1967			
	January 31	April 28	July 31	October 31
Total time and savings deposits	4.31	4.19	4.29	4.33
Savings deposits	3.91	3.91	3.91	3.91
Consumer-type time deposits—less than $100,000	4.83	4.77	4.83	4.85
Business-type time deposits—$100,000 and over	5.19	4.45	4.89	5.09

Source: Federal Reserve *Bulletin*. January 1968, p. 47.

over the first half of 1968. Again, as in the first part of 1967, banks did not reduce i^t enough so that the t-ratio declined. As other market rates fell, banks were able to reduce i^t. However, they maintained offering yields on time deposits high enough relative to other market rates to attract an increased volume of time deposits.

In early October credit market interest rates reversed and began to rise. Banks responded, as the hypothesis predicts, by raising i^t. The t-ratio continued to increase, reaching 1.35 by mid-December. By late November, banks raised their offering rates to the Q ceilings, $i^t = Q^*$. Credit market interest rates on financial assets competitive with time deposits continued to shoot up rapidly. The $\varepsilon(i^t, i^f)$ became zero, and $\varepsilon(t, i)$ became negative. By mid-December the decline in the t-ratio predicted by the hypothesis had begun. With the competitive ability of banks effectively constrained by Regulation Q ceiling rates, the t-ratio exhibited a sharp decline throughout 1969.[21]

Additional information on the response of commercial banks to changes in credit market interest rates may be gained by examining some of the results of the Federal Reserve System's surveys of changes in time and savings deposits at commercial banks.[22] Table 4.10 gives the percentage of member banks raising or lowering their offering rates on classes of time deposits over the period from May 1966, through October 1967.

As shown in Figure 4.7, during the period from May 1966, through late 1966 credit market interest rates rose sharply. Referring to Table 4.10, it can be seen that commercial banks responded by raising the yields they offered on time deposits. From May, 1966 to January 1967, 54 per cent of the reporting member banks raised the rates they offered on consumer-type time

[21] From a peak of $204.9 billion in December 1968, total time deposits declined to $192.0 billion in February 1970. The outstanding volume of large certificates of deposit decreased from about $23.5 billion to $10.5 billion over the same period.

[22] The results of these surveys are reported in the following issues of the Federal Reserve *Bulletin:* April, July, August, 1966; April, July, September, 1967; January, July, 1968; March, May, July, October, 1969; March, May, September, 1970.

deposits, and 71 per cent raised the rates they offered on business-type time deposits (certificate of deposits of over $100,000).

In mid-December 1966, credit market interest rates began a sharp decline which lasted until about mid-June 1967. From January 1967 to April 1967, banks responded by markedly lowering the rates they offered on time deposits. Forty-nine per cent of the member banks with deposits of $100 million and over lowered rates offered on business-type time deposits. Table 4.11 shows that the most common rate paid on business-type time deposits fell from 5.19 per cent in January 1967, to 4.45 per cent by late April.

After mid-June, interest rates began another period of steep increase. The banks reversed their policy of lowering yields on time deposits and began to raise yields (i^t). Referring again to Table 4.10, we see that from late April to the end of July, 34.5 per cent of the large member banks raised rates on business-type deposits and 15 per cent raised rates on consumer-type time deposits. Table 4.11 shows that the most common rate on business-type time deposits of $100,000 and over rose from 4.45 to 4.89 per cent.

As credit market interest rates continued to rise through October 1967, the banks continued to competitively respond by raising yields. From the end of July to the end of October, 35.5 per cent of the large member banks raised offering yields on business-type deposits; and the most common rate on these deposits rose from 4.89 per cent to 5.09 per cent.

Credit market interest rates continued to rise sharply from October 1967, through June 1968. Banks continued to respond to the competitive pressure of rising market yields by raising the rates they offered on time deposits. As shown in Table 4.12 from July 31, 1967 to January 31, 1968, about 65 per cent of the commercial banks with over $100 million deposits raised their most common offering rate on business-type time deposits over $100,000. From January 31 to April 30, 1968, 40 per cent made further upward revisions in their rates, and over the next three months 45 per cent further raised their rates. Table 4.13 shows that by July 31, 1968, the most common interest rate paid by banks on large time deposits of business had risen to 5.88 per cent from 4.89 per cent a year earlier.

From June through mid-October 1968, market interest rates turned downward. Banks reacted by reducing the yields they were offering on time deposits. Thirty-seven per cent of the banks lowered their rates on business time deposits, and the most common rate paid eased to 5.71 per cent by the end of October 1968.

After October, credit market rates began another sharp upward climb. As can be seen in Table 4.13, banks responded by raising offering rates on time deposits. By January 31, 1969, the most common rate on large CD's had risen to 5.98 per cent.

Currency Ratio

The public's decision as to its allocation of its money balances between currency and bank money is summarized in the k-ratio. The dependence of the k-ratio is expressed in relation (4.5):

$$k = f(q, Y/Y_p,\ Tx,\ s,\ W). \qquad (4.5)$$

TABLE 4.12

INSURED COMMERCIAL BANKS CHANGING THE MOST COMMON RATE PAID ON NEW TIME AND SAVINGS DEPOSITS, IPC, SELECTED PERIODS
(PER CENT)

Periods	Per Cent of Banks Surveyed Raising or Lowering Rates	Consumer-Type Time Deposits*		Business-Type Time Deposits†		Savings Deposits
		Size of Bank		Size of Bank		Size of Bank
		All Sizes	Total Deposits of $100 Million and Over	All Sizes	Total Deposits of $100 Million and Over	All Sizes
July 31, 1967, to January 31, 1968	Raising rates	28.2	24.5	31.9	64.5	7.3
January 31 to April 30, 1968	Raising rates	8.0	3.9	21.1	40.2	2.4
April 30 to July 31, 1968	Raising rates	10.1	3.7	25.3	45.2	3.6
July 31 to October, 1968	Lowering rates	2.6	0.4	16.2	37.1	0.8
October 31, 1968 to January 31, 1969	Raising rates	5.4	2.0	25.2	57.2	2.8
January 31 to April 30, 1969	Raising rates	4.9	1.7	22.5	30.7	2.4
April 30 to July 31, 1969	Raising rates	4.2	1.7	20.2	23.8	2.7
July 31 to October 31, 1969	Raising rates	1.1	0.8	17.0	20.6	1.7

* Certificates of deposit less than $100,000.

† Certificates of deposit over $100,000.

Source: Federal Reserve *Bulletin*, July 1968, pp. 600, 601; March 1969, pp. 206, 207; May 1969, p. 418; July 1969, p. 590; October 1969, p. 814; March 1790, p. 223.

TABLE 4.13

AVERAGE OF MOST COMMON INTEREST RATES PAID ON TIME AND SAVINGS DEPOSITS, IPC, AT INSURED COMMERCIAL BANKS

Type of Deposit	Most Common Rate							
	1968				1969			
	Jan. 31	April 30	July 31	Oct. 31	Jan. 31	April 30	July 31	Oct. 31
Total time and savings deposits	4.39	4.44	4.50	4.50	4.54	4.55	4.53	4.51
Savings deposits	3.90	3.91	3.92	3.93	3.93	3.94	3.94	3.95
Total consumer-type time deposits	4.92	4.94	4.97	4.97	4.98	4.99	4.99	4.99
Business-type time deposits—								
less than $100,000*	4.91	4.90	4.94	4.93	4.95	4.97	4.96	4.96
negotiable CD's (over $100,000)	5.40	5.72	5.88	5.71	5.98	6.05	6.09	6.05

* Includes CD's and small-denomination time deposits, open account, other than those in passbook or statement form.

Source: Federal Reserve *Bulletin*, July 1968, pp. 588, 589; March 1969, p. 195; May 1969, p. 412; July 1969, p. 584; October 1969, p. 808; March 1970, p. 216.

In (4.5) the currency ratio is stated to depend upon the factors

q = measure of net service charges on demand deposits,
Tx = public's tax liabilities,
Y/Y_p = ratio of net national product to permanent net national product,
s = mobility of the population and such factors as seasonal patterns introduced by vacation schedules,
W = nominal wealth of the nonbank public.

Historical Background. The public's decision as to the allocation of its money balances between currency and demand deposits has at times exercised an important influence on the money supply process. In the early part of the 1930's the k-ratio doubled, going from an average of .159 in 1929 to .324 in 1933. From 1933 to the end of the 1930's the k-ratio fell sharply, reaching an average of .213 in 1939–1940.

From the early 1940's through the war years the k-ratio again rose sharply. In the post-war period the k-ratio declined rapidly, reaching .258 in 1955. From 1955 through 1962 the yearly average for the k-ratio showed little change. Since 1962 the k-ratio has begun a slow upward trend reaching .292 in 1969, about the same as its average level in 1949–1950.[23]

The k-Ratio and Interest Rates. The k-ratio is defined as the ratio of currency (C^p) to demand deposits (D^p). The quantity of demand deposits the public desires to hold is partly dependent upon the yields available on time deposits and other credit market assets, and may be partly sensitive to interest rates. If it is assumed that the public's demand for currency does not depend upon the interest rate, then the elasticity of the k-ratio with respect to interest rates may be written as

$$\varepsilon(k, i) = -\ \varepsilon(D^p, i).$$

Since

$$\varepsilon(D^p, i) < 0,$$

then

$$\varepsilon(k, i) > 0.$$

The elasticity of D^p with respect to the interest rate depends partially upon the yields on time deposits. As the yields on time deposits rise, the public may be willing to hold a smaller amount of demand deposits relative to their holdings of currency. For example, the rise in the k-ratio in the 1962–1969 period may partly reflect the rising yields on time deposits.

The extent of the dependence of the k-ratio on interest rates is an

---

[23] For an analysis of factors influencing the historical behavior of the currency ratio, see Phillip Cagan, "The Demand for Currency Relative to the Total Money Supply," *Journal of Political Economy*, August 1958, pp. 303–328.

empirical question.[24] To avoid further complicating the analysis of the money supply process, we shall make the assumption that $\varepsilon(k, i)$ is small in numerical value. Hence, in the following discussion the possible influence of changes in interest rates on the multipliers through the dependence of the k-ratio on interest rates is omitted. If the reader wishes to include interest rate effects on the k-ratio, they may be added in a straight-forward manner to the analysis presented in this book.

Dependence of the Multipliers: A General View

The multipliers associate a definite amount of the aggregates M^1, M^2, and bank credit with any given stock of base. The values assumed by all three multipliers depend upon the values of a vector of policy parameters, a vector of bank behavioral parameters, and a vector of behavioral parameters determined by the public.

Let

$$X_1 = \begin{bmatrix} r^t \\ r^d \\ \rho \\ d \\ Q \\ \pi_2 \end{bmatrix} = \text{vector of policy parameters,}$$

$$X_2 = \begin{bmatrix} v \\ e \\ b \\ i^t \end{bmatrix} = \text{vector of behavioral parameters determined by actions of the banks,}$$

$$X_3 = \begin{bmatrix} t \\ k \\ \pi_1 \\ \delta \end{bmatrix} = \text{vector of behavioral parameters determined by actions of the public.}$$

---

[24] Ronald Teigen, using quarterly data for the period 1/53 through IV/64, found there was a significant positive relationship between changes in the currency ratio and the yields on Treasury bills and a weighted average rate on time deposits at banks and savings and loans. See Teigen, "An Aggregated Quarterly Model of the U.S. Monetary Sector, 1953–1964," *Targets and Indicators of Monetary Policy*, *op. cit.*, pp. 180–181.

For a more recent discussion, see J. Carl Poindexter, Jr., "The Currency-Holding Behavior of the Public and the Strength of Monetary Controls," New York University Graduate School of Business Administration, *The Bulletin*, No. 67, November 1970.

Then in general form we can write the functional dependence of the multipliers in the form

$$m = f(X_1, X_2, X_3).$$

The derived quantities, the multipliers, are very important in the analysis of the money and bank credit processes. The multipliers link changes in the net source base to changes in the stocks of money (M^1, and M^2) and bank credit. The size of the multipliers determines the amount of money and bank credit that will be supplied to the economy for any given stock of base. Hence the effect of policy actions by the Federal Reserve also depends upon the multipliers. For example, if the value of the money multiplier falls sharply between two points in time, then the increase in the money supply resulting from an increase in B^a is smaller than previously. Without taking the change in the multiplier into account, the Federal Reserve might view its open market operations increasing the base as simply trying to "push on a string."

By explicitly deriving the multipliers, the framework of the hypothesis permits us to analyze and predict changes in the multipliers. Changes in behavioral actions of the banks and the public as they affect the money and bank credit process can be taken into account. As an illustration, a severe liquidity crisis in the financial markets and/or a sharp downturn in economic activity might lead to a considerable rise in the public's desired currency ratio and a rise in the banks' desired excess reserve ratio. These factors would lower the value of the multipliers. The Federal Reserve would observe that the same percentage change in B^a as before, under these changed economic conditions, had very little effect in expanding the money supply. This does not mean the Federal Reserve can no longer exercise control over the money stock by expanding B^a. The Federal Reserve has not suddenly been put in the proverbial position of "pushing on a string." This change in the economic environment, reflected in the lower value of the money multiplier, means simply that the same degree of expansion of the money stock cannot be expected from the same degree of expansion of the base as previously.

Adjustment Mechanism

The mechanism by which the financial system moves toward an equilibrium position—a point at which the public's and banks' actual ratios equal their desired ratios—is a portfolio adjustment process. Economic units are viewed as seeking those combinations (portfolios) of assets within their wealth constraint that they most prefer to hold. Banks, nonbank financial intermediaries, other business firms, and individuals restructure their portfolios of real and financial assets in response to changes in yields, prices, and other factors. Therefore, when an adjustment process is mentioned, it should be understood as referring specifically to a portfolio adjustment process by the banks and the public.

A policy action by the Federal Reserve alters the composition of the stock of assets held by banks and the public and/or alters the values of parameters such as r^d, r^t, and Q^* that enter into the decision functions of the banks and the public. The commercial banks are viewed as holding a portfolio of assets which consists of borrowed reserves, nonborrowed reserves, and earning assets. The proportion of their total assets which banks desire to hold in each of the three categories is functionally dependent upon such factors as the market interest rate, the discount rate (ρ), and the legal reserve requirement ratios r^d and r^t.

Similarly, asset behavior of the public with regard to their composition of money balances and bank deposits is summarized in the currency (k) and time deposit (t) ratios. The public is viewed as making portfolio decisions as to whether to hold their money balances as currency or deposits at commercial banks (summarized in the k-ratio), and whether to hold their bank deposits in the form of demand deposits or time deposits (summarized in the t-ratio). A change in the actual k or t-ratio from the desired k or t-ratio, or a change in one of the factors which functionally determine the desired or equilibrium values of the k or t-ratio, will result in a portfolio adjustment process on the part of the public.

As an illustration, suppose the Federal Reserve System makes an open market purchase of government securities from the banks. The banks' holdings of base (reserves) are increased. This appears as a rise in the banks' actual excess reserve ratio (e-ratio). The Federal Reserve action has altered the banks' asset portfolio. Assuming that the banks' demand for excess reserves is a stable function of interest rates, a portfolio adjustment is undertaken by the banks. The banks are holding a larger portion of their assets in nonearning assets (reserves) than they desire to hold given the prevailing yields on loans and municipal securities. The banks expand their holdings of earning assets and, in the process by which the banks adjust their asset portfolios, the nonbank public's holdings of bank money (D^p) rises. The increase in D^p alters the public's actual k-ratio and t-ratio. The change in the k-ratio and t-ratio from their desired values then leads to a portfolio adjustment by the public, which feeds back into the money supply and bank credit processes.

Changes in Regulation Q ceiling rates affect the response of the yields that banks offer on time deposits to changes in market yields on other assets (i^f). Through the dependence of the t-ratio on i^t, the t-ratio is influenced by changes in Regulation Q. Changes in the Treasury's administration of its cash balances affect D^t and hence alter the d-ratio.

Actual and Desired Ratios

At any point in time any of the ratios in this chapter may be calculated by collecting the necessary data and performing the required arithmetic. For example, the value of the banks' borrowing ratio at a point in time may be determined by dividing member bank borrowings by all commercial banks' total nonbank deposit liabilities. The r, b, k, t, and d-ratios calculated in this manner are the *actual* ratios at that point in time.

However, the desired r, b, k, t, and d-ratios are determined by the public, banks, and the Treasury. As an illustration, the ratio of borrowings from Federal Reserve Banks to nonbank deposit liabilities which the banks *desire* to maintain depends upon the interest rate, discount rate, and other factors such as the administration of the discount window. Likewise, the public's *desired* allocation of their bank deposits between demand and time deposits depends upon factors such as the yields that banks are offering on time deposits and the yields that are available on alternative assets. At any point in time, we can calculate the actual values of these ratios, but these actual values are not necessarily the desired values.

Likewise, a definite amount of base is supplied to the banks and the public by the actions of the monetary authorities. However, it is not necessarily true that the amount of base held is the amount the banks and the public desire to hold given their holdings of other assets and the prices of other assets. Let us denote desired holdings with an asterisk (*). Then actual holdings of net source base equal desired holdings only when

$$B^a = B^{a*},$$
$$V = V^*,$$
$$R^m = R^{m*},$$
$$C^p = C^{p*}.$$

If desired holdings of base are unequal to actual holdings, then the actual r-ratio and actual k-ratio will not be equal to the banks' desired r-ratio (r^*) or the public's desired k-ratio (k^*). For example if

$$R^{m*} > R^m, \qquad V^* = V,$$

then

$$r^* > r.$$

Nonmember banks are holding the amount of base (vault cash) that they desire to hold given their deposit liabilities. However, member banks desire to hold a larger amount of base (reserves), given their deposit liabilities, than they now hold. Hence, member banks attempt to increase their holdings of reserves, and the result is a decrease in bank deposits.

Likewise, if $r^* = r$. but $C^p > C^{p*}$, the nonbank public is holding less base (currency) than it desires to hold. The public attempts to build up its holdings of currency to the desired level C^{p*} by exercising its instant repurchase agreement with the banks, exchanging bank money for currency. Banks adjust their portfolios to the drain of base out of the banks, and bank deposits fall. Hence, the k-ratio changes, approaching the public's desired k-ratio.

If $r^* = r$ and $k^* = k$, but the public desires to hold a greater amount of time deposits relative to demand deposits, $t^* > t$, then an adjustment process will result. The public uses demand deposits to buy time deposits. This action by the public results in $r^* < r$, and banks adjust their portfolios. In the adjustment process the amount of bank credit and bank money change until $t^* = t$, $r^* = r$, and $k^* = k$.

Although at any point in time when the ratios in the multiplier are measured and the desired ratios are not equal to the actual ratios, the adjustment of actual ratios to desired ratios is rapid. For example, suppose member banks compute their ratio of excess reserves to deposits and find that it exceeds or falls short of their desired e-ratio they then rapidly adjust this ratio by buying or selling federal funds, altering their borrowings from Federal Reserve Banks, or buying or selling securities.

Chapter Five

Dependence of the Multipliers on the Bank Credit Market Interest Rate

The interest rate (i) is a composite interest rate index of the yields on loans and other financial assets traded in the government securities, municipal bond, mortgage, and loan markets in which commercial banks traditionally operate. In the money supply and bank credit processes, the dependence of the excess reserve ratio (e), borrowing ratio (b), and the time deposit ratio (t) on the interest rate (i) imposes a dependence of the money and bank credit multipliers on the interest rate.

The elasticities of the multipliers with respect to interest rates in a general form are as follows:

$$\varepsilon(m, i) = \varepsilon(m, e) \cdot \varepsilon(e, i) + \varepsilon(m, b) \cdot \varepsilon(b, i) + \varepsilon(m, t) \cdot \varepsilon(t, i).$$

The total elasticities of the multipliers *with respect to* the interest rate depend upon (1) the respective elasticities of the excess reserve ratio, borrowing ratio, and time deposit ratio *with respect to* the interest rate, and (2) the elasticities of the multipliers *with respect to* these ratios, which summarize the behavior of the banks and the public.

From our previous discussion the following signs may be specified:

$$\varepsilon(e, i) < 0, \qquad \varepsilon(m, e) < 0,$$
$$\varepsilon(b, i) > 0, \qquad \varepsilon(m, b) > 0.$$

Initial Conditions[1]

To specify the sign of the elasticities of the terms in the expression for $\varepsilon(m, i)$ and to specify also the sign of the elasticity of the t-ratio with respect

[1] For an introductory discussion of initial conditions and their importance in explanations of economic events, see Appendix I at the end of this chapter.

to the interest rate, we must consider the initial conditions or constraints previously introduced.

1. As market interest rates rise (fall) the e-ratio declines (rises), hence

$$\varepsilon(m, e) \to 0 \qquad \text{as interest rates rise,}$$
$$|\varepsilon(m, e)| \qquad \text{increases (declines) as interest rates fall (rise).}$$

2. As market interest rates rise (fall), the b-ratio rises (falls), hence

$$\varepsilon(m, b) \qquad \text{increases (falls) as interest rates rise (fall).}$$

3. The total cost to member banks of borrowing from the Federal Reserve includes the discount rate and any additional costs due to administration of the discount window (π_2). This is expressed as follows:

$$\varepsilon(b, i) \to 0 \qquad \text{as } \pi_2 \text{ increases.}$$

4. When banks are constrained by Regulation Q, as market interest rates rise, banks can no longer respond in a competitive manner by raising the yields they offer on time deposits. This is summarized as

$$\varepsilon(i^t, i^f) > 0 \qquad i^t \text{ is sufficiently below } Q^*,$$
$$\varepsilon(i^t, i^f) \to 0 \qquad \text{as } i^t \text{ approaches } Q^*,$$
$$\varepsilon(i^t, i^f) = 0 \qquad \text{when } i^t = Q^* \text{ and } i^f \text{ is sufficiently above } i^t.$$

Relation between the Elasticities for the Different Multipliers

The sign of the elasticity of the money multiplier with respect to the t-ratio is opposite to the sign of the elasticity of the M^2 and bank credit multipliers:

$$\varepsilon(m^1, t) < 0$$
$$\varepsilon(m^2, t),\ \varepsilon(m^2 - 1, t) > 0.$$

Also, it has been shown (on page 37) that the following ordering relation holds:

$$\varepsilon(m^2 - 1, t) > \varepsilon(m^2, t).$$

With respect to the excess reserve ratio and the borrowing ratio, the following results may be derived:

$$|\varepsilon(m^1, e)| = |\varepsilon(m^2, e)| < |\varepsilon(m^2 - 1, e)|,$$
$$\varepsilon(m^1, b) = \varepsilon(m^2, b) < \varepsilon(m^2 - 1, b).$$

The elasticity of the bank credit multiplier with respect to the e-ratio and b-ratio is greater in absolute value than the elasticity of either the money or M^2 multipliers. The elasticities of the M^2 and money multipliers, with respect to the borrowing ratio and excess reserve ratio, are equal.

Relative Responses of the M^2 and Bank Credit Multipliers to Changes in Interest Rates

To examine the implications of the hypothesis for changes in interest rates on m^2 and $m^2 - 1$, let us write out the elasticities of these multipliers with respect to interest rates as

$$\varepsilon(m^2, i) = \frac{\partial m^2}{\partial i} \cdot \frac{i}{m^2},$$

$$\varepsilon(m^2 - 1, i) = \frac{\partial(m^2 - 1)}{\partial i} \cdot \frac{i}{m^2 - 1}.$$

Since under the constraint of the hypothesis

$$\frac{\partial m^2}{\partial i} = \frac{\partial(m^2 - 1)}{\partial i},$$

we may derive the following ordering relation between the responses of the bank credit and M^2 multiplier with respect to interest rates:[2]

$$\varepsilon(m^2 - 1, i) > \varepsilon(m^2, i).$$

Three Cases for the Elasticities of the Multipliers with Respect to Interest Rates

In order to summarize the discussion in this chapter, three cases are presented. When moving from one case to the next, basic initial conditions are altered. These examples illustrate the crucial importance of clearly specifying initial conditions. They also show the effects on the derivable consequences of the hypothesis of altering these conditions.

For the following cases, and in the rest of the book, a basic assumption about bank behavior is specified:

> Commercial banks attempt to maximize profits subject to the constraints under which they must operate.

---

[2] The reader may note that, although the absolute changes in m^2 and $m^2 - 1$ for a given change in i are the same, since $m^2 - 1$ is smaller than m^2, for a given absolute change, the percentage change in $m^2 - 1$ is larger than the percentage change in m^2.

An important point to note is that if banks do not behave as "profit maximizers," this does not mean the hypothesis must be discarded. Such a circumstance would only imply that the derivable consequences of the hypothesis would be modified.

Case I

Initial conditions:

(1.1) Market interest rates, relative to past historical averages, are at low levels.
(1.2) Yields that banks are offering on time deposits are well below Regulation Q ceiling rates.

Under initial condition (1.1), the banks' desired e-ratio is large and their desired b-ratio small in numerical value. Also, because of the low yields available on market assets, banks would tend to vary i^t in response to i^f only enough to maintain their existing stock of time deposits. Hence, under case I conditions

$$\varepsilon(m, b) \rightarrow 0,$$
$$\varepsilon(t, i) \rightarrow 0.$$

Therefore, the last two terms in the total elasticity of the multipliers approach zero, and the elasticity of the multipliers with respect to interest rates reduces approximately to the following:

$$\varepsilon(m, i) = \varepsilon(m, e) \cdot \varepsilon(e, i).$$

Since the sign of the elasticity of the e-ratio with respect to interest rates is negative, the total elasticities of all three multipliers with respect to interest rates have a positive sign:

$$\varepsilon(m, i) > 0.$$

From the previous analysis (page 100), we have the condition that

$$|\varepsilon(m^1, e)|, |\varepsilon(m^2, e)| < |\varepsilon(m^2 - 1, e)|.$$

The following ordering relation results:

$$0 < \varepsilon(m^1, i), \varepsilon(m^2, i) < \varepsilon(m^2 - 1, i).$$

The ordering relation between the money and M^2 multipliers depends upon whether $\varepsilon(t, i)$ is positive or equal to zero. If we assume that as interest rates rise, banks are willing to raise i^t to induce some increase in the t-ratio, so that $\varepsilon(t, i) > 0$, then the following ordering relations result:

$$0 < \varepsilon(m^1, i) < \varepsilon(m^2, i) < \varepsilon(m^2 - 1, i).$$

Case II

Initial conditions:

(2.1) Market interest rates rise from low levels to medium levels.

(2.2) As market interest rates rise, banks raise i^t, and i^t approaches Regulation Q ceiling rates.

(2.3) As the level of member bank borrowing rises, Federal Reserve Banks begin to exercise closer administrative control over member bank borrowings. $\pi_2 > 0$.

A major change in initial conditions for case II involves altering the assumption about the level of interest rates. At the start of case II it is assumed that interest rates have risen from the low levels associated with case I conditions. Interest rates are assumed to rise through case II, reaching, at the end of case II, high levels relative to their past historical averages.

As market interest rates rise from the low levels of case I, banks' desired holdings of excess reserves relative to deposit liabilities, fall, and banks' desired borrowings to deposit ratio rises. At the medium range of interest rates, characteristic of case II, the banks' desired e-ratio is smaller and their desired b-ratio larger than under case I initial conditions. In the first phase of case II, as interest rates rise, the b-ratio begins to exert a larger influence, hence increasing the numerical value of the $\varepsilon(m, i)$.

As yields available on earning assets rise, the banks bid aggressively for time deposits by raising the yields they offer:

$$\varepsilon(i^t, i^f) > 0,$$
$$\varepsilon(t, i) > 0.$$

The rising t-ratio dampens the interest-rate-induced increase in the money multiplier, but accelerates the rate of increase of the M^2 and bank credit multipliers.

As the volume of member bank borrowings continues to rise, the Federal Reserve Banks begin to exercise tighter administrative control over member bank use of the discount window. The response of member bank borrowings to increases in the interest rate decreases, approaching in limit zero. Thus,

$$\varepsilon(b, i) \to 0;$$

and as a result

$$\varepsilon(m, b) \cdot \varepsilon(b, i) \to 0.$$

As market rates continue to rise and banks respond by raising i^t, the yields offered by banks on time deposits approach Regulation Q ceiling rates:

$$i^t \to Q^*,$$

and therefore

$$\varepsilon(t, i) \to 0.$$

As the constraint of Q^* becomes effective, the interest-rate-induced rise in the M^2 and bank credit multipliers is dampened, and the dampening effect of a rising t-ratio on the money multiplier is reduced.

At the *upper end* of case II, initial conditions are:

$$\varepsilon(b, i) \to 0,$$
$$\varepsilon(t, i) \to 0,$$
$$\varepsilon(m, e) \to 0.$$

The total interest elasticities of all three multipliers approach zero:

$$\varepsilon(m^1, i),\ \varepsilon(m^2, i),\ \varepsilon(m^2 - 1, i) \to 0.$$

Case III

Initial conditions:

(3.1) Interest rates rise to high levels.

(3.2) The yields that banks are offering on time deposits are at the Regulation Q ceiling rates.

(3.3) The Federal Reserve Banks are exercising close administrative control over member bank borrowings so that the total cost of member bank borrowings considerably exceeds the discount rate.

When, relative to past average levels, interest rates are at very high levels the banks' opportunity cost of holding excess reserves becomes very high, and the e-ratio becomes small. Under initial condition (3.3) the response of the aggregate level of member bank borrowings to increases in interest rates is curtailed. Therefore, under case III conditions

$\varepsilon(m, e) \cdot \varepsilon(e, i)$ is approximately zero,
$\varepsilon(m, b) \cdot \varepsilon(b, i)$ is approximately zero.[3]

[3] It is the aggregate level of member bank borrowings that has a fixed upper level. The b-ratio is the ratio of member bank borrowings to deposits. Therefore, if deposits continue to rise, it is possible that the calculated value of $\varepsilon(b, i)$ may become negative.

Under initial condition (3.2), banks are unable to respond competitively to the negative influence of rising market rates on time deposits:

$$\varepsilon(i^t, i^f) = 0.$$

The $\varepsilon(t, i^f)$ dominates the response of the t-ratio and hence the sign of the elasticity of the t-ratio with respect to the interest rate becomes negative:

$$\varepsilon(t, i) < 0.$$

Restating the expression for the total elasticities of the multipliers, we have

$$\varepsilon(m, i) = \varepsilon(m, e) \cdot \varepsilon(e, i) + \varepsilon(m, b) \cdot \varepsilon(b, i) + \varepsilon(m, t) \cdot \varepsilon(t, i).$$

We see that since the numerical values of the first two terms of the expression become small, the sign and numerical value of the term $\varepsilon(m, t) \cdot \varepsilon(t, i)$ dominates the sign and numerical value of the total elasticities of the multipliers with respect to the interest rate index (i).

For the m^1 multiplier, since

$$\varepsilon(m^1, t) < 0,$$
$$\varepsilon(t, i) < 0,$$

then the elasticity of the M^1 multiplier with respect to the interest rate is positive:

$$\varepsilon(m^1, i) > 0.$$

For the m^2 and bank credit multipliers, since

$$\varepsilon(m^2, t) > 0,$$

then the elasticities of the M^2 and bank credit multipliers with respect to the interest rate are negative:

$$\varepsilon(m^2, i) < 0,$$
$$\varepsilon(m^2 - 1, i) < 0.$$

Also, since the elasticity of the bank credit multiplier with respect to the t-ratio is greater than the elasticities of m^2 and m^1 with respect to the t-ratio, the following ordering relation prevails:

$$| \varepsilon(m^2 - 1, i) | > | \varepsilon(m^2, i) | > | \varepsilon(m^1, i) |.$$

The initial condition (3.2), in which i^t is sufficiently close to Regulation Q so that $\varepsilon(i^t, i^f) = 0$, has very important implications for the derivable consequences of the hypothesis. Under initial condition (3.2) the sign of the elasticity of the t-ratio with respect to the index of credit market interest rates (i) is reversed from case I and case II. With initial condition (3.2) the elasticity of the t-ratio with respect to interest rates becomes negative. Increases in market interest rates are accompanied by a decrease in the ratio of time to demand deposits held by the public. Hence the signs of the elasticities of the M^2 and bank credit multipliers with respect to the interest rate are reversed (negative) compared to case I or case II.

Limits on Case III Conditions. As the t-ratio falls, the effect of the t-ratio on the size of the elasticities of the multipliers with respect to the t-ratio is reduced. These results can be stated as follows:

$$\varepsilon(m, t) \to 0 \quad \text{as} \quad t \to 0.$$

Therefore, as market interest rates continue to rise, and the restraint of Q^* results in a sharp decline in the t-ratio, the elasticities of the multipliers with respect to interest rates again approach zero. This is the limit on case III:

$$t \to 0,$$
$$\varepsilon(m^1, i), \varepsilon(m^2, i), \varepsilon(m^2 - 1, i) \to 0.$$

As interest rates come down from peak levels, banks may maintain i^t at levels relative to i^f so that the t-ratio rises. The fall in interest rates permits banks to compete for time deposits. The rising t-ratio results in an increase in the M^2 and bank credit multipliers, but a fall in the money multiplier.

Graphical Representation. The relationships between the interest elasticities of the multipliers under the three cases of differing initial conditions are shown in Figure 5.1. As the economy moves into the initial conditions of case II, the elasticities of M^2 and bank credit with respect to the interest rate continue to rise; but $\varepsilon(m^1, i)$ begins to decline. This change reflects the increased influence of the $\varepsilon(t, i)$ on the multipliers. As market interest rates increase, the banks raise their offering yields on time deposits to induce the public to alter its desired t-ratio. Since the $\varepsilon(m^1, t)$ is opposite in sign to the $\varepsilon(m^2, t)$ and $\varepsilon(m^2 - 1, t)$, the numerical value of the elasticities of the M^2 and bank credit multipliers continue to increase. However, this effect of interest rates on the t-ratio decreases the numerical value of the $\varepsilon(m^1, i)$.

When $i^t \to Q^*$, the $\varepsilon(t, i)$ decreases, and hence the divergence between the numerical values of the elasticities of the three multipliers is reduced. At this point, the $\varepsilon(m^2, i)$ and $\varepsilon(m^2 - 1, i)$ cease to increase and begin to decline, approaching zero as banks' offering rates on time deposits approach Regulation Q limits.

The $\varepsilon(m^1, i)$ remains positive as the economy moves through case II initial conditions. This reflects the continued influence of the $\varepsilon(b, i)$ and $\varepsilon(e, i)$ on the multipliers. In the first phase of case II, the response of the borrowing ratio and excess reserve ratio to interest rates offsets much of the negative influence of the $\varepsilon(t, i)$ on the numerical value of $\varepsilon(m^1, i)$. As banks reduce their e-ratio and as the Federal Reserve Banks exercise greater administrative control of member bank borrowings, the influence of the e-ratio and b-ratio on the elasticities of the multipliers with respect to interest rates is reduced.

When the economy moves into what are characterized as case III

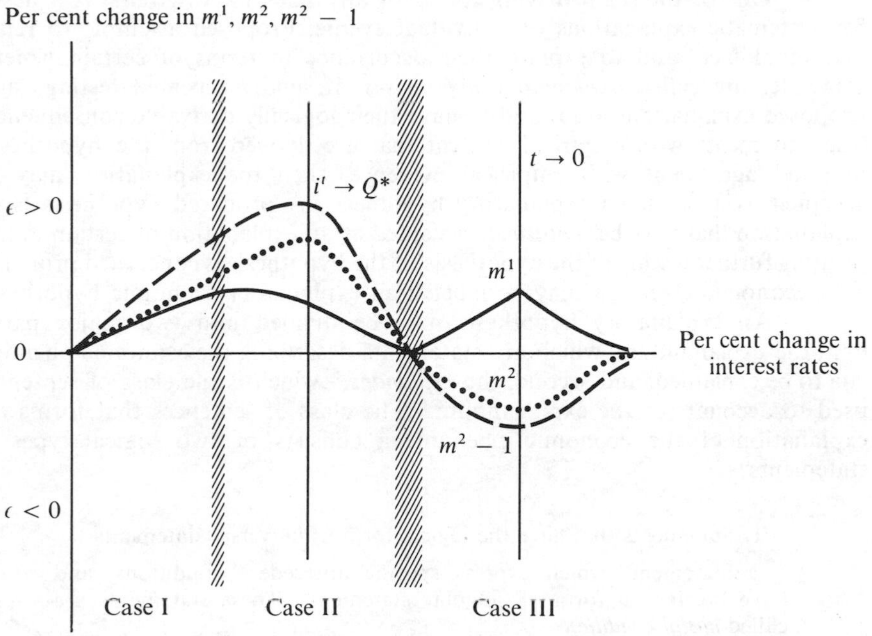

Figure 5.1 Interest Elasticities of the Multipliers

initial conditions, the *e*-ratio and *b*-ratio exercise only a small influence on the numerical value of the elasticities of the multipliers with respect to interest rates. The $\varepsilon(t, i)$ dominates the sign and numerical values of $\varepsilon(m, i)$. Since under these conditions the elasticity of the *t*-ratio with respect to interest rates becomes negative, the $\varepsilon(m^1, i)$ begins to increase and $\varepsilon(m^2, i)$ and $\varepsilon(m^2 - 1, i)$ continue to decline.

As the decline in the *t*-ratio continues (denoted by $t \to 0$) the influence of the *t*-ratio on the multipliers is reduced. Hence, all three multipliers become less sensitive to changes in interest rates. The decreased influence of changes in interest rates is shown in Figure 5.1 as the changes in all multipliers resulting from a change in interest rates again approach zero.

Appendix I

Initial Conditions

In this chapter and the remaining chapters, the concept of initial conditions will be used. To explain the basic idea of initial conditions and their importance, we shall digress for a few pages and discuss the concept of an explanatory economic hypothesis.[4]

---

[4] For a more complete discussion of this material see Ernest Nagel, *The Structure of Science* (New York: Harcourt, Brace and Company, Inc., 1961), and Morris Cohen and Ernest Nagel, *An Introduction to Logic and Scientific Method* (New York: Harcourt, Brace and World, Inc., 1934), especially Chapter XI.

One of the main driving forces of any scientific discipline is a desire for systematic explanations of individual events. Proposed attempts to relate individual facts and to explain their occurrence in terms of certain general principles are called *explanatory hypotheses*. If, under repeated testing, such proposed explanations are found to have their logically derivable consequences (the statements with empirical content that are derived from the hypothesis) in good agreement with empirical evidence, then the explanation may be accepted as a proffered explanatory hypothesis. A proffered hypothesis is an explanation that may be *tentatively* accepted as an explanation of certain events pending further testing of the hypothesis. If the hypothesis is concerned primarily with economic events, it may be labeled an explanatory economic hypothesis.

An explanatory hypothesis may be divided into two major parts: first, the explanandum, which are statements describing the economic phenomena to be explained, and second, the *explanans*,[5] which is the class of sentences used to account for the explanandum.[6] The class of sentences that forms the explanation of the economic phenomena consists of two logical types of statements:

1. Statements that have the logical form of universal statements.
2. Statements which express specific antecedent conditions, and have the logical form of singular statements. These statements are called *initial conditions*.

The general distinction between singular statements and universal statements can be illustrated by an example.[7] A singular statement is of the form:

"The puddle of water on my driveway this morning is frozen."

This statement refers to a particular instance of the item water at a specific time and at a specific place. I can, by certain well-specified means of observation ascertain whether this is a true or false statement.

Previously, I have observed similar occurrences of this phenomenon. Referring to my high school physics courses, I might now formulate a general statement as a possible explanation, not only of this specific occurrence of the freezing of water, but also of all other occurrences of the freezing of water. Such a statement might be of the form:

"All water freezes at 32° Fahrenheit."

---

[5] Other terms, used by some authors, are explicandum and explicans.

[6] See Carl G. Hempel and Paul Oppenheim, "The Logic of Explanation" in *Readings in the Philosophy of Science*, Herbert Feigl and May Brodbeck, eds. (New York: Appleton-Century-Crofts, Inc., 1953), pp. 319–324.

[7] The reader should be cautioned that this is only a very brief and general statement of the differences between singular and universal statements. For a more thorough discussion see a book on propositional logic such as William H. Halberstadt, *Introduction to Logic* (New York: Harper & Brothers, 1960), or Alfred Tarski, *Introduction to Logic and to the Methodology of the Deductive Sciences*, 3rd ed. (New York: Oxford University Press, Galaxy Books, 1965).

Let

$$W = \text{water},$$

$$F = \text{freezes at } 32^\circ \text{ Fahrenheit},$$

$$(x) = \text{universal quantifier}.$$

A universal statement has the logical form

$$(x)\,(W_x \supset F_x).$$

The above notation is read "for every x, if x is water (W_x) then this implies ($\supset$) that x freezes at 32° Fahrenheit (F_x)." The statement refers to all instances of the occurrence of the item water, not to any particular occurrence.

I have formulated a very simple explanation of not only one specific example of water turning into ice, but of all possible cases in which water becomes ice. Operating on this hypothesis, I might decide that, since the weatherman has forecast temperatures below freezing, it would be a good idea to fill my car radiator with anti-freeze. In the process of filling my radiator, some anti-freeze goes into the radiator and some spills onto the driveway. The next morning when I go outside, there are puddles of water on the driveway that are not frozen. I quickly check the temperature. It is 20° Fahrenheit. Have I observed a falsification of my hypothesis?

The answer is no. The crux of the problem is that I had never formulated a fully developed hypothesis. Logicians would be quick to point out the logical error that a singular statement had been deduced from a universal statement. The physicist would point out that the applicability of the general statement "Water freezes at 32° Fahrenheit" depends upon the existence of specific initial conditions. From the statement "Water freezes at 32° Fahrenheit" you can deduce that the puddles of water on your driveway would be frozen if and only if the water was free from impurities. Since anti-freeze was spilled all over the driveway the night before, we should not expect ice. To deduce prediction statements about singular events, singular statements expressing the initial conditions must be conjoined with the universal statement. If these initial conditions are changed, then the predictable consequences of the explanatory hypothesis change.

Let U denote the class of universal statements, and let I designate the class of singular statements (initial conditions) in the explanans. The explanans then may be expressed as the logical conjunction of I and U expressed by $I \cdot U$. Using both the initial conditions and the universal statements, definite singular statements, called prediction statements (S), are derived by rules of logic. This may be expressed as

$$I \cdot U \supset S.$$

This symbolic representation may be read "the logical conjunction of the set of initial conditions and universal statements implies the set of singular statements S." The set of statements S are logical consequences of the hypothesis. They express what the hypothesis predicts, and hence are called prediction statements.

If an economic hypothesis is to serve as an explanation of the explanandum (singular statement about the occurrence of phenomena), then the derivable consequences of the hypothesis must say something about the explanandum. For example, the hypothesis developed in this book is designed to explain such economic phenomena as changes in the magnitudes of the money stock, M^2, bank credit, and the response of credit market interest rates to changes in B^a during specified periods of time. Hence, the derivable consequences of the hypothesis must yield statements about these economic quantities.

The explanandum serves as a potential falsifier of the hypothesis. If the explanandum does not contradict the prediction statements derived from the explanatory hypothesis, then the hypothesis may be said to be confirmed. *Confirmed* is quite a different assertion from *proved* or *shown to be true*. Because of the presence of universal statements in any hypothesis, such an explanation can never be shown to be true by any finite number of confirming instances. When applying or testing a hypothesis, the application or test involves the statement of initial conditions as well as the theory embodied in the hypothesis. We emphasize again that the prediction statements are derived from the conjunction of the universal statements and initial conditions. The initial conditions are an integral part of the explanation. If one or more of the initial condition statements are replaced with different statements which are not equivalent, then what is derived from the full explanans will change.

An example of an initial condition already introduced is the statement of the relationship between Regulation Q ceiling rates and the yields on other market assets. It has been assumed that if, when market interest rates rise, MR_T exceeds MC_T, then banks will raise their offering rates (i^t) on time deposits. Hence we derived the result that

$$\varepsilon(t, i) > 0.$$

However, if bank offering yields are at Regulation Q ceiling rates, $i^t = Q^*$, then banks are unable to raise i^t. Under these initial conditions we derived the prediction statement that

$$\varepsilon(t, i) < 0.$$

The initial condition about Regulation Q ceilings and i^t (a singular statement about an observable condition during a specific period of time) imposes a constraint on the hypothesis. As we proceed, it will become clear that, if this initial condition is altered, the logically derivable prediction statements of the hypothesis for changes in M^1, M^2, and bank credit are markedly changed. The use of initial conditions takes into account that the responses of the banks and the public to certain factors such as policy actions by the Federal Reserve will not be the same under all conditions.

As another example, the banks' reaction to increases in market interest rates will also depend upon whether the Federal Reserve Banks are "exercising the discipline of the discount window." If, when a hypothesis is applied to a specific set of events, the derivable consequences of the hypothesis are not in agreement with empirical evidence, then this is grounds for disconfirmation of the theory embodied in the hypothesis if and only if the assumed initial conditions are also shown to be in good agreement with empirical evidence. If the spread between the discount rate and the yield on financial assets traded on the bank credit market widens, and the ratio of member bank borrowings to total nonbank deposits (*b*-ratio) does not increase, this is not necessarily evidence against the general proposition $\varepsilon(b, i) > 0$. If the Federal Reserve through its administration of the discount window is effectively increasing the implicit borrowing cost at the window, then the hypothesis with this additional initial condition does not predict a rise in member bank borrowings.

> The indispensability of initial conditions for the deductive explanation of individual occurrences is obvious as a point in formal logic. For it is logically impossible to deduce a statement instantial in form from statements that have the form of a universal conditional. (For example, it is impossible to derive an instantial statement of the form "*x* is *B*" from a universal conditional of the form "For any *x*, if *x* is *A* then *x* is *B*.") But obvious though the point may be, it is an important one that is frequently neglected in discussions of scientific procedure. Its neglect is at least partly responsible for the cavalier way in which broad generalizations are sometimes used to account for detailed matters of fact (especially in the study of human affairs) and for the low esteem which observers sometimes have for painstaking investigations of what are the actual facts. It is, however, often difficult to make concrete uses of laws and theories, simply because the specific initial conditions for their application are inaccessible and therefore unknown. And, conversely, mistaken explanations and false predictions are frequently proposed because the general assumptions that are employed, though sound enough in themselves, are applied to situations which do not constitute appropriate initial conditions for those assumptions.[8]

[8] Nagel, p. 32.

Chapter Six The Bank Credit Market

Equilibrium on the market for bank credit requires that the amount of earning assets demanded by commercial banks (E^d) be matched by the amount of earning assets supplied to the banks (E^s). The amount of (E^s) is composed of the dollar value of the public's desired loan liabilities to the banks (L) and the portion of the stock of government securities (S) sold to the banks:

$$E^s = L + S. \tag{6.1}$$

The public's supply of earning assets to the banks is expressed as a function of the interest rate on these assets (i); transitory income (Y/Y_p); real stock of nonhuman wealth, including the stock of government debt outstanding (W/P_a); price expectations (α); the expected rate of return on real capital (β); the interest rate (i_θ) on financial assets other than bank earning assets; and the outstanding stock of U.S. government securities (S^G):[1]

$$E^s = f(i, Y/Y_p, W/P_a, \alpha, \beta, i_\theta, S^G). \tag{6.2}$$

The postulated relations between these factors and E^s are

$$\frac{\partial E^s}{\partial i}, \frac{\partial E^s}{\partial S^G} < 0,$$

$$\frac{\partial E^s}{\partial (Y/Y_p)}, \frac{\partial E^s}{\partial (W/P_a)}, \frac{\partial E^s}{\partial \alpha}, \frac{\partial E^s}{\partial \beta}, \frac{\partial E^s}{\partial i_\theta} > 0.$$

[1] The stock of government securities is composed of the stock of U.S. government debt obligations (S^G) and the stock of municipal securities. The amount of government securities the public is willing to supply to the banks depends partly upon the size of the stock of U.S. government debt obligations (S^G). This dependence becomes important, as will be shown later, because an open market operation by the Federal Reserve results in a change in the outstanding stock of U.S. government securities (S^G).

The public's supply of earning assets to the banks should not be confused with the public's demand for money. The public's supply of loan liabilities to the banks represents the public's demand for bank *credit*. Banks purchase earning assets from the public with bank money (D^P), so at the time of the transaction, every bank purchase of securities or loans from the public raises the public's money holdings by an equal amount. But this does not imply anything about the behavioral functions involved. Particularly it does not imply an identity of the public's supply of earning assets and the public's demand for money. For example, the public's supply of earning assets (E^s) is postulated to be positively related to the expected rate of return on real capital. Economic theory, however, postulates that the public's demand for money is negatively related to the rate of return on real capital.[2]

The commercial banks' demand for earning assets depends upon the amount of base and the value of the bank credit multiplier. Therefore, the banks' demand for earning assets may be expressed as

$$E^d = (m^2 - 1)B^a.$$

The equilibrium condition on the bank credit market is that the stock of earning assets that banks desire to hold equals the stock of assets the public desires to supply to the banks ($E^d = E^s$). We can write the equilibrium condition for the bank credit market as follows:

$$(m^2 - 1)B^a = E^s. \tag{6.3}$$

In the process of adjustment by which equilibrium is reached in the credit market, the outstanding stock of publicly held government securities is absorbed into the asset portfolio of the banks and the public; the volume of loans extended by the commercial banks changes; and interest rates are adjusted on bank loans, government securities, and other financial assets traded on the credit market.

The Bank Credit Market Interest Rate

The bank credit market interest rate is determined by the interaction of the banks and the public, and is therefore dependent upon those same factors that influence the banks' demand for earning assets and the public's supply of earning assets to the banks. The dependence of the interest rate on these factors may be expressed as basic relation (6.4).

$$i = f(B^a, r^d, r^t, \rho, Q^*, k, d, \pi_1, \pi_2; Y/Y_p, W/P_a, \alpha, \beta, i_\theta). \tag{6.4}$$

The first set of factors includes those items upon which the banks' demand for earning assets depends, but which are not dependent upon the

---

[2] See Karl Brunner, ed., "Monetary Analysis and Federal Reserve Policy" *Targets and Indicators of Monetary Policy* (San Francisco: Chandler Publishing Co., 1969), pp. 269–271.

interest rate (i). The second set of factors includes those items upon which the public's supply of earning assets is dependent.

The short-run or partial equilibrium condition on the bank credit market is that the dollar volume of banks' desired holdings of earning assets is equal to the dollar volume of assets (loan liabilities and government securities) which the public desires to supply to the commercial banks. In the portfolio adjustment process by which the stock of assets traded on the credit market is absorbed into the portfolios of the banks and the public, interest rates on these assets adjust, and the composite interest rate is determined by the adjustment process.

The Response of the Bank Credit Market Interest Rate to Changes in B^a

An increase or decrease in the base (in a dynamic context, an increase or decrease in the growth of the base) results in a change in the composition of the asset portfolios of the economic units that operate in the credit market. For example, an increase in the base results in banks and/or the public holding more of this particular type of asset relative to their holdings of other assets. As the banks and the public react to this change in the composition of their stock of assets, the bank credit market interest rate changes.

The response of the interest rate (i) to changes in B^a, in terms of elasticities may be expressed as follows:[3]

$$\varepsilon(i, B^a) = \frac{-1}{\varepsilon(m^2 - 1, i) - \varepsilon(E^s, i)}$$

The predicted response of the interest rate to changes in the net source base depends on two major factors. The first factor, $\varepsilon(m^2 - 1, i)$, expresses the percentage change in the quantity of earning assets demanded by banks resulting from a one per cent change in the interest rate. The second factor, $\varepsilon(E^s, i)$, gives the percentage change in the quantity of loan liabilities and securities the public is willing to supply to the banks given a one per cent change in the interest rate.

Figure 6.1 shows graphically the derivation of the banks' demand curve for earning assets. Graph II gives the relation between the bank credit multiplier $(m^2 - 1)$ and bank credit (E). Using the definition

$$\frac{E}{m^2 - 1} = B^a,$$

we see that the line drawn in graph II represents the net source base.

---

[3] The interested reader may check this by taking logs of both sides of the expression $B^a = E^s/(m^2 - 1)$ and differentiating with respect to i.

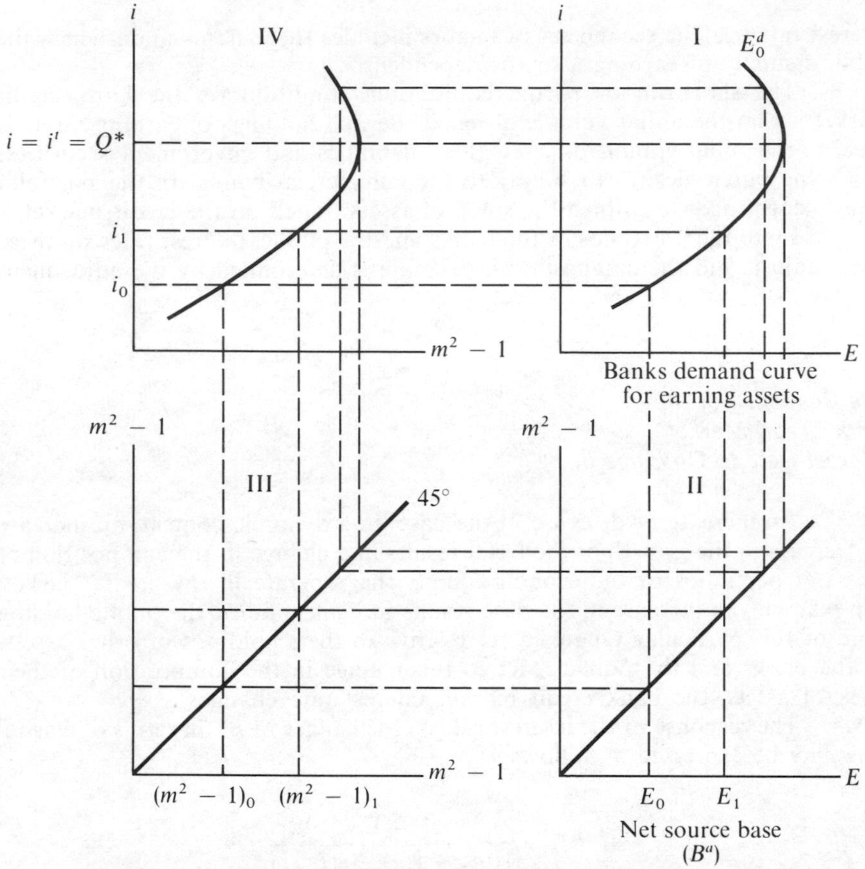

Figure 6.1 Derivation of the Banks' Demand Curve for Earning Assets

Graph IV expresses the relation between the bank credit multiplier and the interest rate. As discussed in the previous chapter, the dependence of the bank credit multiplier on the interest rate follows from the dependence of the excess reserve ratio, borrowing ratio, and time deposit ratio on the interest rate. The curve in graph IV was drawn by using the results derived in cases I–III at the end of the previous chapter. Following the curve, we see that, at low levels of the interest rate and with i^t well below Regulation Q ceilings, an increase in the interest rate leads to a relatively large increase in the bank credit multiplier. As the interest rate rises to high levels, and as the yields offered by banks on time deposits approach Regulation Q, ($i^t \rightarrow Q^*$), the increase in $m^2 - 1$ resulting from a rise in the interest rate becomes smaller. As i^t gets close to Regulation Q, the change in $m^2 - 1$, following a rise in the interest rate, approaches zero—(case II). When the interest rate rises to high levels and $i^t = Q^*$, then the sign of the response of $m^2 - 1$ to a rise in interest rates is reversed. The curve bends backward, showing that an increase in interest rates—resulting in a fall in the t-ratio—reduces the value of the multiplier.

The banks' demand curve for earning assets (E^d) may be derived by picking an interest rate i_0. Given i_0, there will be a definite value for the multiplier $(m^2 - 1)_0$; and given the stock of base $B_0{}^a$, there is a definite amount of earning assets E_0 that banks desire to acquire. At higher level i_1 of the market interest rate, there is associated a greater value $(m^2 - 1)_1$ for the multiplier. Given the same amount of base $(B_0{}^a)$, the banks desire to hold a larger dollar value E_1 of earning assets.

The banks' demand curve for earning assets is drawn in graph I. For a given amount of net source base, as the interest rate on earning assets rises, banks desire to acquire a larger portfolio of loans and securities. After the point at which $i = i^t = Q^*$, the continued rise in the interest rate leads to an outflow of time deposits and the t-ratio falls, resulting in a decrease in the total quantity of earning assets that banks desire to hold, given that the amount of base is unchanged.

To determine the bank credit market interest rate and the amount of bank credit, the public's supply curve of earning assets to banks must be combined with the banks' demand curve for earning assets. In Figure 6.2, the public's supply curve of earning assets (E^s) is drawn showing that as the interest rate falls, other factors constant, the quantity of earning assets the public supplies to banks increases.

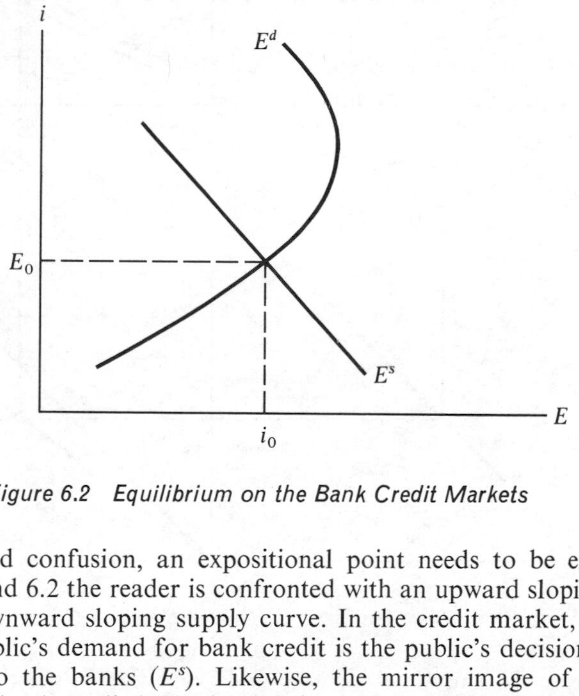

Figure 6.2 Equilibrium on the Bank Credit Markets

To avoid confusion, an expositional point needs to be emphasized. In Figures 6.1 and 6.2 the reader is confronted with an upward sloping demand curve and a downward sloping supply curve. In the credit market, the mirror image of the public's demand for bank credit is the public's decision to supply earning assets to the banks (E^s). Likewise, the mirror image of the banks' supply curve of bank credit is the banks' demand for earning assets (E^d). The slopes of the credit market supply and demand curves therefore depend upon from which side of the market we view the process. Because we are emphasizing bank behavior, the supply and demand conditions in the credit market are specified in terms of E^s and E^d.

The banks' demand curve (E^d) is not horizontal, but has an upward slope. To induce the banks to demand a larger volume of earning assets (supply more credit), the interest rate must rise. Banks are not viewed as passively accommodating the demand for bank credit. Suppose the public's supply of earning assets to banks increases (E^s shifts to the right). Then, other factors remaining constant, the amount of bank credit increases only if the interest rate (i) rises.

Figure 6.3 shows the effect of an increase in the base on the banks' demand curve for earning assets. The increase in B^a is shown in graph II by rotating the curve which expresses the relationship between E and $m^2 - 1$, to every value of the bank credit multiplier there is associated a larger quantity of earning assets demanded by banks.

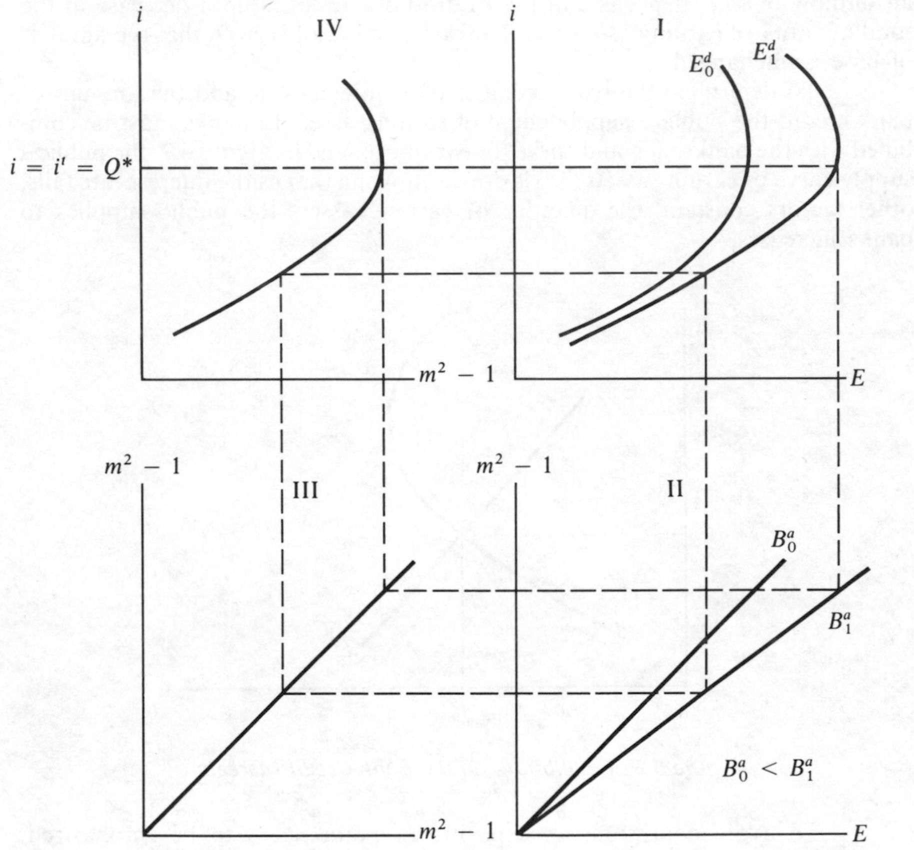

Figure 6.3 Effect of an Increase in B^a on Banks' Demand Curve for Earning Assets

Figure 6.4 shows an increase in B^a resulting in the banks' desiring to hold a larger stock of earning assets at the interest rate (i_0) than the amount they hold (E_0). However, E_0 is the amount of liabilities the public desires to incur to the banks at the cost i_0. To induce the public to supply more earning assets, the banks lower the rates they charge on bank loans and increase the prices they offer for government securities. In the adjustment process the stock of bank credit rises to E_1, and the interest rate falls to i_1.

The short-run effect of an increase (decrease) in the net source base is to decrease (increase) the bank credit market interest rate and expand (contract) the stock of earning assets (loans and securities) held by the commercial banks.

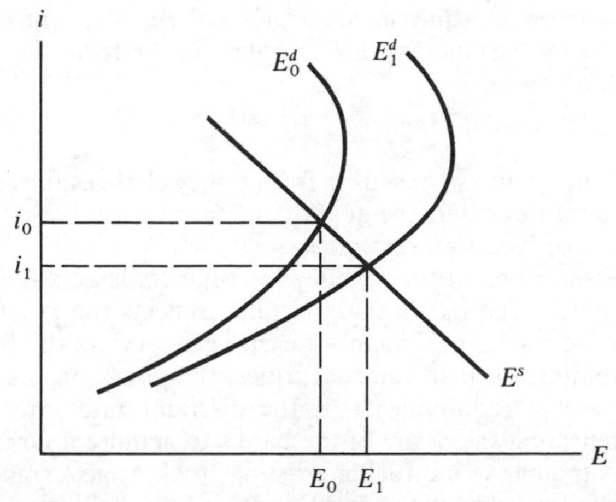

Figure 6.4 Short-run Change in Bank Credit and the Interest Rate Resulting from an Increase in B^a.

The short-run changes in the interest rate result from the commercial banks' attempt to adjust their portfolios of earning assets to the change in the quantity of B^a supplied to them. In terms of elasticities, the short-run elasticity of the interest rate (i) with respect to B^a is negative:

$$\varepsilon(i, B^a) < 0 \qquad \text{short-run.}$$

The numerical value of $\varepsilon(i, B^a)$ depends upon the numerical values of the two elasticities that appear in the denominator. The larger the banks' and the public's response to interest rate changes, the greater the numerical value of $\varepsilon(m^2 - 1, i)$ and $\varepsilon(E^s, i)$, and hence the smaller the percentage response of the interest rate to a given percentage change in the base. If the public and banks are relatively insensitive to changes in the interest rate, then $\varepsilon(m^2 - 1, i)$ and $\varepsilon(E^s, i)$ are small in value, and the adjustment process resulting from changes in the net source base leads to relatively large percentage changes in the interest rates on the bank credit market.

For example, assume that $\varepsilon(E^s, i)$ is small in numerical value and the Federal Reserve increases the base by an open market purchase of securities from the banking system. Given this initial condition, in order to induce the public to increase its supply of loan liabilities and to transfer a portion of the smaller stock of outstanding securities to the banks, the banks must lower the interest rate they charge on bank loans and must raise the price they offer to pay for securities more than under initial conditions where E^s is more sensitive to changes in interest rates.

Response of the Interest Rate to Other Policy Actions

Reviewing the basic relations derived in Chapter 4 and the definition of the bank credit multiplier, one can see that $m^2 - 1$ is dependent upon the policy parameters, reserve requirements (r^d, r^t) and the discount rate (ρ). Since the banks' demand for earning assets E^d is given in the form

$$E^d = (m^2 - 1)\,B^a,$$

a change in the value of $m^2 - 1$ resulting from policy changes in reserve requirements or the discount rate alters the quantity of earning assets that banks desire to hold at all levels of credit market rates.

An increase in one of these policy instruments lowers the value of the bank credit multiplier. The fall in the multiplier reflects the portfolio decision by the banks to hold a smaller amount of earning assets. As the banks attempt to reduce their holdings of loans and securities, the yields on these assets rise. Likewise, when reserve requirements or the discount rates are lowered, the multiplier rises, reflecting the desire of the banks to acquire a larger amount of earning assets. As the banks bid for the existing stock of government securities and attempt to induce the public to increase their loan liabilities to banks, the interest rate falls.

The effect on the banks' demand for earning assets can be shown with the graphs in Figure 6.1. Changes in reserve requirements, the discount rate, and Regulation Q ceiling rates on time deposit yields would appear as a shift in the curve drawn in graph IV. The relation expressed in graph IV between the interest rate and the multiplier was drawn on the assumption that, as the interest rate changes, the other factors influencing the value of the bank credit multiplier remained constant. However, due to the dependence of the r-ratio on reserve requirements, the dependence of the borrowing ratio and excess reserve ratio on the level of the discount rate, and the t-ratio on Regulation Q rates, changes in these policy instruments alter the relation between the interest rate and the multiplier.

For example, an increase in reserve requirements raises the reserve ratio. Banks desire to hold a smaller volume of earning assets at every level of the yields on these assets. An increase in r^d, r^t, or ρ is shown in Figure 6.5.

The curve in graph IV shifts to the left, as the value of the multiplier is smaller for any given interest rate. This is shown in graph I by a shift to the left to $E_2{}^d$ of the banks' demand curve for earning assets.

As illustrated in Figure 6.6, changes in the Regulation Q ceiling rates on time deposits cause a somewhat different movement in the curve in graph IV. An increase in Regulation Q shifts the curves in Figure 6.6 to the right, just as would a decrease in reserve requirements or the discount rate. However, instead of a parallel shift in the curve in graph IV, as is the case for a decrease in r^d, r^t, or ρ, the increase in Regulation Q causes the curve to shift right by a greater amount at interest rates close to $i^t = Q^*$ than at rates well below $i^t = Q^*$. The explanation for this difference is quite straightforward. If interest rates are well below Regulation Q ceiling rates, then an increase in Regulation Q ceiling rates has very little effect on increasing the competitive ability of commercial banks as they bid for time deposits.

However, when $i = i^t$ close to Q^*, a rise in Q^* is an important factor permitting banks to respond to an increase in market yields. This can be clearly seen in Figure 6.6 at the point where $i^t = Q_1{}^*$. If the market rate (i) rises above i^t, then under $Q_1{}^*$ the banks cannot effectively compete for time deposits, the t-ratio falls, and the amount of credit extended by the banks falls. If at this

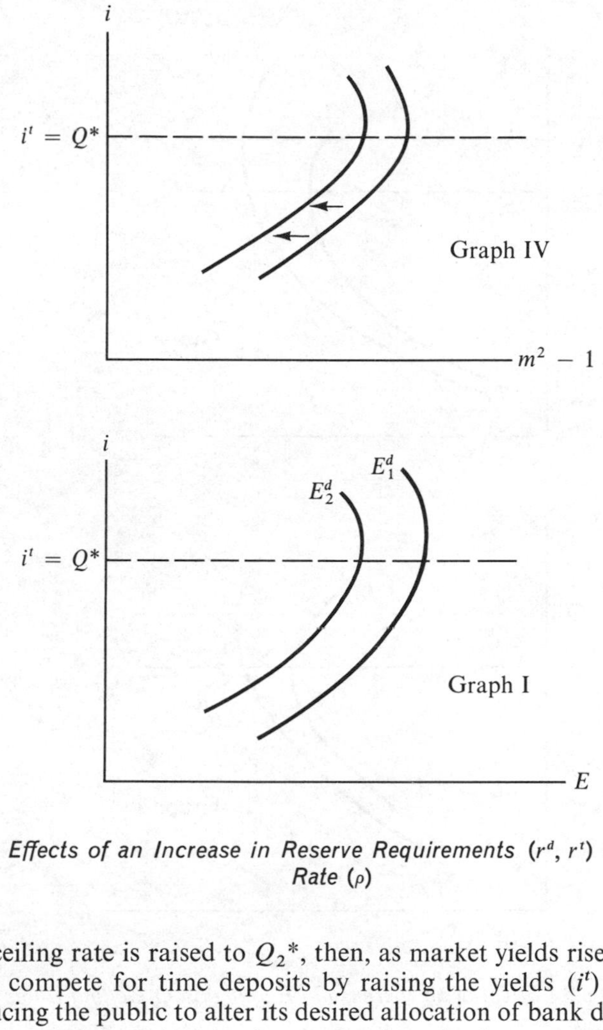

Figure 6.5 Effects of an Increase in Reserve Requirements (r^d, r^t) or the Discount Rate (ρ)

point the ceiling rate is raised to $Q_2{}^*$, then, as market yields rise up to $i^t = Q_2{}^*$, banks can compete for time deposits by raising the yields (i^t) they offer and hence inducing the public to alter its desired allocation of bank deposits between time and demand deposits. As the t-ratio rises, banks are willing and *able* to increase their holdings of earning assets; and bank credit expands rather than falls.

Elasticities

The response of the interest rate (i) to changes in r^d, r^t, and ρ may be expressed in terms of elasticities as follows:

$$\varepsilon(i, x) = \frac{-\varepsilon(m^2 - 1, x)}{\varepsilon(m^2 - 1, i) - \varepsilon(E^s, i)},$$

where x is used as a general symbol for r^d, r^t, or ρ.

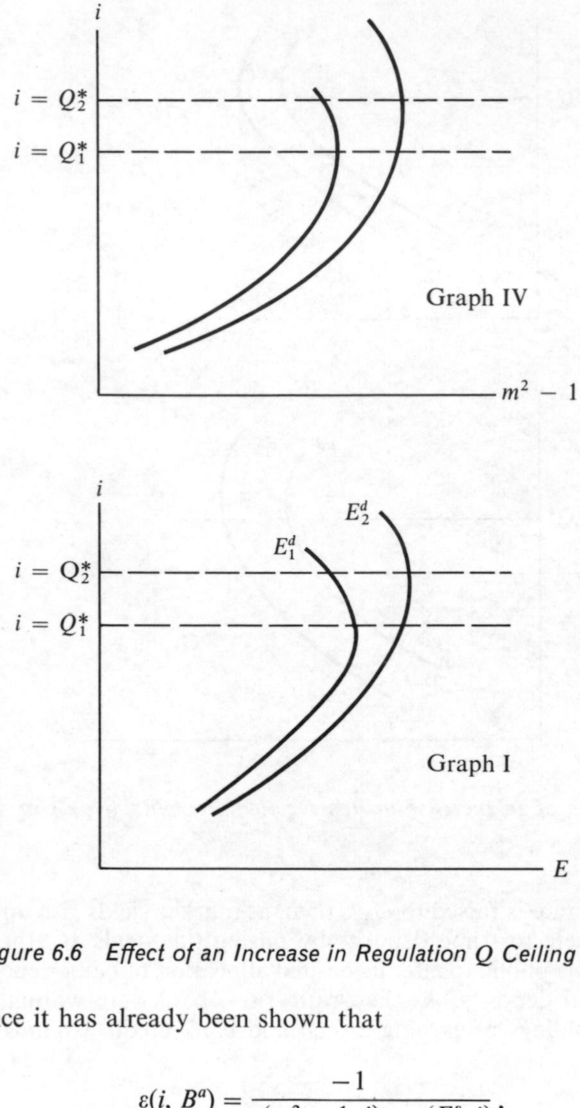

Figure 6.6 Effect of an Increase in Regulation Q Ceiling Rates

Since it has already been shown that

$$\varepsilon(i, B^a) = \frac{-1}{\varepsilon(m^2 - 1, i) - \varepsilon(E^s, i)},$$

we may express the $\varepsilon(i, x)$ in the following manner:

$$\varepsilon(i, x) = \varepsilon(m^2 - 1, x) \cdot \varepsilon(i, B^a).$$

From the previous discussion, it follows that an increase (decrease) in reserve requirements or the discount rate lowers (raises) the value of the bank credit multiplier:

$$\varepsilon(m^2 - 1, x) < 0.$$

Also, from earlier discussion we can see that the short-run effect of an increase in B^a is to lower credit market interest rates and that a decrease in B^a raises credit market interest rates. Therefore

$$\varepsilon(i, B^a) < 0.$$

Combining these two results on the signs of the components of the elasticity of interest rates with respect to r^d, r^t, and ρ, the conclusion follows that

$$\varepsilon(i, x) > 0.$$

An increase (decrease) in reserve requirements or the discount rate raises (lowers) short-term interest rates.

Interest Rate Effects of a Change in B^a Resulting from Open-Market Operations Compared to Interest Rate Effects of Changes in Other Policy Instruments

An open market purchase or sale of Government securities by the Federal Reserve results in an equal and opposite change in the amount of securities held by the public and banks. In the portfolio adjustment process following an open market purchase (sale) there is a smaller (larger) stock of interest-bearing assets available to satisfy the portfolio demands of the banks and the public. A change in reserve requirements, the discount rate, or Regulation Q does not involve a direct reduction or increase in the stock of securities held by the public sector. Hence, an open market operation would be expected to have a greater effect on credit market interest rates than a corresponding change in one of the other policy instruments of the Federal Reserve System.

Graphically, the short-run partial equilibrium results can be illustrated as in Figure 6.7.

In Figure 6.7 the public and banks' stock demand for securities is given by D_1. The stock supply of securities is shown by S_1. An open market purchase of Government securities by the Federal Reserve increases the base and hence increases the public and banks' stock demand for securities to D_2. However, corresponding to the purchase is a decrease in the stock of securities to S_2 (where the decrease $S_1 - S_2$ equals the volume of securities purchased by the Fed). The market interest rate on securities falls to i_3.[4]

In the case in which a corresponding increase in the stock demand for securities is induced by a decrease in reserve requirements, D_1 shifts to D_2.

---

[4] The reader is cautioned that these are only short-run partial equilibrium results. The fall in the interest rate to i_3 may induce an increased flow supply of new securities which, over time, will increase the stock of securities.

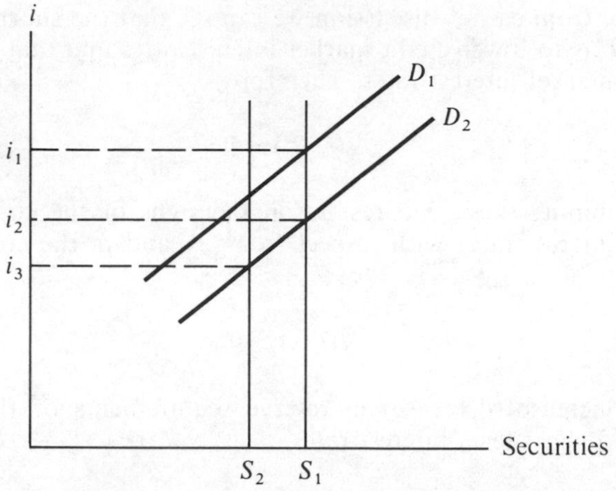

Figure 6.7 Open market purchase

However, there is no corresponding decrease in the stock of securities which remains at S_1. Consequently, the interest rate on securities falls only to i_2 instead of i_3, as shown in Figure 6.8.

Using the above results, the following relationship between the elasticity of interest rates with respect to B^a and with respect to other policy instruments follows:

$$|\varepsilon(i, B^a)| > |\varepsilon(i, x)|.$$

Note that these are elasticities and hence that they express a relationship between *percentage* changes. The above relationship states that a one per cent change in B^a leads to a greater percentage change in credit market interest rates than a one per cent change in reserve requirements, the discount rate, or Regulation Q. For example, a rise in reserve requirements on demand deposits from

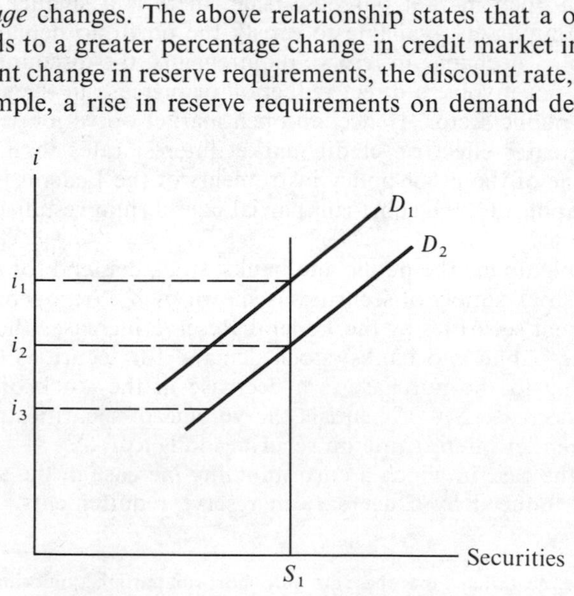

Figure 6.8 Decrease in reserve requirements

$14\frac{1}{2}$ per cent to 15 per cent is about a 3.5 per cent increase in r^d. A corresponding equal percentage change in a net source base of $75 billion would represent a sale of about $2.6 billion of Government securities by the Federal Reserve System.

Consideration of Feedback and Long-Run Effects of Changes in B^a on Interest Rates

So far, our analysis has covered only the short-run interest rate effects of changes in one of the policy instruments. These results are only partial equilibrium conditions; they do not take into account the spill-over effects into the real sector of changes in the money stock resulting from changes in the rate at which base is supplied to the economy. Consequently, feedback effects to the bank credit market from changes in the real sector induced by monetary influences have not yet been taken into consideration. To analyze the feedback and long-run effects of changes in the policy instruments on the interest rate, the hypothesis must be broadened to include propositions about the real sector. Important consequences for the predicted response of interest rates to changes in the policy instruments emerge from such an analysis.[5]

A policy-induced change in the net source base can be accomplished in a very short time via open market operations. The short-run impact effect of such policy-induced changes in B^a will be movements of interest rates in the opposite direction to the change in B^a. However, the increased or decreased stock of base must be assimilated into the asset portfolios of the banks and the public.

The market interest rate (i) may be expressed as a combination of two components α and β, where

$$\alpha = \text{expected rate of change of prices,}$$

$$\beta = \text{expected rate of return on real capital,}$$

$$i = \alpha + \beta.$$

The expected rate of return on real capital (β) is taken as a positive function of the demand for real output (y). As the amount of real output demanded increases, other factors influencing β held constant, the expected rate of return on real capital increases.

For example, assume that the base is increased via an open market purchase. There is an increase in the banks' demand for earning assets. As the banks attempt to acquire a larger stock of earning assets, the index of credit market interest rates (i) falls and money and bank credit expand. The bank

---

[5] For a more complete discussion see Karl Brunner and Allan Meltzer, "The Meaning of Monetary Indicators," *Monetary Process and Policy: A Symposium*, G. Horwich, ed. (Homewood, Ill.: Richard D. Irwin, Inc., 1967), pp. 187–217.

credit market approaches a new partial equilibrium position. The short-run elasticity of the interest rate with respect to B^a is negative.

However, the fall in the interest rate and the increase in the money stock spills over into the real sector in the form of an increase in total spending. The increased flow of total spending has an impact on real output and prices. As real output rises, the expected rate of return on real capital rises. This result reenters the credit market in the form of an expansion in the public's demand for bank credit. To the extent that the monetary authorities do not attempt to peg market interest rates by continuing to increase the base, the money stock expansion-induced increase in demand for credit results in a rise in the level of credit market interest rates.

The increase (decrease) in total spending generated by an expansion (contraction) in the monetary aggregates following an increase (decrease) in the growth of the base has an effect on the rate of change of real output (y) and prices (P). If we let Y denote total spending in current market prices ($Y = Py$), then the response of prices to changes in Y may be expressed in terms of elasticities as follows:

$$\varepsilon(P, Y) = 1 - \varepsilon(y, Y).$$

Under most conditions, an increase in total spending results in some increase in prices. The elasticity of prices with respect to total spending is greater than zero:

$$\varepsilon(P, Y) > 0.$$

The numerical value of the $\varepsilon(P, Y)$ depends upon the relation between the current level of real output and the productive capacity of the economy. When the quantity of real output that is being produced is much below the productive capacity of the economy, the response of prices to an increase in total spending is small. As the level of real output increases and the economy approaches full employment of its resources, the response of prices to changes in the flow of total spending increases.

The relationship between changes in prices and changes in the net source base may be expressed in terms of elasticities as follows:

$$\varepsilon(P, B^a) = \varepsilon(P, Y) \cdot \varepsilon(Y, M) \cdot \varepsilon(M, B^a).$$

The percentage change in the general level of prices resulting from a percentage change in B^a depends upon the responsiveness of money to base, total spending to changes in money, and prices to total spending.

As the economy approaches full employment, the response of real output to continued growth of total spending decreases

$$\varepsilon(y, Y) \to 0,$$

and hence $\varepsilon(P, Y)$ increases:

$$\varepsilon(P, Y) \to 1 \text{ as } y \to \text{full employment}.$$

As the economy approaches full employment, a policy leading to an expansion of the money stock, through its impact on total spending, results in more rapid increases in the price level. Over a longer period of time, as prices rise (fall) more rapidly than in the past, the public revises its expectations about the future rate of change of prices. These expectations affect the demand for credit and hence interest rates. Therefore, price expectations generated as a result of an expansionary monetary policy lead, over a longer period of time, to rising market interest rates. In the expression for the nominal interest rate:

$$i = \alpha + \beta.$$

This is reflected in a change in α.

There is considerable disagreement among economists as to the length of time it takes for the public to revise its expectations about the future rate of change of prices. However, almost all economists seem to agree that the effect of changes in the price level on interest rates is a longer-run phenomenon than the impact effect of changes in B^a on interest rates, and the feedback effects (β) of changes in real output on interest rates. The lag between price level changes and interest rate changes may also be variable, decreasing as the rate of change of prices increases.

William P. Yohe and Denis S. Karnosky have presented evidence indicating that the length of time it takes changes in market prices to be built into price expectations and hence to influence nominal interest rates depends upon the rate at which prices are increasing.[6]

Their evidence indicates that, although the long-term yields are somewhat less sensitive to price expectations than the short-term yields, the time it takes for changes in price expectations to be reflected in market interest rates decreases as the rate of change of prices increases.

> The total price expectations effect is much larger in the 1961–1969 period (a period that after 1964 was characterized by a rapidly rising price level) than in the earlier period (1952–1960). In the 1961–1969 period the total effect on short-term interest rates is about 90 per cent of the annual rate of change in prices. The total effect on long-term rates is about 80 per cent of the rate of price change.[7]

Many economists might disagree with the Yohe-Karnosky results on the rapid response of nominal interest rates to changes in market prices. However, many economists would agree that, over the long run, changes in the price level affect the demand for credit and hence affect the level of market interest rates (i). Over a longer period of time, the price expectations generated as a result of an expansionary monetary policy lead to an increase in α and hence a rise in interest rates. Conversely, a restrictive monetary policy (a decrease in the growth rate of B^a), over the long run, causes a downward revision in α by the public and hence a fall in market interest rates.

---

[6] William P. Yohe and Denis S. Karnosky, "Interest Rates and Price Level Changes, 1952–1969," Federal Reserve Bank of St. Louis *Review*, December 1969.

[7] Yohe and Karnosky, p. 29.

The influence of prices on market interest rates was noted as far back as 1811:

> It was material to observe, that there had, since the beginning of the war, been a continual fall in the value of money: he meant, of money commonly so-called, whether consisting of cash or paper. This had been estimated by some at 60 or 70 per cent, and certainly was not less than 40 and 50 per cent; which was, on the average, 2 or 3 per cent per annum: it followed from hence, that if, for example, a man borrowed of the Bank 1000£ in 1800, and paid it back in 1810, having detained it by means of successive loans through that period, he paid back that which had become worth less by 20 or 30 per cent than it was worth when he first received it. He would have paid an interest of 50£ per annum for the use of this money; but if from this interest were deducted the 20£ or 30£ per annum, which he had gained by the fall in the value of the money, he would find that he had borrowed at 2 or 3 per cent, and not at 5 per cent as he appeared to do . . . . Accordingly, in countries in which the currency was in a rapid course of depreciation, supposing that there were no usury laws, the current rate of interest was often, as he believed, proportionably augmented.[8]

> Suppose money to be in process of depreciation by means of an inconvertible currency, issued by a government in payment of its expenses. This fact will in no way diminish the demand for real capital on loan; but it will diminish the real capital loanable, because, this existing only in the form of money, the increase of quantity depreciates it.
>
> We thus see that depreciation, merely as such, while in process of taking place, tends to raise the rate of interest: and the expectation of further depreciation adds to this effect; because lenders who expect that their interest will be paid, and the principal perhaps redeemed, in a less valuable currency than they lent, of course require a rate of interest sufficient to cover this contingent loss.
>
> So that in this case increase of currency really affects the rate of interest, but in the contrary way to that which is generally supposed; by raising, not by lowering it.[9]

Taking into account the feedback effects from the real sector and the long-run effects of base-induced changes in prices and price expectations, in the new equilibrium position on the credit market, interest rates may be higher than before an increase in the base. Under these conditions

$$\varepsilon(i, B^a) > 0 \qquad \text{long-run.}$$

Graphically, the public's supply curve of earning assets to banks (E^s) may be derived as shown in Figure 6.9. In Figure 6.9 the term *ri*, which denotes

---

[8] Henry Thornton, *Two Speeches of Henry Thornton, Esq. on the Bullion Report, May 1811*, in F. A. v. Hayek, ed., *An Enquiry into the Nature and Effects of the Paper Credit of Great Britain*, (New York: Augustus M. Kelley, 1962), pp. 335–336.

[9] John Stuart Mill, *Principles of Political Economy* (First Edition 1843; New York: Augustus M. Kelley, 1961), p. 646.

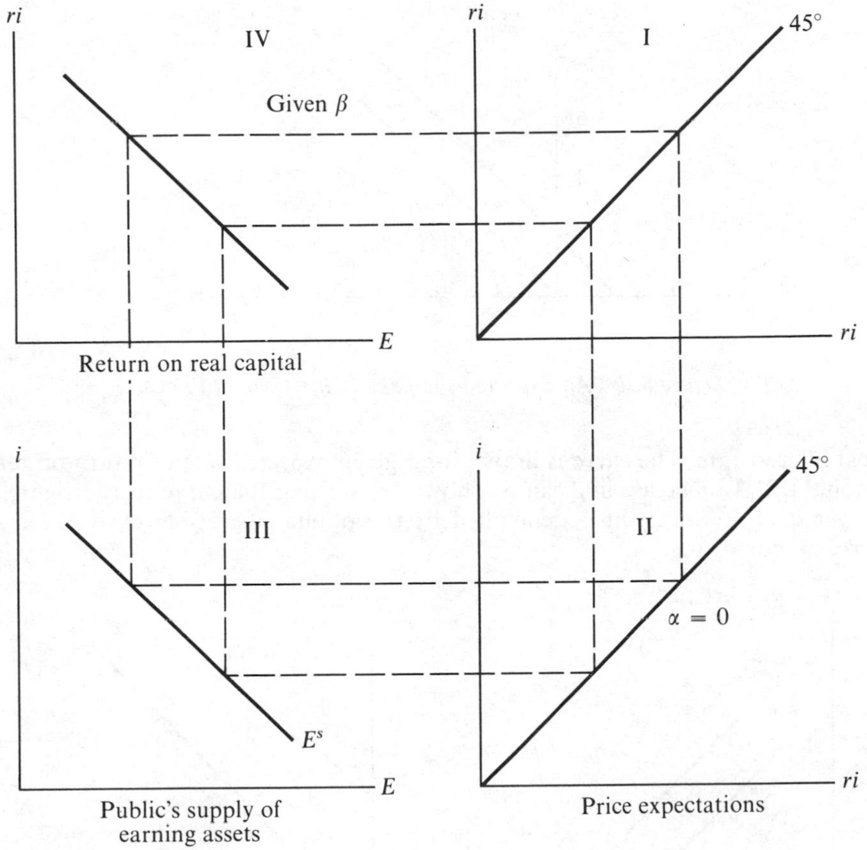

Figure 6.9 Public's Supply Curve of Earning Assets

the real interest rate, is introduced. The real interest rate is the nominal or market interest rate (i) with the influence of price expectations removed:

$$i - \alpha = ri \qquad \text{real interest rate.}$$

Graph II shows the relation between the market or nominal interest rate (i) and the real interest rate (ri). The curve is drawn on the assumption that prices are expected to remain constant over the life of the financial asset, $\alpha = 0$.

Figure 6.10 shows first the case in which $\alpha = 0$ and then the case in which $\alpha = 2$ (prices are expected to rise 2 per cent over the life of the security).

We can see that when the nominal market rate (i) equals 2 per cent, then given an expected 2 per cent increase in prices, the real rate (ri) equals zero. Lower nominal rates are associated with negative real rates.

Graph II in Figure 6.9 can therefore be used to show the effects of changes in price expectations. An increase in α results in a shift to the left in the curve, and correspondingly a decrease in α causes the curve to shift to the right.

Graph IV of Figure 6.9 expresses a relation between the quantity of earning assets supplied by the banks to the public in response to changes in the

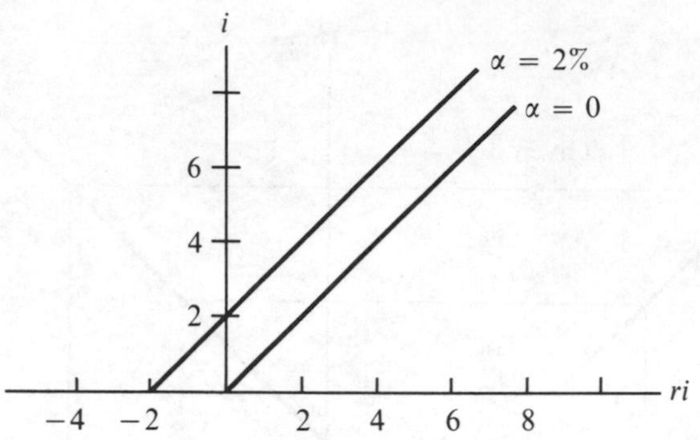

Figure 6.10 An Expected Increase in the Level of Prices

real interest rate. The curve is drawn for a given expected rate of return on real capital (β). An increase in β can be shown by shifting the curve to the right; a larger quantity of credit is demanded by the public at every level of the real cost of borrowing.

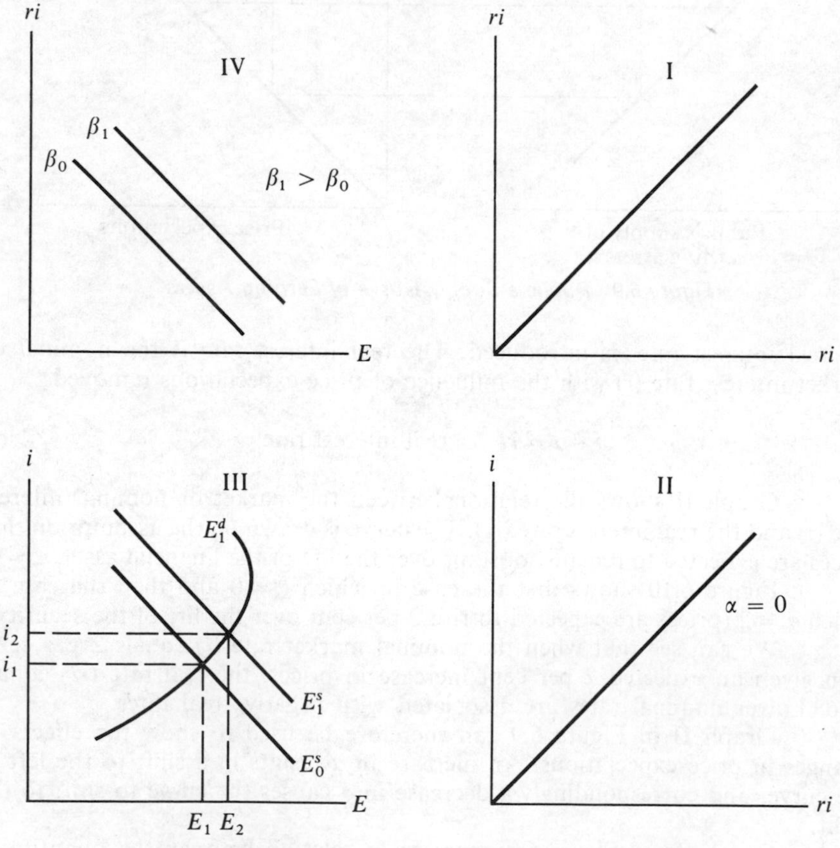

Figure 6.11 Effect of an Increase in the Rate of Return on Real Capital on E^s

Full Interest Rate Effects of an Increase in B^a

As discussed earlier, an increase in B^a results in an increase in the banks' demand for earning assets. As the banks attempt to acquire a larger volume of earning assets, the yields on these assets fall. Figure 6.4 shows the short-run effects of an increase in B^a. The interest rate falls from i_0 to i_1, and bank credit rises from E_0 to E_1.

The banks, when acquiring the additional earning assets $E_1 - E_0$, purchase these assets (loans and securities) by producing bank money (D^P), and hence the money stock increases. The increase in the money supply results in an increase in total spending, which in the real sector is reflected in a rise in real output demanded. The increase in the quantity of real output demanded raises the expected rate of return on real capital (β), which results in a shift to the right of the public's supply curve of earning assets to banks, as shown in Figure 6.11.

The increase in the expected rate of return on real capital, shown in graph IV, results in an increased demand for credit by the public, shown in graph III by a shift to the right of the public's supply curve of earning assets from $E_0{}^s$ to $E_1{}^s$. To induce the banks to acquire more earning assets (extend a greater volume of credit), the public must raise the yields offered on these assets. The interest rate increases and the amount of bank credit expands.

Fueled by a continued increase in the money stock, total spending

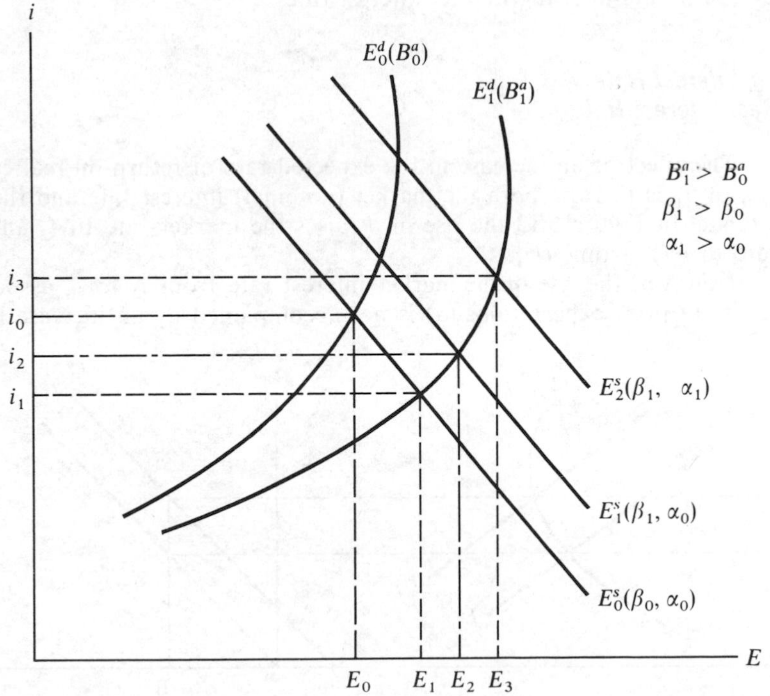

Figure 6.12 Short-Run and Long-Run Effects of an Increase in B^a Interest Rates

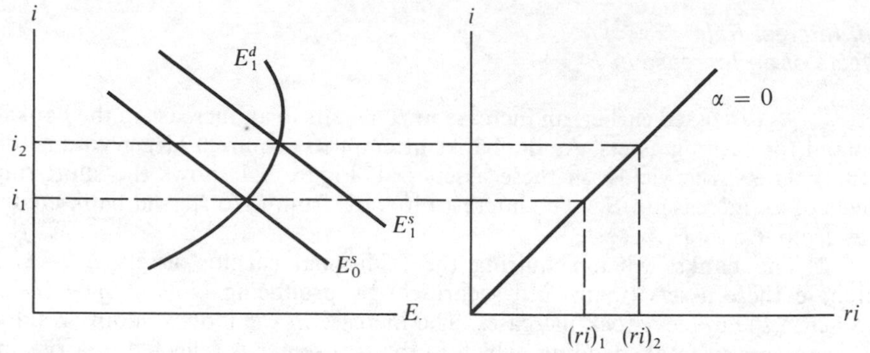

Figure 6.13 Market Rates and Real Rates when β Increases

continues to expand and the price level begins to rise. As prices rise, individuals revise upward their expectations about the future level of prices. This raises α, and the public's supply curve of earning assets again shifts to the right. Combining these results with the banks' demand curve for earning assets gives the situation shown in Figure 6.12.

Bank credit expands to E_3, and the bank credit market interest rate rises to i_3. Notice that the market rate i_3 is above the initial rate i_0 which prevailed before the increase in B^a. Although the impact effect of an increase in the base is to lower interest rates, over the longer run a maintained expansion of the base results in rising market interest rates.

Market Interest Rate and Real Interest Rate

The effect of an increase in the expected rate of return on real capital from β_0 to β_1 is to raise both the market (nominal) interest rate and the real interest rate. In Figure 6.13 the rise in β raises the market rate to i_2 and the real rate to $(ri)_2$ from $(ri)_1$.

However, the rise in the market interest rate from i_2 to i_3 associated with a rise in price expectations (α) is not accompanied by an increase in the

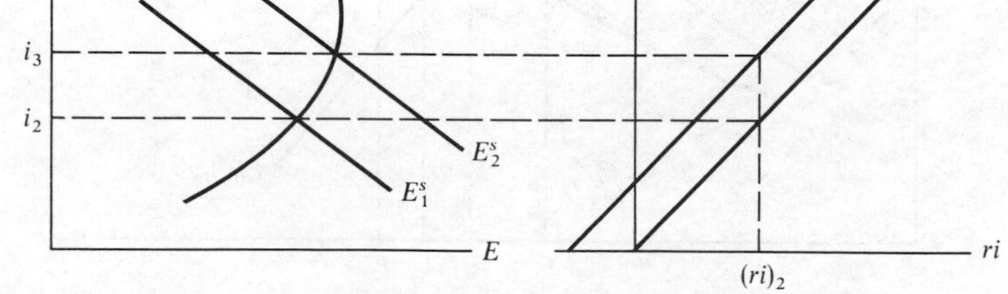

Figure 6.14 Market Rates and Real Rates when α Increases

real interest rate. As shown in Figure 6.14, the market rate rises to i_3 but the real rate remains at $(ri)_2$.[10]

Summary

To analyze the interest rate effects of a change in the magnitude or rate at which base is supplied to the economy we must consider three effects:

1. The impact or short-run effect of changes in B^a on credit market interest rates. The impact effect is

$$\varepsilon(i, B^a) < 0.$$

2. Feedback effects from the real sector to the credit market. The feedback effects of increases (decreases) in B^a act to raise (lower) interest rates.

3. Long-run or price expectation effects of a change in the base. This depends upon the change in the price level resulting from the effects in the real sector of base-induced changes in the monetary aggregates. These effects operate to raise (lower) interest rates as the base expands (contracts).

Appendix

SUMMARY TABLE OF THE BASIC RELATIONS INVOLVED IN THE HYPOTHESIS

$M^1 = D^p + C^p$		money	(3.1)
	D^p = demand deposits held by the public		
	C^p = currency held by the public		
$M^2 = M^1 + T$		money + time deposits	(3.2)
	T = time deposits		
$E = L + S - (N + D^t)$		bank credit	(3.3)
	L = loans held by commercial banks		
	S = security holdings by commercial banks		
	N = capital accounts of commercial banks		
	D^t = Treasury deposits at commercial banks		

[10] Taking into consideration the effect of inflation on real money balances, the real rate of interest would be expected to fall. The decline in real money balances and the resulting decline in wealth stimulates increased saving which causes the real rate to fall and the market rate to rise by less than the expected rate of inflation. See Robert Mundell, "Inflation and Real Interest," *Journal of Political Economy* (June 1963), pp. 280–284.

$B = A + B^a$ — source base (3.4)

A = sum of discounts and advances made to member banks by the Federal Reserve Banks

$B^a = B - A$ — net source base (3.5)

$k = \frac{C^p}{D^p}$ — currency ratio (3.8)

$k = f(q, Y/Y_p, Tx, s, W)$ (5.4)

q = measure of net service charges on demand deposits

Y/Y_p = ratio of net national product to permanent net national product

Tx = tax liability of the public

s = mobility of the population and such factors as seasonal patterns introduced by vacation schedules

W = nominal nonhuman wealth of the non-bank public

$t = \frac{T}{D^p}$ — time deposit ratio (3.9)

$t = f(i^f, i^t, W/P_a, Y/Y_p)$ (4.3)

i^f = index of yields on assets other than time deposits traded on bank credit market

i^t = index of yields on time deposits

W/P_a = real value of the stock of nonhuman wealth held by the public

$i^t = f(i^f, Q^*)$ — index of yields on time deposits (4.4)

i^f = a composite index of interest rates on financial assets traded on the credit market

Q^* = Regulation Q ceiling rates on time deposits

$d = \frac{D^t}{D^p}$ — Treasury deposit ratio (3.10)

D^t = Treasury deposits at commercial banks

D^p = Demand deposits held by the nonbank public

$b = \frac{A}{D^p + D^t + T}$ — borrowing ratio (3.11)

$b = f(i, \rho, \pi_2)$ (4.2)

π_2 = index of other factors which affect member bank borrowing from the Federal Reserve Banks

ρ = discount rate
i = index of bank credit market interest rates

$$R = R^r + R^e + V$$ reserves held by commercial banks (3.12)

R^r = required reserves
R^e = excess reserves
V = vault cash of nonmember banks

$$r = \frac{R}{D^p + D^t + T}$$ reserve ratio (3.14)

$$e = \frac{R^e}{D^p + D^t + T}$$ excess reserve ratio (3.15)

R^e = excess reserves

$$e = f(i, \rho, \pi_1)$$ (4.1)

i = index of yields on assets traded on the bank credit market
ρ = rediscount rate
π_1 = factors influencing the demand for excess reserves such as, the variance of interest rates, the variance of currency flows between the banks and the public, and banks' anticipations about the average level and variance of the reserve ratio.

$$v = \frac{V}{D^p + D^t + T}$$ nonmember bank vault cash ratio (3.16)

V = vault cash holdings of nonmember banks

$$\delta = \frac{D^m}{D^p + D^t}$$ (3.17)

D^m = member bank demand deposits subject to reserve requirements

$$\tau = \frac{T^m}{T}$$ (3.18)

T^m = member bank time deposits subject to reserve requirements

$$r = r^d\,\delta u + r^t\,\tau(1 - u) + e + v$$ (3.19)

r^d = weighted average legal reserve requirements on member bank demand deposits
r^t = weighted average legal reserve requirements on member bank time deposits

$$u = \frac{1 + d}{1 + t + d}$$

$m^1 = \dfrac{1 + k}{(r - b)(1 + t + d) + k}$	money multiplier
$m^2 = \dfrac{1 + k + t}{(r - b)(1 + t + d) + k}$	money plus time deposits multiplier
$m^2 - 1 = \dfrac{(1 + t) - (r - b)(1 + t + d)}{(r - b)(1 + t + d) + k}$	bank credit multiplier
$E^s = L + S$	public supply of earning assets to banks

$$E^s = f(i, Y/Y_p, W/P_a, \alpha, \beta, i_\theta, S^G) \tag{6.2}$$

α = price expectations
β = expected rate of return on real capital
S^G = stock of U.S. government securities

$$(m^2 - 1)B^a = E^s \tag{6.3}$$

equilibrium condition for bank credit market

Chapter Seven

Effects of Federal Reserve Policy Actions

Within the framework of the hypothesis used in this book, Federal Reserve policy actions influence the money supply process through two major channels. The first is through the effect of open market operations on the net source base. The second is through changes in the equilibrium values of the multipliers. The influence of changes in reserve requirements, the discount rate, and Regulation Q are impounded in changes in the multipliers.[1] Because of the dependence of the excess reserve ratio, borrowing ratio, and time deposit ratio on interest rates, open market operations may also affect the money and bank credit multipliers.

Open Market Actions

An open market operation by the Federal Reserve System may be thought of as an act of exchange in which base money is exchanged for Government securities. Such a purchase increases the amount of base held by the banks and the nonbank public; a sale decreases the base. Corresponding to the open market policy-induced change in the net source base is an equal change in the opposite direction of the dollar amount of government securities held by banks and the nonbank public.

The Federal Reserve acquires a given volume of Government securities from banks and the public by bidding up the price of government securities (alternatively forcing down their yields). It thus induces the public and the banks to alter their portfolio of assets. At the higher price of government securities, the public is temporarily willing to exchange them for demand deposits; the banks are willing to exchange them for excess reserves.

[1] In other formulations of the hypothesis in which the concept of the base is more broadly defined, such policy actions may appear as changes in the base. For example, if the monetary base concept is used instead of B^a, then reserve requirement changes and member bank borrowings would alter the monetary base. See Appendix II, Chapter 3.

Following the open market purchase by the Federal Reserve, at the lower interest rate on government securities, the banks and the public are willing to hold the smaller stock of government securities. The interest rate on government securities is, however, only one interest rate entering into the determination of the composite bank credit market interest rate (i), which determines the equilibrium values of the e, b, and t-ratios and hence the equilibrium values of the money and bank credit multipliers.

If the banks sell the entire volume of government securities purchased by the Federal Reserve, the instantaneous impact of the open market policy action is to increase the commercial banks' excess reserve ratio. Assuming that commercial banks were initially holding the ratio of excess reserves to deposits that they desired to hold, then this policy-induced change in their asset portfolios leaves them holding a greater amount of excess reserves than they desire relative to other assets, given the prevailing market interest rate and prices of other financial and real assets. A portfolio adjustment process will follow.

In this adjustment process, the banks attempt to acquire a larger portion of the stock of other assets. The commercial banks attempt to acquire a larger stock of earning assets by bidding for municipal securities and inducing the public to increase its demand for commercial bank loans. As a consequence, the composite interest rate (i) decreases. After the adjustment process, the yields on assets other than government securities will have fallen, and the rate on banks' loans will have decreased. Banks and the public will be willing to hold the smaller total stock of securities at lower interest rates. For the commercial banks, the likely result of the adjustment process is that they are holding a larger volume of loans and other securities, a smaller volume of government securities, and a larger amount of excess reserves than before the policy-induced change in their asset portfolio.[2]

If an open market purchase or sale of securities by the Federal Reserve *does not affect the equilibrium values of the* e, b, t, k, *and* r*-ratios* (i.e., the multipliers m^1 and m^2 may be considered constants), and if the system was in equilibrium, then the multipliers return to their predisturbance values (their values prior to the open market operation). Following an open market purchase (sale) B^a is larger (smaller), and the stocks of money and bank credit increase (decrease). The elasticities of M and E with respect to a change in B^a are equal to one. A percentage change in the net source base leads to an equal percentage change in the stocks of money and bank credit.

However, since the magnitudes of M^1, M^2, and E are not the same, a given change in B^a leads to different *absolute* changes in M^1, M^2, and E. If the magnitude of M^1 is less than the magnitude of bank credit, a change in B^a leads to a greater dollar change in bank credit (E) than M^1, even though the percentage changes are the same.

---

[2] The final outcome of the adjustment process depends on the bidding of the banks and the public for the existing stock of securities and the willingness of the public to incur additional liabilities to the commercial banking system. Under certain conditions, the banks or the public may be unable to increase their portion of the total stock of securities; the end result would be that each sector holds the same portion of the existing stock of assets as before the open market purchase but at higher prices.

Interest Rate Effects on Open Market Operation

Once we introduce the conditions that (1) changes in the net source base affect interest rates, and (2) the elasticities of the e, b, and t-ratios with respect to the interest rate are not equal to zero, then the elasticities of M^1, M^2, and E with respect to changes in B^a are no longer necessarily equal to one. Changes in credit market interest rates caused by changes in B^a alter the equilibrium values of the multipliers.

Let

$$\varepsilon(i, B^a) = \text{elasticity of interest rates with respect to } B^a,$$
$$\varepsilon(m, i) = \text{elasticity of the multipliers with respect to } i.$$

The effect of interest rate changes induced by changes in the base on M^1, M^2, and bank credit can be expressed in a general form as follows:

$$\varepsilon(m, i) \cdot \varepsilon(i, B^a)$$

The elasticities of M^1, M^2, and E with respect to B^a, taking into account interest rate effects, are as follows:

$$\varepsilon(M^1, B^a) = 1 + \varepsilon(m^1, i) \cdot \varepsilon(i, B^a),$$
$$\varepsilon(M^2, B^a) = 1 + \varepsilon(m^2, i) \cdot \varepsilon(i, B^a),$$
$$\varepsilon(E, B^a) \quad = 1 + \varepsilon(m^2 - 1, i) \cdot \varepsilon(i, B^a).$$

Writing the elasticities in this form makes explicit that the percentage changes in the monetary aggregates and bank credit depend not only upon the percentage change in B^a but also upon the response of interest rates to changes in B^a and the response of the banks and the nonbank public to base-induced changes in interest rates. Under the condition that the multipliers are completely insensitive to changes in the interest rate (the case in which $\varepsilon(m, i) = 0$), the elasticities of money, M^2, and bank credit with respect to B^a are equal to one.

Chapter 5 showed that the signs and numerical values of the elasticities of the multipliers with respect to the composite interest rate (i) depend upon (1) the relevant initial conditions about the level of interest rates, (2) the relationship between the yield that banks are offering on time deposits and Regulation *Q* ceiling rates, and (3) the reactions of the Federal Reserve Banks to a rising level of member bank borrowings. In Chapter 6 the sign and numerical value of $\varepsilon(i, B^a)$ were shown to depend upon (1) the elasticities of the banks' asset demand and the public's asset supply functions with respect to the interest rate (i), and (2) upon whether we are considering a partial equilibrium (short-run situation) or are taking into account the full feedback effects from the real sector (and hence considering the long-run response of interest rates to maintained expansions or contractions of the base). Therefore, the derivable consequences of an open market operation for the monetary aggregates and bank credit depends upon what assumptions are made about the initial conditions under which the open market operation is carried out.

Predicted Consequences of an Open Market Operation

To demonstrate the workings of the hypothesis, we shall analyze in three different cases, the predicted short-run and long-run effects of open market operations on the monetary aggregates and bank credit. The cases will be labeled cases I–III to correspond to cases I–III in Chapter 5, where the elasticities of the money and bank credit multipliers with respect to the interest rate (i) were discussed.

Case Ia: Short-Run

Initial conditions:

(1.1a) Interest rates, relative to their past levels, are low.
(1.2a) $\varepsilon(i, B^a) < 0$.
(1.3a) The yields banks are offering on time deposits are sufficiently below Regulation Q ceiling rates so that banks can respond competitively to rising market interest rates.

Initial condition (1.2a) states that changes in the net source base result in changes in the opposite direction in short-term interest rates. Condition (1.3a) means that banks' response to rising market yields on other assets offsets the negative influence on the t-ratio of the rise in market yields relative to i^t.

Under the initial conditions of Case Ia, as discussed in Chapter 5, the total elasticities of the multipliers with respect to interest rates are dominated by the $\varepsilon(m, e) \cdot \varepsilon(e, i)$. The sign of the elasticities of the multipliers with respect to interest rates is positive:

$$\varepsilon(m, i) > 0.$$

Rewriting the expressions for the elasticities of M^1, M^2, and E with respect to the net source base

$$\varepsilon(M, B^a) = 1 + \varepsilon(m, i) \cdot \varepsilon(i, B^a),$$
$$\varepsilon(E, B^a) = 1 + \varepsilon(m^2 - 1, i) \cdot \varepsilon(i, B^a);$$

we conclude that, since under the short-run conditions of case Ia

$$\varepsilon(i, B^a) < 0,$$

the following results hold under case Ia initial conditions:

$$\varepsilon(M^1, B^a) < 1,$$
$$\varepsilon(M^2, B^a) < 1,$$
$$\varepsilon(E, B^a) < 1.$$

Also, as shown in Chapter 5 under case I conditions, the following ordering relation prevails:

$$\varepsilon(m^1, i) < \varepsilon(m^2, i) < \varepsilon(m^2 - 1, i).$$

Therefore, the following ordering relation between M^1, M^2, and E with respect to interest rates is derived:

$$\varepsilon(M^1, B^a) > \varepsilon(M^2, B^a) > \varepsilon(E, B^a).$$

Under the initial conditions of case Ia low interest rate regime in which banks are not constrained by Regulation Q, a 1 per cent change in the net source base results in a less than 1 per cent change in the same direction of M^1, M^2, and bank credit. When the Federal Reserve System expands the base by purchasing government securities, the short-term interest rate falls. Banks increase their holdings of excess reserves relative to deposit liabilities. Since in case Ia the e-ratio is large and exercises a significant influence on the values of the multipliers, the rise in the e-ratio reduces the multipliers and hence base-induced increases in the stocks of money and bank credit are dampened.

The relative percentage responses of M^1, M^2, and E to changes in B^a are not of the same magnitude. Bank credit and M^2 are less sensitive to changes in the base than is the narrowly defined money stock. A 1 per cent increase (decrease) in B^a leads to a larger percentage increase (decrease) in M^1 than in the money stock defined to include time deposits and a larger percentage increase (decrease) in M^2 than bank credit.

The difference in the relative responses of M^1, M^2, and E hinges on the difference in the responses of the multipliers to changes in interest rates. The numerical value of the elasticity of $m^2 - 1$ with respect to the excess reserve ratio is greater than m^2 or m^1. Also, the elasticities of m^2 and $m^2 - 1$ with respect to the t-ratio are opposite in sign to the response of the money multiplier. Under a regime of extremely low levels of interest rates relative to past levels of interest rates, banks tend to be quite sensitive to a small percentage increase in interest rates. A policy-induced decrease in B^a, resulting in an increase in interest rates may result in a marked decline in banks' desired excess reserve-to-deposit ratio (e) and some rise in the t-ratio. The interest rate effects of the decrease in B^a operate to offset more of the base-induced decrease in bank credit than money.

Case Ib: Long-Run

In case Ib we retain initial conditions (1.1a) and (1.3a). The only change made is that now the long-run interest rate effects resulting from a change in B^a are taken into account. The new condition is stated as

(1.2b) $\varepsilon(i, B^a) > 0.$

This change reflects the discussion in Chapter 6 of short-run and long-run interest rate effects of a change in B^a.

Using condition (1.2b), we can now trace the impacts on M^1, M^2, and E of a change in B^a. For M^1,

$$\varepsilon(m^1, i) > 0,$$
$$\varepsilon(i, B^a) > 0.$$

Therefore

$$\varepsilon(m^1, i) \cdot \varepsilon(i, B^a) > 0.$$

Therefore the elasticity of M^1 with respect to the net source base is greater than one.

$$\varepsilon(M^1, B^a) > 1.$$

From M^2 and bank credit we have a similar result:

$$\varepsilon(m^2, i) > 0,$$
$$\varepsilon(i, B^a) > 0.$$

Hence the elasticities of M^2 and E with respect to the net source base are greater than one.

$$\varepsilon(M^2, B^a) > 1,$$
$$\varepsilon(E, B^a) \quad > 1.$$

Since, as shown under case Ia, with the initial conditions (1.1a) and (1.3a),

$$\varepsilon(m^1, i) < \varepsilon(m^2, i) < \varepsilon(m^2 - 1, i);$$

then

$$\varepsilon(M^1, B^a) < \varepsilon(M^2, B^a) < \varepsilon(E, B^a).$$

The reader should note that this reverses the results derived in case Ia.

In case Ia the short-run base-induced changes in interest rates acted to dampen the response of the monetary aggregates and bank credit to changes in the net source base. In case Ib, as a result of altering initial condition (1.2a), the long-run interest rate effects of a change in B^a act to increase the elasticities of M^1, M^2, and E with respect to B^a. In the short-run the base-induced decrease in the interest rate acts to dampen the percentage changes in these aggregates resulting from an increase in B^a. Over the long run taking the effects of the increase in monetary aggregates on total spending into account and the feedback from the real sector to the bank credit market into account, interest rates on the bank credit market rise, resulting in a rise in the multipliers and hence a further increase in the monetary aggregates and bank credit.

Case IIa: Short-Run

Initial Conditions:

(2.1a) Interest rates are at about the average of their past levels and in a medium range.
(2.2a) $\varepsilon(i, B^a) < 0$.
(2.3a) Banks offering yields on time deposits (i^t) approach Regulation Q ceiling rates and the numerical value of $\varepsilon(i^t, i^f)$ decreases.
(2.4a) As the level of member bank borrowing rises, Federal Reserve Banks begin to exercise closer administrative control over member bank borrowing. $\pi_2 > 0$.

Case IIa, like case Ia, is a short-run analysis. This is reflected in initial condition (2.2a), which is identical to initial condition (1.2a).

Case IIa alters the initial conditions concerning the level of interest rates and the relationship between the yields offered by banks on time deposits (i^t) and the ceiling rates (Q) imposed by the Federal Reserve System.

In order to trace through the results under case IIa, this case is divided into two phases.

Phase I. It is assumed the banks are still able to vary i^t so as to offset the negative influence of a rise in market yields on the t-ratio. Also, it is assumed that the total cost of member bank borrowing from Federal Reserve Banks remains below market interest rates.

As interest rates rise the banks reduce their holdings of excess reserves relative to deposits, and the influence of the e-ratio on the multipliers is reduced from case Ia. This result is expressed as

$$\varepsilon(m, e) \to 0 \qquad \text{as interest rates rise.}$$

With market yields exceeding the total cost of borrowing from the Federal Reserve Banks, the member banks expand their borrowings. The b-ratio comes to exercise a more important influence on the multipliers:

$$\varepsilon(m, b) > 0 \qquad \text{increases as interest rates rise.}$$

To take advantage of higher yields on earning assets, the banks raise the yields they offer on time deposits to induce the public to increase its t-ratio. These results are expressed as

$$\varepsilon(i^t, i^f) > 0,$$
$$\varepsilon(t, i) > 0.$$

As we proceed through phase I, the decline in $\varepsilon(m, e)$ and the rise in $\varepsilon(m, b)$ come to offset one another and the $\varepsilon(t, i)$ dominates the total interest elasticity of the multipliers. Since

$$\varepsilon(m^1, t) < 0,$$
$$\varepsilon(m^2, t),\ \varepsilon(m^2 - 1, t) > 0,$$

the rise in the t-ratio, induced by banks' actions with respect to the yields they are willing and able to offer on time deposits, reduces the numerical value of the money multiplier but raises the value of the M^2 and the bank credit multipliers.

Phase II. Banks have raised their offering yields on time deposits close to Regulation Q ceiling rates. Also, the Federal Reserve has begun to exercise tighter control over the aggregate level of member bank borrowing.

Under initial condition (2.4a) as the level of member bank borrowing rises, the Federal Reserve Banks begin to exercise closer administrative control over member bank borrowing, and

$$\pi_2 > 0,$$
$$\varepsilon(b, i) \to 0.$$

To take advantage of higher yields available on earning assets, the banks raise their offering yields on time deposits. However, as i^t approaches Regulation Q ceiling rates, the ability of banks to offset the negative influence of rising market yields on the public's desired t-ratio is constrained, and

$$\varepsilon(t, i) \to 0.$$

Consequently, under these initial conditions at the *upper end* of case IIa, the elasticities of the multipliers with respect to the interest rate approach zero. Restating the expressions:

$$\varepsilon(M^1, B^a) = 1 + \varepsilon(m^1, i) \cdot \varepsilon(i, B^a),$$
$$\varepsilon(M^2, B^a) = 1 + \varepsilon(m^2, i) \cdot \varepsilon(i, B^a),$$
$$\varepsilon(E, B^a) + 1 + \varepsilon(m^2 - 1, i) \cdot \varepsilon(i, B^a).$$

We conclude that as interest rates rise from low levels to medium levels and as $i^t \to Q^*$, the differences between the elasticities of the monetary aggregates and bank credit with respect to B^a are reduced:

$$\varepsilon(m, i) \to 0$$
$$\varepsilon(M^1, B^a), \varepsilon(M^2, B^a), \varepsilon(E, B^a) \to 1.$$

Under the initial conditions of case IIa, as the level of market rates rises, short-run interest rate effects induced by changes in the supply of net source base have progressively less of a dampening effect on the percentage change in M^1, M^2, and E for a given percentage change in B^a.

As $\varepsilon(m, i) \to 0$, the percentage responses of the monetary aggregates and bank credit approach equality. Precisely, the difference in the percentage changes in M^1, M^2, and E generated by an open market operation are due to different responses of the multipliers to given interest rate changes. As the total response of the multipliers to changes in the interest rate becomes small, the divergence in percentage changes in the money stock, M^2, and bank credit resulting from increases or decreases in the net source base disappear.

The difference between the relative responses of money and bank credit in phase I and phase II of Case IIa may be illustrated using a couple of graphs previously introduced. We use the graph showing the relationship between E and M^1 developed in Chapter 4 in Figures 4.5 and 4.6. Also, we use the graph that illustrates equilibrium on the bank credit market, developed in Chapter 6 in Figures 6.1, 6.2, and 6.3. Combining these graphs, the effect of decrease in B^a under phase II conditions is illustrated in Figure 7.1. A subscript Q_1 is attached to the banks' demand curve for earning assets to denote that E^d_{Q1} is drawn assuming a given value for Regulation Q ceiling rates. The reader may want to review pages 116–117 and 120–121 in Chapter 6 for the discussion of the effect of Regulation Q on the shape of the banks' demand curve. The starting positions for our graphical analysis are denoted with an asterisk (*).

A decrease in B^a shifts the banks' demand curve for earning assets to the left from $^*E^d_{Q_1}$ to $E^d_{Q_1}$. Under phase II initial conditions, the total interest rate effect on the multipliers of the decrease in B^a is approximately zero. Hence, the interest rate on the bank credit market rises from $^*i$ to i_1 and the bank credit and money (M^1) decrease from $^*E$ to E_1 and $^*M$ to M_1 respectively.

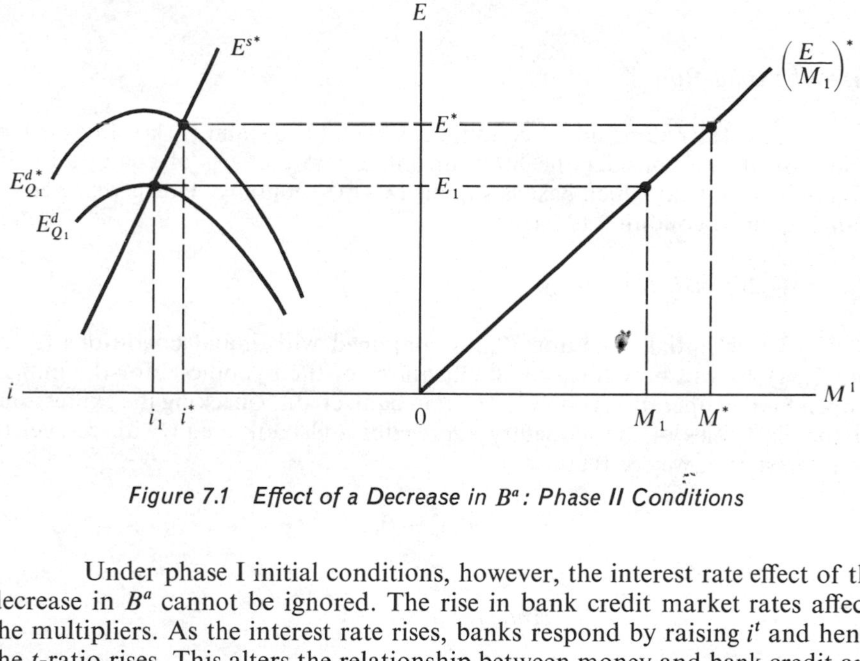

Figure 7.1 Effect of a Decrease in B^a: Phase II Conditions

Under phase I initial conditions, however, the interest rate effect of the decrease in B^a cannot be ignored. The rise in bank credit market rates affects the multipliers. As the interest rate rises, banks respond by raising i^t and hence the t-ratio rises. This alters the relationship between money and bank credit and results in a rotation of the line E/M^1 (as discussed in Chapter 4 and illustrated in Figure 4.6). Since under these conditions, $\varepsilon(m^2 - 1, i) > 0$, the portion of the banks' demand curve which is cut by the supply curve has a different shape. This difference is illustrated by the dotted line on the demand curve in Figure 7.2.

In the situation illustrated in Figure 7.2 money and bank credit decline. However, the decrease in bank credit is *less* and the decrease in money is *greater* than under phase II conditions. Due to the interest rate effects on the multipliers, bank credit declines to E_2 instead of E_1, money declines to M_2 instead of M_1. Market rates rise only to i_2 instead of i_1 as in phase II conditions.

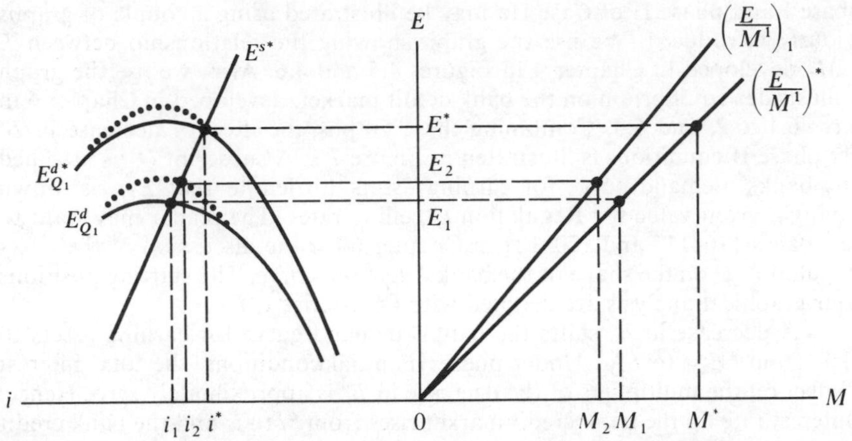

Figure 7.2 Effect of a Decrease in B^a Phase I Conditions

Case IIb: Long-Run

Case IIb retains initial conditions (2.1a), (2.3a), and (2.4a). In case IIb, as in case Ib, we consider the long-run interest rate effects of changes in the magnitude or rate at which base is supplied to the economy. This is reflected by changing initial condition (2.2a) to

(2.2b) $\varepsilon(i, B^a) > 0.$

Using initial condition (2.2b) conjoined with initial conditions (2.1a) and (2.3a), we can now trace the implications of the hypothesis for the impact of open market operations on M^1, M^2, and bank credit. Checking the expressions for the elasticities of the monetary aggregates and bank credit with respect to the interest rate, we see that:

$$\varepsilon(m, i) \rightarrow 0.$$

Therefore

$$\varepsilon(m, i) \cdot \varepsilon(i, B^a) \rightarrow 0;$$

and consequently the elasticities of the stocks of money and bank credit with respect to B^a approach one:

$$\varepsilon(M, B^a) \rightarrow 1,$$
$$\varepsilon(E, B^a) \rightarrow 1.$$

These results lead to an interesting implication. Although we reversed the initial condition (2.2) about the direction of the response of interest rates to changes in B^a, the same limiting results emerge under case IIb as under case IIa. In both cases, although the short- and long-run effects of changes in B^a on the interest rate may be opposite in direction, to the extent that initial conditions (2.1), (2.3), and (2.4) hold, as interest rates rise to the upper end of their medium range, the total interest elasticity of the multipliers decreases approaching zero, and the feedback effect of base-induced changes in interest rates on the multipliers become very small.

Case IIIa: Short-Run

Initial conditions:

(3.1a) Interest rates relative to their past levels are high.
(3.2a) $\varepsilon(i, B^a) < 0$.
(3.3a) i^t sufficiently close to Q^* so that $\varepsilon(i^t, i^f)$ approaches zero.
(3.4a) The Federal Reserve Banks are exercising close administrative control over member bank borrowings, hence the total cost of member bank borrowings considerably exceeds the discount rate.

Initial condition (3.3a) states that the yields offered by banks on time deposits are close to the Regulation Q ceiling rates. This means that the ability of banks to raise i^t in response to an increase in yields (i^f) on other market assets is constrained.

The result of imposing initial condition (3.3a) is that

$$|\varepsilon(t, i^f)| > |\varepsilon(t, i^t) \cdot \varepsilon(i^t, i^f)|,$$

and hence

$$\varepsilon(t, i) < 0.$$

Under initial condition (3.3a) the elasticity of the t-ratio with respect to the interest rate has an opposite sign (negative) compared to our previous two cases. For case I initial conditions, interest rates are at low levels and i^t is sufficiently below Regulation Q ceiling rates so that as market interest rates rise, the t-ratio rises. In case II initial conditions, as market rates rise and i^t approaches Q^*, the $\varepsilon(t, i)$ remains positive but decreases in numerical value. As i^t approaches closer to Q^*, the $\varepsilon(t, i) \rightarrow 0$. Under the initial conditions of case III, because of Regulation Q constraints, $\varepsilon(i^t, i^f)$ approaches zero and the sign of the elasticity of the t-ratio with respect to the interest rate is reversed, becoming negative.

Under high levels of interest rates, initial condition (3.1a), and the constraint on member bank borrowings imposed by (3.4a), the first two sets of terms in the expression for the total elasticities of the multipliers with respect to interest rates,

$$\varepsilon(m, i) = \varepsilon(m, e) \cdot \varepsilon(e, i) + \varepsilon(m, b) \cdot \varepsilon(b, i) + \varepsilon(m, t) \cdot \varepsilon(t, i)$$

become small in numerical value and the last set of terms dominates the sign and size of the total elasticity of the multipliers. Since, under case III initial conditions, the elasticity of the t-ratio with respect to the interest rate is negative, and as previously $\varepsilon(m^1, t) < 0$, it follows that

$$\varepsilon(m^1, i) > 0,$$

and we conclude that

$$\varepsilon(M^1, B^a) < 1.$$

For the M^2 and bank credit multipliers we conclude that since

$$\varepsilon(m^2, t) > 0, \qquad \varepsilon(t, i) < 0,$$

then the sign of the elasticity of the money defined to include the time deposits multiplier is negative:

$$\varepsilon(m^2, i) < 0.$$

From the expressions

$$\varepsilon(M^2, B^a) = 1 + \varepsilon(m^2, i) \cdot \varepsilon(i, B^a),$$
$$\varepsilon(E, B^a) = 1 + \varepsilon(m^2 - 1, i) \cdot \varepsilon(i, B^a),$$

the conclusion is reached that

$$\varepsilon(M^2, B^a) > 1,$$
$$\varepsilon(E, B^a) > 1.$$

Relationship between Elasticities of M^2 and Bank Credit with Respect to B^a

Under the initial conditions of case IIIa

$$\varepsilon(m^2, i), \varepsilon(m^2 - 1, i) < 0;$$

and as shown previously

$$|\varepsilon(m^2 - 1, i)| > |\varepsilon(m^2, i)|.$$

Comparing the expressions for the elasticities of M^2 and bank credit with respect to the net source base, the following result emerges:

$$\varepsilon(E, B^a) > \varepsilon(M^2, B^a).$$

Under the initial conditions of case IIIa, the impact effect of an increase in the base is to lower credit market interest rates. The decrease in credit market interest rates makes time deposits more attractive than other assets. The public's demand for time deposits increases and the t-ratio rises. The increase in the t-ratio raises the equilibrium values of the bank credit and M^2 multipliers and reinforces the increase in M^2 and E resulting from an increase in the base.

The rise in the time deposit ratio lowers the M^1 multiplier, and this process dampens the rate of increase of M^1.

When the rate at which base is supplied by the central bank decreases, the impact effect raises credit market yields. Because banks' offering rates on time deposits are at Q ceilings, no change in the yields that banks are offering on time deposits can occur, and the t-ratio decreases. The decline in the t-ratio results in a fall in m^2 and $m^2 - 1$, and this reinforces the rate of decrease of M^2 and bank credit resulting from the decrease in B^a. However, the reduction in the t-ratio raises the money multiplier (m^1) and acts to dampen the rate of decrease of M^1.

The effect of a decrease in B^a, under case IIIa conditions, can be illustrated with the same graphs used in Figures 7.1 and 7.2. Since, under case IIIa initial conditions the interest rate effect of the decrease in B^a operated to decrease the t-ratio, the bank credit multiplier falls and the money multiplier rises, hence the line (E/M^1) rotates to the right. The banks' demand curve must be redrawn to show that banks are constrained by Regulation Q. The demand curves labeled $^*E^d_{Q2}$ represent this condition. These effects are illustrated in Figure 7.3.

A comparison of Figure 7.3 and Figure 7.2 shows the difference in the effects of a decrease in B^a on money and bank credit under differing initial conditions. In the situation illustrated by Figure 7.2, banks are free to vary i^t and hence (E/M^1) rotates to the left.

In Figure 7.3 banks are constrained by Regulation Q ceilings. Hence, a decrease in B^a results in bank credit falling to E_3, a greater amount than E_2 (the result of Figure 7.2) or E_1 (the result under the absence of interest rate effects on the multipliers). Money falls to M_3, a lesser amount than M_1 (the result under the absence of interest rate effects on the multipliers) or M_2 (the result of Figure 7.2). The bank credit market interest rate rises to i_3 under case IIIa conditions, a higher level than i_2, or i_1 (the absence of interest rate effects on the multipliers). In summary, a comparison of Figures 7.1–7.3 shows that a decrease in B^a leads to the greatest decrease in money (M^1) under phase I conditions of case IIa. However, these conditions, lead to the smallest relative decline of bank credit (E).

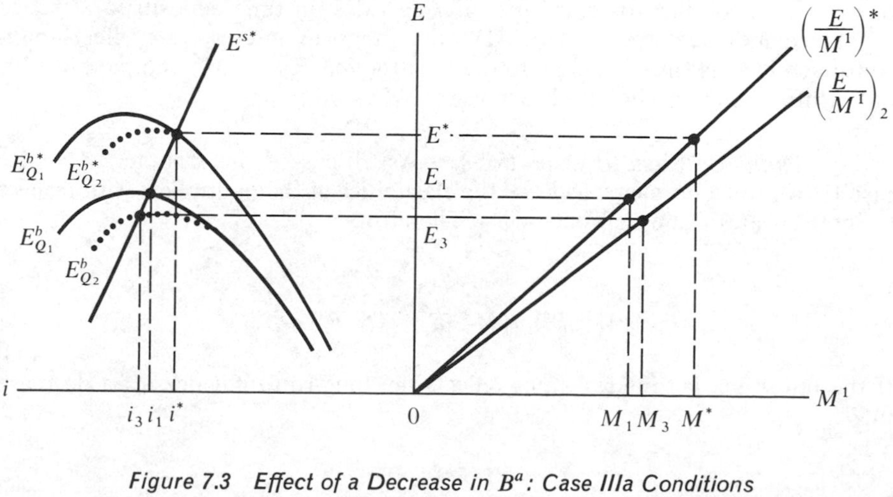

Figure 7.3 Effect of a Decrease in B^a: Case IIIa Conditions

Case IIIb: Long-Run

In case IIIb the initial conditions (3.1a), (3.3a), and (3.4a) are retained, but initial condition (3.2a) is replaced:

(3.2b) $\varepsilon(i, B^a) > 0.$

Since under case IIIb initial conditions, the following results apply:

$$\varepsilon(m^1, i) > 0,$$
$$\varepsilon(i, B^a) > 0;$$

then

$$\varepsilon(M^1, B^a) > 1.$$

Since, due to the constraint of Regulation Q,

$$\varepsilon(m^2, i), \qquad \varepsilon(m^2 - 1, i) < 0;$$

then, using condition (3.2b), we conclude:

$$\varepsilon(M^2, B^a) < 1,$$
$$\varepsilon(E, B^a) < 1.$$

Under the initial conditions of case IIIb the long-run interest rate effects of changes in the base operate, as in case Ib, to increase the elasticity of M^1 with respect to B^a. However, in case IIIb, due to the constraint of Regulation Q, the long-run interest rate effects of a change in B^a operate to decrease the elasticity of M^2 and E with respect to B^a. This is the reverse of case Ib. The difference lies in initial conditions (1.3) and (3.3). In case I banks are able to vary i^t to offset the negative influence of a rise in i^f on the t-ratio. In case IIIb banks are constrained from raising offering rates on time deposits, and hence $\varepsilon(t, i)$ becomes negative. In case IIIb the long-run interest rate effects of a continued increase in B^a operate to dampen the increase in M^2 and bank credit, but reinforce the base-induced increase in M^1.

Limits on Case III Conditions. As discussed in Chapter 5 under case III for the multipliers, as $t \to 0$ the elasticities of the multipliers with respect to interest rates again approach zero. Therefore

$$t \to 0,$$
$$\varepsilon(M^1, B^a),\ \varepsilon(M^2, B_p),\ \varepsilon(E, B^a) \to 1.$$

If the fall in market interest rates reflects the long-run influences of a decrease in B^a,

$$\varepsilon(i, B^a) > 0,$$

then the following are the derivable results for the elasticities of M^1, M^2, and bank credit with respect to B^a:

$$\varepsilon(M^1, B^a) > 1,$$
$$\varepsilon(M^2, B^a) < 1,$$
$$\varepsilon(E, B^a) < 1.$$

As interest rates begin to fall, as discussed in Chapter 5, the banks may maintain the spread between i^t and i^f so that the t-ratio rises. The money multiplier falls and the M^2 and bank credit multipliers rise.

In the first phase of the downturn in interest rates, the banks' reaction to the large existing spread between i^t and the available returns on earning assets may act to dampen the rate of decrease of M^2 and bank credit resulting from a decline in B^a, but reinforce the downward pressures on the money stock.

Over Time

If the Federal Reserve pursues a maintained policy of expansion or contraction, the analysis might move between cases characterized by short-run conditions to cases characterized by long-run conditions. Figure 7.1 illustrates an example in which, beginning in initial conditions of case Ia (low levels of interest rates and i^t well below Q^*), the Federal Reserve pursues a maintained expansionary policy. In Figure 7.4 the upper graph shows the elasticities of M^1 and bank credit with respect to B^a. The lower graph expresses the elasticity of the interest rate (i) with respect to the net source base.

Following through Figure 7.4, as the Federal Reserve begins its expansionary policy in case Ia, interest rates are quite responsive to changes in B^a, and $\varepsilon(i, B^a) < 0$. Interest rate effects of changes in B^a have a significant dampening effect on the percentage responses of money and bank credit to expansions or contractions of B^a.

As the Federal Reserve continues its expansionary policies, the impact effects of an increase in B^a come to be partly offset by feedback effects from the real sector—for example, the rising expected rate of return on real capital. The $\varepsilon(i, B^a)$ remains negative but decreases in numerical value from case Ia. As $\varepsilon(i, B^a) \rightarrow 0$, the $\varepsilon(M^1, B^a)$ and $\varepsilon(E, B^a)$ rise.

With continued expansion of B^a, the feedback effects from the real sector come to dominate the response of interest rates, and the elasticity of the interest rate with respect to B^a becomes positive. The economy moves into case Ib conditions. The rise in interest rates resulting from a continued increase in B^a reinforces the expansionary effect of B^a on M^1 and E.

As feedback effects in the form of the expected rate of return on real capital and price expectations come to exercise a larger influence on market interest rates, $\varepsilon(i, B^a)$ increases. As the expansion of B^a continues, the economy enters case IIb conditions. Now the constraint of Regulation Q becomes important in determining the $\varepsilon(M^1, B^a)$ and $\varepsilon(E, B^a)$. As the yields that banks are offering on time deposits approach Q^* ceiling rates, the elasticities of the multipliers with respect to the interest rate approach zero and hence $\varepsilon(M^1, B^a)$ and $\varepsilon(E, B^a)$ approach 1.

The economy now moves into case III conditions—high levels of interest rates and the constraint of Regulation Q. Let us now assume the Federal Reserve engages in massive open market operations that have the impact effect of temporarily lowering credit market interest rates. The result is depicted by case IIIa conditions. The temporary fall in interest rates permits banks to compete for time deposits, and $\varepsilon(E, B^a) > 1$ and $\varepsilon(M^1, B^a) < 1$.

This would only be a temporary position. To keep credit market rates at their existing levels, the Federal Reserve would have to accelerate the growth rate of the base. This policy generates increasing upward pressures on prices and hence upward pressures on market interest rates.

In a short period of time, the elasticity of credit market interest rates

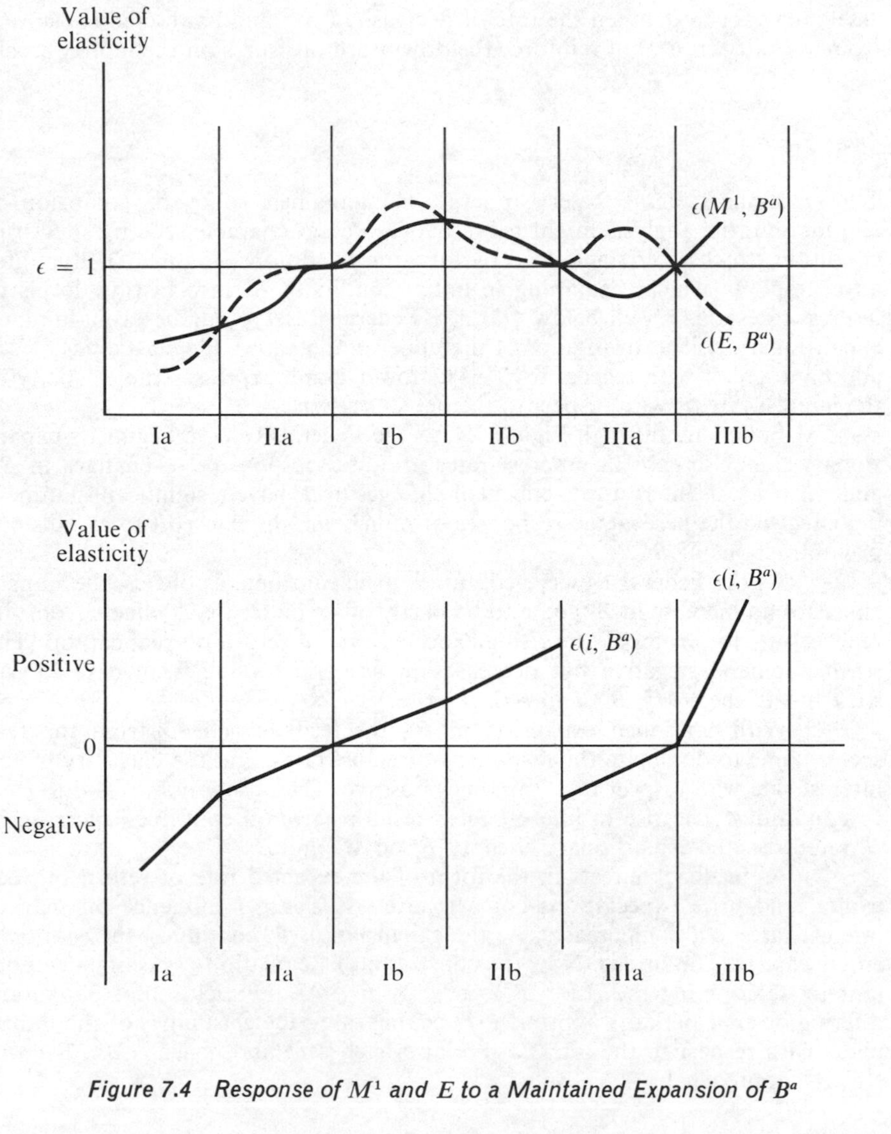

Figure 7.4 Response of M^1 and E to a Maintained Expansion of B^a

with respect to B^a become positive. In the face of rapidly rising interest rates, in order to continue to increase their time deposit liabilities the banks are forced to rapidly increase their offering rates on time deposits. The yields on time deposits (i^t) soon reach Regulation Q ceiling rates.[3] The economy moves into case IIIb conditions.

Rising interest rates and a rapidly expanding supply of base accelerate the growth rate of M^1. However, the rising interest rates, operating to reduce the t-ratio, dampen the effects of an accelerating supply of B^a on bank credit.

If the Federal Reserve then begins by open market sales to reduce the growth rate of the base, the short-run effect will be to raise interest rates. The rise in interest rates further reduces the t-ratio, and the contractionary effect of the reduction in the growth of B^a on M^2 and E is reinforced. Of the three aggregates, the short-run effects of this tighter monetary policy are greatest on bank credit.

As the Federal Reserve maintains a slower growth rate of B^a, market interest rates begin to fall. With banks again able to compete for time deposits, the t-ratio rises and the corresponding rise in the M^2 and bank credit multipliers offset part of the effects of the decrease in B^a on M^2 and bank credit. However, the rise in the t-ratio results in a decrease in the money multiplier which reinforces the downward pressures on the money stock resulting from the reduction in B^a.

Reserve Requirements and the Rediscount Rate

A change in member bank weighted average legal reserve requirements (r^d, r^t) and changes in the discount rate (ρ) have their impact on money and bank credit by changing the values of parameters of the multipliers and hence altering the equilibrium values of the money and bank credit multipliers. A change in r^d, r^t, or ρ does not alter the net source base B^a (B^a has been adjusted by removing member bank borrowings from the broader concept of the base B).

When the Board of Governors changes effective legal reserve requirements, this policy action alters the amount of reserves that member banks must hold given their deposit liabilities. In terms of the multipliers, a change in reserve requirements is reflected in a change in the reserve ratio, which was defined as

$$r = u\,\delta\, r^d + (1 - u)\tau\, r^t + e + v.$$

For example, an increase in reserve requirements leads to a portfolio adjustment process on the part of the commercial banking system. Given their existing liabilities, banks are no longer satisfied with the structure of their asset portfolios. They attempt to restructure their asset portfolios to contain more

---

[3] For example, in December 1965, Regulation Q ceiling rates were raised from $4\frac{1}{2}$ to $5\frac{1}{2}$ per cent. However, by early July 1966 the new issue rate on CD's was again at Regulation Q ceiling rates.

base (reserves) relative to their deposit liabilities. This adjustment process leads to a decrease in the stocks of money and bank credit.

A change in the discount rate alters the amount of base that member banks desire to borrow from the Federal Reserve Banks. For example, if other factors affecting the b-ratio remain unchanged, a decrease in the discount rate makes reserves borrowed from the Federal Reserve Banks a more attractive means of supporting deposits for member banks. The banks' desired ratio of borrowings to deposits (b-ratio) rises, and this is reflected in an increase in the multipliers.

Changes in the discount rate also affect the potential reserve adjustment costs to banks. If the discount rate is lowered, then the cost to a member bank of making short-term reserve adjustments is reduced. Therefore, as the discount rate is changed, this policy action affects member banks' desired holdings of excess reserves relative to deposit liabilities. A reduction (increase) in potential reserve adjustment costs reduces (raises) the banks' desired e-ratio.

For example, when the Federal Reserve Banks increase their discount rates, this increases the member banks' desired ratio of excess reserves to deposits and decreases their desired borrowings-to-deposits ratio. In the portfolio adjustment process following the policy-induced change in ρ, member banks attempt to increase their holdings of excess reserves relative to deposits and reduce their borrowings from the Federal Reserve. In the credit market, the member banks attempt to shift part of their holdings of securities to the public and nonmember banks and/or reduce their flow of credit to the public sector. The credit market interest rate rises in response to this adjustment process.

In terms of the multipliers, the increase in the e-ratio leads to an increase in the r-ratio and, combined with the decrease in the borrowing ratio, $(r - b)$ increases. Consequently, the equilibrium values of the multipliers decrease. An increase in the discount rate, other factors constant, exerts a dampening influence on the money supply process. In the case of a decrease in ρ, the equilibrium value of the e-ratio decreases, the b-ratio increases, thus the equilibrium values of the multipliers rise, and the resulting adjustment process exerts an expansionary influence on the growth of money and bank credit.

Since a change in reserve requirements or the discount rate does not affect B^a, the response of money and bank credit to changes in these policy instruments depends upon the response of the multipliers to changes in the policy instruments. Expressing the responses of the monetary aggregates and bank credit in percentage terms, we can write in elasticity notation the response of M^1, M^2, and E as follows:

$$\varepsilon(M^1, x) = \varepsilon(m^1, x)\,\frac{1}{B^a},$$

$$\varepsilon(M^2, x) = \varepsilon(m^2, x)\,\frac{1}{B^a},$$

$$\varepsilon(E, x) = \varepsilon(m^2 - 1, x)\,\frac{1}{B^a},$$

where x is a general symbol for r^d, or r^t, or ρ.

The elasticities of the multipliers with respect to reserve requirements may be written as follows:

$$\varepsilon(m, r^d) = \varepsilon(m, r) \cdot \varepsilon(r, r^d),$$
$$\varepsilon(m, r^t) = \varepsilon(m, r) \cdot \varepsilon(r, r^t).$$

The response of the multipliers to changes in the discount rate depends upon the response of both the *e*-ratio and the *b*-ratio to changes in the discount rate. The elasticity of the multipliers with respect to the discount rate may be expressed as follows:

$$\varepsilon(m, \rho) = \varepsilon(m, e) \cdot \varepsilon(e, \rho) + \varepsilon(m, b) \cdot \varepsilon(b, \rho).$$

Based on previous discussion, the signs of the terms appearing in the above expressions can be specified in the following manner:

$$\varepsilon(m, r) < 0, \qquad \varepsilon(r, r^t) > 0, \qquad \varepsilon(m, b) > 0,$$
$$\varepsilon(r, r^d) > 0, \qquad \varepsilon(e, \rho) > 0, \qquad \varepsilon(b, \rho) < 0.$$

Given this information, it follows that

$$\varepsilon(m, r^d), \qquad \varepsilon(m, r^t), \qquad \varepsilon(m, \rho) < 0.$$

An increase in reserve requirements or the discount rate decreases the values of the multipliers.

Inclusions of Interest Rate Effects

To complete the analysis of the effects of changes in reserve requirements and the discount rate, we must consider interest rate effects of these policy actions. In the portfolio adjustment process by which banks react to changes in these policy instruments, the interest rate (i) changes. Since the equilibrium values of the multipliers also depend upon the interest rate (i), possible interest rate effects must be added to the expressions for the elasticities of M^1, M^2, and E. This can be taken care of by expanding the previous expressions in the following manner:

$$\varepsilon(M, r^d) = [\varepsilon(m, r) \cdot \varepsilon(r, r^d) + \varepsilon(m, i) \cdot \varepsilon(i, r^d)] \frac{1}{B^a}$$

$$\varepsilon(E, r^d) = [\varepsilon(m^2 - 1, r) \cdot \varepsilon(r, r^d) + \varepsilon(m^2 - 1, i) \cdot \varepsilon(i, r^d)] \frac{1}{B^a}$$

$$\varepsilon(M, \rho) = [\varepsilon(m, e) \cdot \varepsilon(e, \rho) + \varepsilon(m, b) \cdot \varepsilon(b, \rho) + \varepsilon(m, i) \cdot \varepsilon(i, \rho)] \frac{1}{B^a}.$$

$$\varepsilon(E, \rho) = [\varepsilon(m^2 - 1, e) \cdot \varepsilon(e, i) + \varepsilon(m^2 - 1, b) \cdot \varepsilon(b, \rho) + \varepsilon(m^2 - 1, i) \cdot \varepsilon(i, \rho)] \frac{1}{B^a}.$$

The last product of terms in each of the rather lengthy expressions in the brackets given above takes into account the interest rate effects of changes in the policy instruments.

These expressions have many terms in common. The difference in the percentage response of the three aggregates depends upon the signs and numerical values of the following terms:

1. The elasticities of the multipliers with respect to the r-ratio.
2. The elasticities of the multipliers with respect to the e-ratio and b-ratio.
3. The elasticities of the multipliers with respect to interest rates.

As a first stage in the analysis of the relative responses of M^1, M^2, and bank credit to Federal Reserve policy changes in reserve requirements and the discount rate, let us take the simplest case. This corresponds to case II conditions for the multipliers. As shown in Chapter 5, under the initial conditions characterizing this case, the following results hold:

$$\varepsilon(m^1, i), \varepsilon(m^2, i), \varepsilon(m^2 - 1, i) \to 0.$$

In this case, a percentage change in the interest rate elicits a very small percentage change in all three multipliers.

Therefore, under these initial conditions, the last terms in all three expressions for the elasticities of M^1, M^2, and E with respect to reserve requirements and the discount rate are approximately zero. For example,

$$\varepsilon(m, i) \cdot \varepsilon(i, r^d) \to 0.$$

This result does not mean that the bank credit market interest rate is insensitive to changes in reserve requirements or the discount rate. These results follow because, under the conditions of case II, the elasticities of the e-ratio, b-ratio, and t-ratio with respect to the interest rate are such that the numerical values of the total elasticities of the multipliers with respect to the interest rate become very small.

Under this set of initial conditions, the ranking of the responses of M^1, M^2, and bank credit to Federal Reserve policy actions changing reserve requirements depends upon the responses of the multipliers to the r-ratio. With a little more work, something can be said about the relative responses of the multipliers to changes in the values of these policy instruments. Using the explicit forms for the multipliers and carrying through the necessary math to get explicit expressions for the elasticities, the following results emerge:

$$|\varepsilon(m^1, r)| = |\varepsilon(m^2, r)| < |\varepsilon(m^2 - 1, r)|.$$

Hence the conclusion follows that under conditions in which *the multipliers are relatively insensitive to interest rates*:

$$|\varepsilon(M^1, r^d)| = |\varepsilon(M^2, r^d)| < |\varepsilon(E, r^d)|,$$
$$|\varepsilon(M^1, r^t)| = |\varepsilon(M^2, r^t)| < |\varepsilon(E, r^t)|.$$

The percentage response of bank credit to reserve requirement changes is greater than the percentage responses of M^1 and M^2, which are approximately equal.[4]

The ranking of the percentage responses of M^1, M^2, and bank credit to changes in the discount rate depend upon the responses of the multipliers to changes in the banks' excess reserve and borrowing ratios. Further analysis of the elasticities of the three multipliers with respect to the e-ratio and b-ratio leads to the following results:

$$|\varepsilon(m^1, e)| = |\varepsilon(m^2, e)| < |\varepsilon(m^2 - 1, e)|,$$
$$\varepsilon(m^1, b) = \varepsilon(m^2, b) < \varepsilon(m^2 - 1, b).$$

Given these results it follows that, under the case $\varepsilon(m, i) \to 0$, the elasticities of M and E with respect to the discount rate can be approximated by the following expressions:

$$\varepsilon(M, \rho) = [\varepsilon(m, e) \cdot \varepsilon(e, \rho) + \varepsilon(m, b) \cdot \varepsilon(b, \rho)] \frac{1}{B^a},$$

$$\varepsilon(E, \rho) = [\varepsilon(m^2 - 1, e) \cdot \varepsilon(e, \rho) + \varepsilon(m^2 - 1, b) \cdot \varepsilon(b, \rho)] \frac{1}{B^a}.$$

Given the previous ordering relations, the following ordering relation prevails:

$$|\varepsilon(M^1, \rho)| = |\varepsilon(M^2, \rho)| < |\varepsilon(E, \rho)|.$$

Under conditions in which the multipliers are relatively insensitive to market interest rates, changes in the discount rate lead to the greatest percentage change in bank credit.

Under conditions in which the multipliers are more sensitive to changes in the interest rate, such as case I, phase I of case II, and case III, then interest rate effects of changes in reserve requirements and the discount rate must be taken into consideration. Under the initial conditions outlined under case I—interest rates at low levels and i^t well below Regulation Q ceilings—the response of the multipliers to interest rates is in the same direction as the movement of interest rates:

$$\varepsilon(m, i) > 0.$$

If a rise (fall) in the interest rate results in a rise (fall) in the values of the multipliers, then

$$\varepsilon(m, i) \cdot \varepsilon(i, x) > 0, \qquad x = r^d, r^t, \rho.$$

Consequently, the increase in the interest rate, resulting from the banks' portfolio adjustment that accompanies an upward revision in member bank reserve requirements or the discount rate, acts to dampen the percentage decrease in M^1, M^2, and bank credit. The elasticities of M^1, M^2, and E with respect to

---

[4] The reader should note that the condition in which the elasticities of M^1 and M^2 with respect to reserve requirements are approximately equal is a limiting case of case II.

reserve requirements and the discount rate would be smaller than in the case in which interest rate effects on the multipliers are much reduced.

Also, since under case I conditions the M^1 multiplier is least sensitive to interest rate changes (see Chapter 5), changes in reserve requirements and the discount rate would tend to have the greatest percentage effect on M^1 compared to money defined to include time deposits and bank credit.

Turning to the situation in which interest rates are at high levels and the banks are effectively constrained by Regulation Q ceiling rates (case III), the ordering among the percentage responses of the stocks of money and bank credit to changes in reserve requirements and the discount rate is reversed from case I. Reviewing, we have the results that, under the initial conditions of case III,

$$\varepsilon(m^1, i) > 0,$$
$$\varepsilon(m^2, i) < 0,$$
$$\varepsilon(m^2 - 1, i) < 0.$$

The signs of the elasticities of the M^2 and bank credit multipliers with respect to interest rates are reversed from under case I conditions. Also, in Chapter 5 it was shown that, under these initial conditions, a 1 per cent rise in the interest rate leads to a greater percentage decline in bank credit than in the aggregate money defined to include time deposits.

With these results, it follows that changes in the interest rate resulting from changes in r^d, r^t, and ρ operate to dampen the change in money (M^1), but reinforce the change in M^2 and bank credit. Contrary to case I, under high levels of interest rates and the effective constraint of Regulation Q, bank credit is more sensitive to changes in reserve requirements and the discount rate; and money (M^1) is less sensitive to changes in these policy instruments.

Summary

One very important point should emerge from a careful reading of Chapter 7. This is that the Federal Reserve System should not necessarily expect its policy actions to have the same relative effect on the monetary aggregates and bank credit. The responses of the monetary aggregates and bank credit to Federal Reserve actions depend crucially upon the initial conditions under which actions, such as the purchase or sale of government securities, changes in reserve requirements, changes in the discount rate, and changes in Regulation Q ceiling rates, are carried out. Some of these basic initial conditions that affect the outcome of Federal Reserve actions are as follows:

1. The level of credit market interest rates relative to their historical average levels.
2. The response of the interest rate to open market operations.
3. The relationship between the yields that banks are offering on time deposits, Regulation Q ceiling rates on time deposit rates, and the level of other credit market interest rates.
4. The policy which the Federal Reserve Banks use to control the aggregate level of member bank borrowings.

Table 7.1 summarizes, in terms of elasticities, the responses of money (M^1), money defined to include time deposits (M^2), and bank credit (E), to changes in the net source base, reserve requirements, and the discount rate under the initial conditions of the three cases developed in Chapter 5 and Chapter 7.

TABLE 7.1

ELASTICITIES OF M^1, M^2, AND BANK CREDIT WITH RESPECT TO B^a, RESERVE REQUIREMENTS AND THE DISCOUNT RATE

Elasticities with Respect to B^a

Short-Run Cases			Long-Run Cases		
$\varepsilon(M^1, B^a) < 1$	Case Ia	$\varepsilon(M^2, B^a) < 1$	$\varepsilon(M^1, B^a) > 1$	Case Ib	$\varepsilon(M^2, B^a) > 1$
		$\varepsilon(E, B^a) < 1$			$\varepsilon(E, B^a) > 1$
$\varepsilon(M^1, B^a) \rightarrow 1$	Case IIa	$\varepsilon(M^2, B^a) \rightarrow 1$	$\varepsilon(M^1, B^a) \rightarrow 1$	Case IIb	$\varepsilon(M^2, B^a) \rightarrow 1$
		$\varepsilon(E, B^a) \rightarrow 1$			$\varepsilon(E, B^a) \rightarrow 1$
$\varepsilon(M^1, B^a) < 1$	Case IIIa	$\varepsilon(M^2, B^a) > 1$	$\varepsilon(M^1, B^a) > 1$	Case IIIb	$\varepsilon(M^2, B^a) < 1$
		$\varepsilon(E, B^a) > 1$			$\varepsilon(E, B^a) < 1$

Elasticities with Respect to
Reserve Requirements and the Discount Rate (x = general symbol for r^d r^t, ρ),

Short-Run Cases*

Case I

$$\varepsilon(M^1, x) = \varepsilon(m^1, x) + \text{dampening interest rate effects}$$
$$\varepsilon(M^2, x) = \varepsilon(m^2, x) + \text{dampening interest rate effects}$$
$$\varepsilon(E, x) = \varepsilon(m^2 - 1, x) + \text{dampening interest rate effects}$$

Case II

$$\varepsilon(M^1, x) \rightarrow \varepsilon(m^1, x)$$
$$\varepsilon(M^2, x) \rightarrow \varepsilon(m^2, x)$$
$$\varepsilon(E, x) \rightarrow \varepsilon(m^2 - 1, x)$$

Case III

$$\varepsilon(M^1, x) = \varepsilon(m^1, x) + \text{dampening interest rate effects}$$
$$\varepsilon(M^2, x) = \varepsilon(m^2, x) + \text{reinforcing interest rate effects}$$
$$\varepsilon(E, x) = \varepsilon(m^2 - 1, x) + \text{reinforcing interest rate effects}$$

* In writing out these cases $\varepsilon(M, B^a) = \varepsilon(m^1, x)\,(1/B^a.)$ However, the $1/B^a$ has been omitted to simplify the notation.

In Table 7.1 the percentage changes in M^1, M^2, and bank credit differ under the three cases. For example, expansionary actions or contractionary actions[5] by the Federal Reserve System have the greatest short-run effect on

[5] When Federal Reserve actions are called expansionary, this refers to policy actions resulting in an increase in the base (or in a dynamic framework, an increase in the rate at which B^a is supplied), and a decrease in reserve requirements or the discount rate. Contractionary Federal Reserve actions refer to the opposite changes in these items. With respect to Regulation Q, one must be very careful. A rise in Regulation Q ceilings would have a contractionary effect on M^1 but an expansionary effect on M^2 and bank credit.

M^1 under the conditions of case II, the absence of interest rate effects on the money multiplier. In the short-run, under conditions in which the multiplier responds to changes in the interest rate, the interest rate effects of Federal Reserve actions act to dampen the impact of Federal Reserve policy actions on the money supply process.

However, M^2 and bank credit are most responsive to Federal Reserve actions in the short-run under case IIIa conditions—interest rates at high levels and the effective constraint of Regulation Q. Under these conditions, interest rate effects of Federal Reserve actions operate to reinforce the impact of policy actions on M^2 and bank credit.

The necessity for clearly stating the initial conditions under which policy actions take place becomes evident if we compare the long-run and short-run effects of open market operations. In cases Ib–IIIb, increases in B^a operate to raise the interest rate. Under these long-run conditions, M^1 is most responsive to Federal Reserve open market operations under case I and case III conditions, instead of as in the short-run case II. Bank credit and M^2 are now most responsive to open market operations under case I conditions—low levels of interest rates and i^t well below Regulation Q. These results follow from the specification that the long-run feedback and price expectations effects of a steady rise (fall) in the base increase (decrease) interest rates.

The analysis developed in this book points out that not only is the response of M^1, M^2, and E to changes in Federal Reserve actions not the same under all initial conditions, but that the *relative* responses of these three aggregates are not necessarily the same. Table 7.2 gives the ranking, in terms of elasticities, of the relative responses of M^1, M^2, and bank credit to changes in the net source base under differing initial conditions. Only under case II conditions, in which the multipliers are insensitive to interest rate changes resulting from changes in B^a, would the percentage responses of all three aggregates to open market operations be expected to be the same.

TABLE 7.2

RELATIVE RESPONSES OF M^1, M^2, AND BANK CREDIT TO CHANGES IN B^a

Short-Run Cases
Case Ia
$\varepsilon(M^1, B^a) > \varepsilon(M^2, B^a) > \varepsilon(E, B^a)$
Case IIa
$\varepsilon(E, B^a) \rightarrow \varepsilon(M^2, B^a) \rightarrow \varepsilon(M^1, B^a)$
Case IIIa
$\varepsilon(E, B^a) > \varepsilon(M^2, B^a) > \varepsilon(M^1, B^a)$
Long-Run Cases
Case Ib
$\varepsilon(E, B^a) > \varepsilon(M^2, B^a) > \varepsilon(M^1, B^a)$
Case IIb
$\varepsilon(E, B^a) \rightarrow \varepsilon(M^2, B^a) \rightarrow \varepsilon(E, B^a)$
Case IIIb
$\varepsilon(M^1, B^a) > \varepsilon(M^2, B^a) > \varepsilon(E, B^a)$

The effects of policy actions by the Federal Reserve on money, money plus time, and bank credit and the relative responses of these aggregates depends upon the existing initial conditions. For example, if market interest rates are rising rapidly and the Federal Reserve engages in a contractionary policy, if banks are not effectively constrained by Regulation *Q* ceilings, then the Federal Reserve should not be surprised to find that, in the short-run, the growth of bank credit is not sharply reduced. If under conditions of high interest rates and the constraint of Regulation *Q* the Federal Reserve attempts to reduce the growth of M^1 by a contractionary policy, the policymakers should not be surprised if the response of M^1 is slower than under other conditions and the response of bank credit is more rapid than under different conditions. Observed divergent movements of M^1, M^2, and bank credit are completely consistent with the derivable implications of the hypothesis. The hypothesis also clearly provides the initial conditions under which such divergent patterns would be expected to occur.

Appendix: Supplemental Evidence

Professor Richard Zecher has recently published a study of some of the implications of four econometric models of the financial sector.[6] The four models studied by Professor Zecher include two versions of a model by Ronald Teigen,[7] the Brookings model financial sector by Frank de Leeuw,[8] and the MIT-FRS group financial sector model.[9]

Because the results of Professor Zecher's study bear directly on the conclusions developed in this book, some of Professor Zecher's results are reported in this appendix.

1. First quarter response of the short-term interest rate (Treasury bill rate) to a \$1.0 billion increase in B^a implied by all the models falls in the range −115 to −236 basis points.

2. Although the adjustment patterns differ among the models, all of the models imply that, in the second and later quarters after the change in B^a, the responses of both the short-term interest rate and the long-term interest rate decay rapidly. The models all imply that lagged effects of B^a on the short-term interest rate and long-term interest rate are important quantitatively, and in the opposite direction in the quarter

---

[6] Joseph R. Zecher, "An Evaluation of Four Econometric Models of the Financial Sector," Dissertation Series Number 1 in Federal Reserve Bank of Cleveland *Economic Papers* (January 1970).

[7] Ronald Teigen, "An Aggregated Quarterly Model of the United States Monetary Sector, 1953–1964," in *Targets and Indicators of Monetary Policy*, ed. by Karl Brunner (San Francisco: Chandler Publishing Co., 1969), pp. 175–218.

[8] Frank de Leeuw, "A Model of Financial Behavior" in The *Brookings Quarterly Econometric Model of the United States* (Chicago: Rand McNally and Co., 1965), pp. 465–530.

[9] Frank de Leeuw and Edward Gramlich, "The FRS–MIT Econometric Model," Federal Reserve *Bulletin* (January 1968), pp. 11–40.

after B^a is changed. If B^a is increased, the short-term interest rate and long-term interest rate will decrease the first quarter and will then increase the second quarter if no further changes in B^a are made.[10]

3. Using B^a to control the term structure of interest rates is effective only in the quarter of the policy action. By the second quarter most of the effect of the policy action disappears and may actually be reversed if income is especially responsive to changes in B^a.

4. The effects of a $1.0 billion increase in nominal income on the short-term interest rate is positive for all models.

5. All four models exhibit a positive relation between changes in the discount rate and the yield on short-term Treasury bills.

6. All four models exhibit a positive relation between changes in reserve requirements and the yield on short-term Treasury bills.

7. The long-run response of the volume of commercial bank loans to nominal income is positive for all models except the FRS–MIT model.

8. The response of the multiplier m to changes in the discount rate or reserve requirements is negative. The response of the multiplier to changes in reserve requirements in absolute value is larger than the response of m to changes in the discount rate.

9. For all four models, in the short run, increases in B^a, reserve requirements, and the discount rate all tend to decrease the multiplier in the first quarter.

10. In the long run, increases in B^a result in increasing the multiplier above its initial level in all models except de Leeuw's (which implies that the long-run $\varepsilon(M, B^a) = 1$). The long-run effects of changes in the discount rate and reserve requirements are in the same direction as the initial change.

11. According to the models, the monetary authorities must choose to control either money or interest rates and let the other one vary with income. None of the models implies that it is possible to use required reserve ratios and B^a to attain independent effects on short-term interest rates and money.

12. A constant interest rate policy has the following characteristics according to these models: (a) control of demand deposits is forfeited in the quarter in which the policy is instituted, (b) control of time deposits is forfeited after the first quarter, and (c) the sharp reversal of the response to B^a after the first quarter, and the resulting shift in the relative influence on the short-term interest rate of the initial changes in B^a and income, make the conduct of an interest rate policy in succeeding quarters increasingly complicated.

---

[10] Similar results were also obtained by using the Ando-Goldfeld model. See Joseph R. Zecher. "Implications of Four Econometric Models for the Indicator Issue," *American Economic Review*, May 1970, pp. 47–54, especially Table 3, p. 50.

Chapter Eight

The Implementation Problem of Monetary Policy

The monetary policy process consists of two broad phases. First, the policymakers must decide which economic variables they ultimately desire to influence. These economic variables, such as prices, output, and employment, will be referred to as the ultimate objectives of policy. Second, policymakers must decide how to manipulate policy instruments, such as open market operations, reserve requirements, and the discount rate, to achieve the desired levels or rates of change of their ultimate objectives. This second phase is the implementation stage of policy.

This chapter presents a general discussion of the implementation problem.[1] Chapter 9 discusses the implications of our money supply hypothesis for the implementation of policy, and Chapter 10 presents a schema for implementing policy.

To begin the discussion, let us first carefully define what we mean by monetary policy instruments, monetary policymakers, and monetary policy.

> *Definition—Monetary Policy Instrument:* A monetary policy instrument is a part of the economic structure such that:
>
> 1. changes in the policy instrument affect the monetary process,
> 2. the policy instrument is under direct administrative control of the monetary authorities.
>
> *Definition—Monetary Policymakers:* Monetary policymakers are those individuals who, acting alone or in groups, have the power to manipulate the monetary policy instruments.

The above definition of monetary policymakers sets them off from the multitude of other individuals who offer advice. The policymakers are the

[1] Two basic references for the problem of economic policy making are: Jan Tinbergen, *Economic Policy: Principles and Design*, (Amsterdam: North-Holland Publishing Co., 1966); and Bent Hansen, *Lectures in Economic Theory: Part II*, *The Theory of Economic Policy and Planning*, (Lund, Sweden; Studentlitteratur, 1967). For the monetary policy problem, a good general treatment is in *The Analytics and Institutions of Money and Banking*, William J. Frazer and William P. Yohe, (New York: D. Van Nostrand and Co., 1966), Chapters 24–26.

persons who not only may discuss what policy should be, but also have the power to actually manipulate the policy instruments.

Within the existing legal and institutional structure of the United States, the monetary policymakers consist of the following:

1. the Federal Reserve Board of Governors,
2. the Federal Open Market Committee (FOMC) which consists of the twelve Presidents of the district Federal Reserve Banks and the Board of Governors, and
3. the Secretary of the Treasury.

The policymakers' direct administrative control over the policy instruments usually results from a legislative act, such as the Federal Reserve Act. However, in some cases, such as the Bank of England, power of control may be the result of tradition.

The set of monetary policy instruments controlled by the Treasury are:

1. Purchase and sale of gold.
2. Treasury balances at the Federal Reserve Banks.
3. Treasury issue of currency.

The set of monetary policy instruments controlled by the Federal Reserve in 1970 consisted of the following:

1. The amount of government securities held by the Federal Reserve System,
2. Member bank reserve requirements on net demand deposits and time deposits,
3. Classification of member bank demand and time deposits for reserve requirement purposes,
4. Classification of member bank liabilities subject to reserve requirements,
5. Ceiling rates on interest that member banks can pay on different classes of time deposit liabilities,
6. The interest rate charged member banks for borrowing from the Federal Reserve Banks (discount rate), and
7. Control over the privilege of member bank borrowing at the discount window.

Other means under the administrative control of the Federal Reserve by which the economic structure might be altered would include the System's decisions as to admission of banks to membership in the Federal Reserve System and rulings on proposed combinations, such as holding companies and mergers of member banks.

The set of monetary policy instruments has not always been as inclusive as it is today. For example, prior to the 1930's the set of monetary policy instruments did not include variable reserve requirements or Regulation *Q* ceiling rates. In the future, by changes in the Federal Reserve Act, the set of monetary policy instruments may be expanded or decreased. Also, this definition of monetary policy instruments rules out certain variables such as the money stock and market interest rates which are not administratively controlled as policy instruments.

The primary responsibility for the deliberate manipulation of policy instruments to achieve ultimate objectives of economic policy rests with the Federal Reserve System. However, certain actions by the Treasury can, unless offset by Federal Reserve actions, affect monetary influences on the economy. The 1930's stand out as an example of Treasury actions exerting a major influence on monetary changes. Since the Federal Reserve also acts as the fiscal agent for the federal government in the sale of new securities, Treasury policy on refundings and raising new cash may affect the conduct of monetary policy. The period from the Second World War to the Accord of 1952 stands as an example of this influence. Also, the occurrence of periods of "even keel" reflects the influence of the Treasury on the Federal Reserve's conduct of monetary policy, especially in the short run.[2] Another example of the interaction between the Treasury and Federal Reserve is the use on occasion of increases or decreases in Treasury balances at Federal Reserve Banks to effect very short-run changes in member bank reserves without engaging in open market operations.

> *Definition: Monetary Policy.* Monetary policy consists of the deliberate manipulation of the monetary policy instruments by the monetary policymakers.

Monetary policy in the United States thus consists of manipulation of monetary policy instruments such as purchase and sale of gold by the Treasury; decisions by the Federal Open Market Committee to buy and sell government securities; and changes in legal reserve requirements, Regulation *Q* ceiling rates, approval of discount rate changes, and other administrative acts by the Federal Reserve Board of Governors.

Incomplete Information

To outline the implementation problem, let us assume that the policymakers have a single ultimate objective; they want prices to increase over a given time period at a rate no greater than some specified rate. The implementation problem is how to manipulate policy instruments so that this desired rate of change of prices can be achieved. The policymakers generally have to pursue an ultimate objective, such as prices, subject to self-imposed constraints. For example, when pursuing the price objective, the growth rate of real output may not be allowed to fall below a certain level, and the level of unemployment may not be allowed to rise above some level. Since policy actions taken to influence the rate of change of prices also affect real output growth and the level of employment, policymakers may not be able to achieve their preferred value for the ultimate objective variable within the specified time period without violating one of these constraints.

---

[2] "Even keel" refers to the practice by which the Federal Reserve System attempts to prevent significant changes in interest rates and other money market conditions during a period of Treasury financing.

An example from recent experience illustrates these points. Beginning in early 1969, the primary objective of monetary policy was to reduce inflation. Suppose that in early 1969 the policymakers desired to reduce the rate of increase of prices to a 2 per cent annual rate by the start of 1971. But actions taken to achieve this goal might imply that by mid-1970 real output growth would be negative and the unemployment rate would be above 7 per cent. These effects on real output and employment might be larger than the policymakers could accept. Consequently, they would be constrained in achieving their most desired value for the rate of change of prices and would have to accept a slower reduction in inflation in order to stay within their self-imposed constraints on real output growth and employment.

If monetary policy could be implemented with complete information about the structure of the economy and therefore exact knowledge of the way in which policy instruments, financial variables, and real variables are interrelated, then the implementation of monetary policy would be much easier. It would only involve manipulating the policy instruments in a way that would have a known and desired effect on the levels and rates of change of the ultimate objectives of monetary policy. The policymakers would know how close they could come, by manipulating the policy instruments, to insuring that the actual rate of change of prices ($\dot{p}$) equals their desired value ($\dot{p}^*$) without violating their constraints. There would be no possibility of a "slip 'twixt cup and lip." The policy instruments could simply be set at definite values and the desired goals of policy would be achieved subject to the existing constraints.

However, because monetary policy must be implemented under less than perfect structural knowledge, the policymakers do not know exactly how close they can come to $\dot{p}^*$ without violating their constraints. As policymakers' information about the influence of policy actions on the economy increases, there should be a reduction in the deviation of the achieved value of $\dot{p} - \dot{p}^*$ from the best that could be reached within the given time period.

Indicators and Operational Targets

The indicator–operational target approach is a pragmatic method of improving the implementation of monetary policy. It starts with the fact that no one has perfect information about the way policy actions filter through the economy, are modified by other factors, and ultimately influence the rate of growth of real output, prices, and employment. Economic research, however, has provided some theoretical and empirical information about the transmission process of monetary policy. The indicator–operational target approach attempts to employ this available information to guide the process by which policy is implemented.

Policymakers are concerned with two major questions when implementing policy. First, what effects are monetary influences exerting on the ultimate policy objectives? Are monetary influences exerting a more, less, or an unchanged expansionary influence on the future rates of change of prices and employment? An indicator provides information about this question. Second, policymakers want to know how they should manipulate their policy instruments to insure that monetary influences are modified to continue exerting the effect desired by the policymakers. An operational target provides a method for answering this second question.

Indicators

An indicator is an economic variable that provides information about the current thrust of the financial sector on future movements in the ultimate policy objectives. Empirical evidence confirms that the effect of monetary policy actions on the ultimate policy objectives is distributed over time. Hence, the Federal Reserve cannot accurately judge the degree of ease or restraint its current policy actions are exerting on the ultimate objectives of policy by looking directly at the ultimate objectives. Current changes in the ultimate objectives primarily reflect the effects of policy actions taken in previous periods.

A further point must be clarified. The monetary policymakers do not need an indicator to tell them their current *intent* of policy. They already know what they intend to accomplish with their policy actions.[3] Policymakers want information about the influence their past policy actions are exerting on the future course of the economy.

The choice of an indicator involves choosing some financial variable that consistently provides reliable information about the current influence of the financial sector on future economic activity. In general terms, this requires that the following relationship holds between the indicator and the ultimate policy objective:

> A change in the magnitude of an indicator is followed by a predictable change in the magnitude of the economic variables that are the ultimate objectives of monetary policy.

An economic variable that meets the above criterion can serve as a scale that permits policy advisers to make meaningful statements about the relative effects of different policy actions on the ultimate policy objectives. It provides a means of relative comparison of different sets of policy actions, not necessarily an absolute means of comparison. For example, suppose that the hypothesis in which the indicator and ultimate objective appear predicts that an increase in the indicator leads to an increase in the growth rate of the ultimate objective variable. Then, if the magnitude of the indicator associated with the set of policy actions P_1 is X_1, and the magnitude of the indicator associated with the set of policy actions P_2 is X_2, and X_1 is greater than X_2, then policy P_1 is said to be relatively more expansionary than policy P_2.

The usefulness of an indicator, let us repeat, hinges on whether or not it consistently supplies reliable information to the policymakers. If at times the ultimate policy objectives move in a direction opposite to the direction predicted

---

[3] Since the intent of current policy is not made public until about 90 days after the FOMC Meeting in the "Record of Policy Actions of the FOMC" appearing in the Federal Reserve *Bulletin*, a measure of policy intent may be of interest to market participants. However, this is a different problem from the one with which this chapter is concerned.

using a given indicator, then the indicator frequently provides false information to the policymakers about the thrust of their policy actions on the ultimate objectives of monetary policy.

Operational Targets

An operational target is an economic variable the Federal Reserve attempts to control directly in its day-to-day money market operations. Following each Federal Open Market Committee (FOMC) meeting, the Committee issues a directive to the New York Federal Reserve Bank. The day-to-day implementation of open market operations is carried out by the Trading Desk at the New York Bank. In general, these directives have traditionally been worded in broad terms such as:

> . . . maintain the prevailing firm conditions in the money and short-term credit markets,

Although the directive may appear to be worded in somewhat ambiguous terms, the Trading Desk does not randomly buy and sell securities. It chooses some financial variable or variables to control and aims its day-to-day operations in the money market at controlling this operational target. The operational target should satisfy three basic criteria as follows:

1. The Federal Reserve should be able to accurately measure the magnitude of the operational target over very short periods of time.
2. By manipulating policy instruments, the Federal Reserve should be able, in a very short period of time, to offset any other factors acting to change the magnitude of the operational target.
3. Changes in the magnitude of the operational target over an intermediate period of time should dominate changes in the magnitude of the economic variable chosen as an indicator.

The question may arise as to why the concept of an operational target has to be introduced once an indicator is chosen. Why cannot the Federal Reserve aim day-to-day operations directly at the indicator? The necessity for the introduction of operational targets, like indicators, arises basically from the lack of complete information. At a minimum, the Trading Desk must have some means of evaluating whether its day-to-day operations in the money market are in accord with the intent expressed by the Federal Open Market Committee. To maximize the effectiveness of its daily operations in the money market, the Federal Reserve needs accurate information regarding the influence of these policy actions. In the short run many other factors influence the movement of intermediate variables such as the money stock and interest rates. If these intermediate variables are used as operational targets, then the short-run influence of other factors frequently causes them to transmit misleading information to the policymakers about the effect their day-to-day policy actions are exerting on the intermediate-term movements of the indicator variables.

Choosing one of the economic variables in the chain from policy actions to ultimate objectives as an operational target of policy actions and a separate variable as an indicator is not a logical necessity. It arises from the fact that economists possess incomplete information about the way the influence of monetary policy actions are passed through the economic system and modified by other factors. An indicator helps the Federal Reserve judge the thrust of monetary influences on the future values of the ultimate objectives. An operational target helps the Federal Reserve maximize its control over the intermediate-term movements of the indicator.

The implementation problem of monetary policy may be diagrammed as in Figure 8.1. The extent of direct control of the Federal Reserve is illustrated

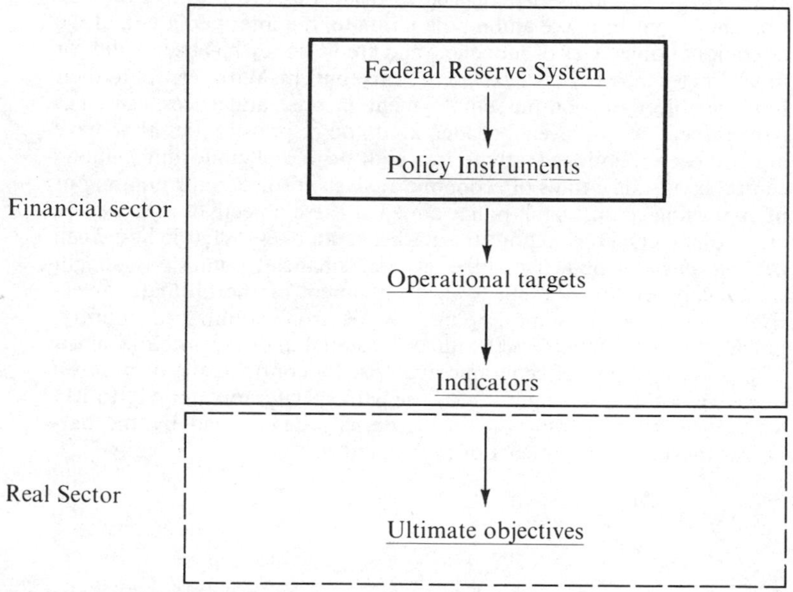

Figure 8.1 Diagram of the Implementation Problem

by enclosing the part of the transmission mechanism under its direct control—policy instruments—in a box. The part of the transmission mechanism lying wholly within the financial sector consists of policy instruments and operational targets. A partial list of the economic variables that have been offered by different economists as candidates for operational targets are free reserves, nonborrowed reserves, member bank basic reserve position,[4] base money, and interest rate on federal funds.

The indicators are shown located as the connecting link between the financial sector and the ultimate objectives of policy which lie in the real sector. Proposed candidates for indicators include market interest rates, money stock (M^1), money defined to include time deposits (M^2), and bank credit. The ultimate

[4] The member banks' basic reserve position is based on a sample of 46 large member banks. It is calculated by subtracting borrowings from the Federal Reserve Banks and net interbank federal funds transactions of the 46 banks from excess reserves. This data appears in the table "Basic Reserve Position, and Federal Funds and Related Items."

objectives of monetary policy—those economic variables that policy is implemented to affect—include such candidates as real income, prices, employment, and balance-of-payments equilibrium.[5]

A statement of these relationships was presented by Robert V. Roosa, an individual who spent a number of years as an advisor in the field of monetary policy.[6] In the Brookings Lectures of 1958–1959, Roosa said:

> My own opportunity for reasonably close observation of central banking, here and abroad, extends back only to the close of World War II. But my more experienced associates assure me that the distinction I want to make among the ultimate, the intermediate, and the operational objectives of monetary and credit policy has been valid for much longer than my own experience can confirm. With respect to their *ultimate* objectives—output, employment, income, and prices, as well as with respect to the even broader kinds of responsibilities that have already been mentioned—there is a high degree of uniformity among central banks. The tools of economic analysis for use in formulating or in appraising central bank policy aimed at these objectives may well be close to universal throughout the market economies. What I should call the *intermediate* objectives—the general financial conditions sought as a means of contributing toward fulfillment of the ultimate objectives—may differ in some important ways from country to country, but for the most part these too may be stated and appraised in terms of a common body of economic analysis. By contrast, the *operational* objectives—the specific guides for use with specific tools in day-to-day central banking operations—are necessarily determined by the particular market arrangements of each country.[7]

---

[5] In the actual behavior of the Federal Reserve, there has not always been a sharp distinction between ultimate objectives (employment and prices) and considerations such as the stability of the financial system. Some evidence indicates that in both the 1933–1939 and 1953–1968 periods the behavior of the Federal Reserve was strongly influenced by a desire to prevent short-run instability in the financial system. See Michael W. Keran and Christopher T. Babb, "An Explanation of Federal Reserve Actions (1933–1968)," Federal Reserve Bank of St. Louis *Review* (July 1969), pp. 7–20.

[6] Mr. Roosa was associated with the Federal Reserve Bank of New York from 1946–1960, and from 1961–1964 served as Under-Secretary of the Treasury for Monetary Affairs.

[7] Robert V. Roosa, "Monetary and Credit Policy," in *Economics and the Policy Maker*, Brookings Lectures 1958–1959, (Washington, D. C.: Brookings Institute, 1959), p. 99.

Chapter Nine

The Implementation of Monetary Policy under Competing Hypotheses

The monetary policymakers may express the policy they desire to follow in general terms as "an easier policy," "no change in policy," or "tighter policy." These statements express the effects the policy makers desire their manipulation of the policy instruments (policy actions) to have on the ultimate policy objectives. For instance, if the Federal Reserve System expresses a desire to move toward an "easier policy," "less restrictive policy," or "more expansionary policy," this generally means that the policymakers want real output and employment to rise in the future at more rapid rates than at present.

Once the policymakers have sorted out their policy preferences they must decide how to implement policy (see Chapter 8). They must gauge what effects their current policy actions are going to have on ultimate objectives and then decide whether to apply more, the same, or less pressure on their operational targets.

Because of lack of complete information about the way policy actions are transmitted to ultimate objectives, proposed explanations (hypotheses) are formulated about the process. An hypothesis is not the transmission process; it is only an attempt to formulate a representation of the process. If an hypothesis is able to withstand repeated attempts to falsify it, it may serve as a valuable aid in the implementation of monetary policy.

The recommendation of a specific economic variable as an operational target and the selection of an indicator generally involves some hypothesis about the way policy actions are transmitted through the financial sector into the real sector. The disagreement among economists as to the appropriate choices of an operational target and an indicator is basically a disagreement as to the correct representation of the monetary policy transmission mechanism.[1]

[1] For an interesting discussion of contrasting views on the indicator problem, see "The Appropriate Indicators of Monetary Policy," Part I by Allan H. Meltzer, pp. 10–31, and Part II by George Horwich and Patric H. Hendershott, pp. 32–52, in Donald P. Jacobs and Richard T. Pratt, ed., *Savings and Residential Financing, 1969 Conference Proceedings* (Chicago: U.S. Savings and Loan League, 1969). The reader should also study the discussion of these two papers on pp. 53–67.

The explanation of the money supply process developed in this book incorporates policy instruments and behavioral actions by the banks, public, and institutional factors. The hypothesis integrates policy actions with movements in the monetary aggregates, bank credit, and market interest rates. Therefore, using this explanatory framework, one can examine the interdependencies of proposed candidates for operational targets and indicators and the implications of using different hypotheses about the transmission of monetary policy.

Explanations of the Transmission Process

Two widely used hypotheses about the transmission of monetary policy may be labeled (1) the Market Interest Rate Hypothesis and (2) the Monetary Aggregate Hypothesis. These two hypotheses are outlined in Figure 9.1. Although

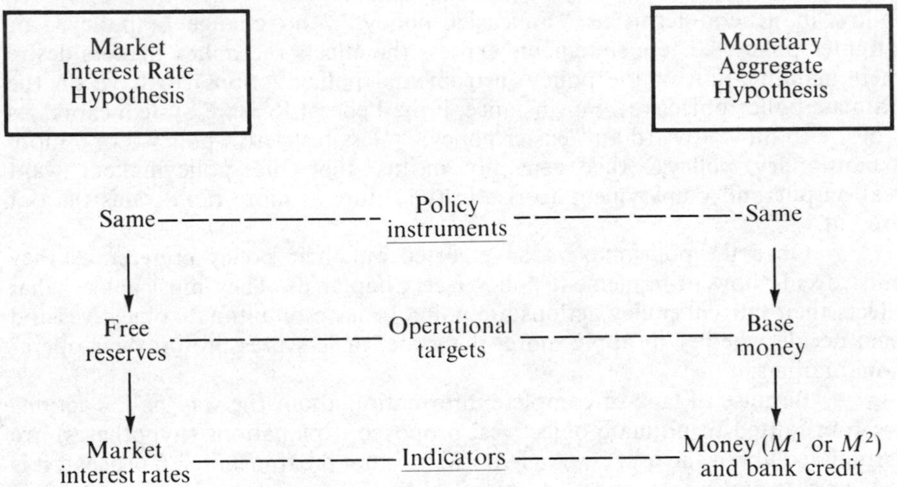

Figure 9.1

there are differences between advocates of the two hypotheses about the relative importance of different policy instruments and ultimate objectives, the sets of policy instruments and ultimate objectives available to policymakers is the same regardless of their hypothesis about the transmission process.[2] The basic

[2] For example, many supporters of the Money Supply Hypothesis have traditionally placed more reliance on open market operations and would advocate very limited use of the other policy instruments, particularly Regulation *Q*.

difference between these two views of the transmission process centers around the way in which changes in the policy instruments filter through the financial system and ultimately affect prices, employment, and output.

The Market Interest Rate Hypothesis asserts: (1) changes in the level of market interest rates are a major factor determining changes in real variables and prices; and (2) the Federal Reserve by its policy actions can determine the level of market interest rates. Therefore, under this hypothesis, market interest rates are chosen as the best summary measure of current financial influences on future changes in the real sector. The operational target becomes some variable which is postulated to best summarize the effects of the day-to-day money market operations of the Federal Reserve on market interest rates. Usually this is some economic variable such as free reserves (referred to as net borrowed reserves when borrowings exceed excess reserves).

We must pause a minute to make an important point. In the outline of the Market Interest Rate Hypothesis, free reserves are specified as the operational target. Many supporters of the main tenets of this hypothesis would probably argue that this is an incorrect or very incomplete specification of the operational target. In actual practice, this is probably a legitimate criticism. We do not claim that free reserves are the only factor that supporters of this hypothesis would consider important at an operational level. However, to simplify the discussion, free reserves have been chosen as a surrogate for a number of short-term money market factors such as the federal funds rate, "tone and feel of the market", member banks' basic reserve position, dealer positions, and the Treasury bill rate. An actual operational strategy might involve consideration of all of these factors.

The Market Interest Rate Hypothesis postulates that the following relationship holds between the indicator and ultimate objectives:

> If the level of the market interest rate associated with the set of policy actions P_1 is higher than the level of the market interest rate associated with policy action P_2, then the expansionary influence of policy action P_1 on the ultimate objectives of policy is *smaller* than policy actions P_2.

The Monetary Aggregate Hypothesis asserts: (1) changes in the growth rates of the monetary aggregates and bank credit are the major factors determining changes in the growth of total spending and hence changes in prices and fluctuations in real output and employment about their long-run equilibrium growth paths; and (2) the Federal Reserve by its policy actions can determine the intermediate-term growth rates of the monetary aggregates and bank credit. Under this hypothesis, one of the aggregates, M^1, M^2, or bank credit is chosen as the indicator of future changes in the real sector. The operational target becomes some variant of the base concept.

The Monetary Aggregate Hypothesis postulates that the following relationship holds between changes in the magnitude of the indicator and the ultimate objectives of policy:

> If the growth rate of a monetary aggregate associated with the set of policy actions P_1 is greater than the growth rate of the same monetary aggregate associated with policy actions P_2, then the expansionary influence of policy actions P_1 on the ultimate objectives of policy is *greater* than policy actions P_2.

Examining Figure 9.1, we can see that some differences of opinion might arise about the influence of Federal Reserve policy. For one thing, the two hypotheses in Figure 9.1 measure the day-to-day influence of Federal Reserve actions by different means. One viewpoint measures them in terms of the supply of base money, the other in terms of the level of free reserves.

A second area of disagreement can develop about how these day-to-day actions are converted into a flow of total spending. One viewpoint is that an increased flow of base into the financial sector is converted into an increased growth of the money stock, which results in an increased flow of total spending, hence influencing employment, prices, and real output. The alternative view (Market Interest Rate Hypothesis) is that an increased level of free reserves is converted in the financial sector into lower market interest rates, which primarily affect investment decisions and hence result in an increased flow of total spending and thereby influence real variables.

Essentially, supporters of the two hypotheses are monitoring the progress of policy by different gauges, where the gauges are attached to the same part of the process. Since the growth of the money stock and market interest rates frequently move in the same direction, this can lead to substantial divergences of opinion about the correct policy action to take to achieve the same ultimate objective.

For example, suppose that the supporters of the Market Interest Rate Hypothesis look at their indicator (the gauge on the financial system) and observe that market rates are rising. They may advise that current policy actions will not be converted into low enough market rates to expand real output and employment. Hence, they would advise that policy instruments be used to raise the level of free reserves.

However, let us assume that the supporters of the Money Supply Hypothesis look at their indicator and observe the growth rate of money is accelerating. They would advise that the current policy actions would be converted into a progressively more rapid flow of total spending. They would advise that the policy instruments be used to slow the growth of the base.

At this point a substantial divergence of opinion about the reason for the change in market interest rates arises between the supporters of the two hypotheses. This difference of analysis has important implications for the conduct of monetary policy. The supporters of the Market Interest Rate Hypothesis contend that Federal Reserve policy actions are dominating the movements in interest rates and that the rise in market rates will result in a slowdown in the real economic activity. The supporters of the Money Supply Hypothesis, however, contend that changes in the public's demand for credit are dominating movements in market interest rates and that Federal Reserve actions through their influence on total spending are influencing the public's demand for credit. The supporters of the Money Supply Hypothesis assert that the market interest rate indicator is not insulated from developments in the real sector. As the real sector heats up (employment, real output, and prices rise), this influences the readings on the market interest rate indicator.

To analyze the importance of this difference of analysis, we shall first discuss the interdependence of free reserves and the net source base. Then the implications for monetary policy of this interdependence are examined.

Interdependence

The interdependence of free reserves (R^f) and the net source base (B^a) can be illustrated by defining each operational target. *In the following presentation the net source base is used and hereafter when the terms "base money" or "base" are used they will refer to net source base.* The same results may be derived by using the monetary base or source base. From the uses side, the net source base is defined in the following manner:

$$B^a = R^m - A + V + C^p,$$

where:

R^m = member banks reserves = $R^r + R^e$
V = vault cash holdings of nonmember banks
A = member bank borrowings from the Federal Reserve Banks
C^p = currency held by the nonbank public
R^e = excess reserves of member banks
R^r = required reserves of member banks

Free reserves (R^f) are defined as follows:

$$R^f = R^e - A.$$

The relationship between the net source base and free reserves can be expressed as follows:

$$B^a = (R^e - A) + R^r + C^p + V = R^f + R^r + C^p + V.$$

Looking at this expression, we can see that if the Federal Reserve alters the free reserves of banks, then, if currency held by the public and vault cash of nonmember banks are held constant, the net source base is changed in the same direction. The operational targets of the two hypotheses outlined in Figure 9.1 are not independent of each other. Actions taken by the Federal Reserve to alter or maintain the existing level of free reserves exert an influence on the base.

To analyze the importance of the interdependence of free reserves, we will use our previous analysis of the bank credit market. In Chapter 6 the credit market equilibrium condition was expressed as:

$$(m^2 - 1)\, B^a = E^s,$$

where $(m^2 - 1)\, B^a$ expressed the banks' demand for earning assets (E^d), and E^s was the public's supply of earning assets. Both E^s and $m^2 - 1$ were shown to depend upon credit market interest rates.

Both E^s and E^d depend upon a number of other factors. For example, the public's supply of earning assets to the banks depends upon the expected rate of return on real capital, price expectations, and alternative costs of borrowing.

The bank's demand for earning assets depends upon the amount and rate of growth of the net source base. In the following illustrations, these factors would appear as shifts in the curves.

A rise in market interest rates could result from either a shift in the bank's demand for earning assets, or a shift in the public's supply of earning assets to banks, or some combination of the two. The effect of a decrease in the banks' demand for earning assets is shown in Figure 9.2. A shift of E^d from E_1^d to E_2^d leads to a decrease in the amount of earning assets banks are willing to acquire at the interest rate i_1. As the credit market adjusts, the market rate rises toward i_2.

Now let us look at an alternative explanation for the rise in market rates. Suppose that the rise in rates was due to a shift in the public's supply of earning assets to banks. This appears as a shift to the right of the public's supply curve from E_1^s to E_2^s, as shown in Figure 9.3. Under these conditions, if the Federal Reserve System does not increase the growth rate of the net source base in response to the rise in interest rates, but permits market interest rates to adjust to clear the credit market, the interest rate rises toward i_2. As the yields on loans and securities rise, the amount of earning assets banks are willing to acquire rises; banks reduce their excess reserves and increase borrowings from Federal Reserve Banks, and raise the yields they offer on time deposits. The new equilibrium quantity of bank credit demanded and supplied is E_3.[3]

Two explanations of the rise in market rates have been presented. The Federal Reserve does not observe the shifts in credit supply and demand curves. All it observes is the increase in the reading on its market interest rate indicator.

Let us assume the Federal Reserve desires no change in the influence of policy. The policymakers may now increase their purchases of securities to

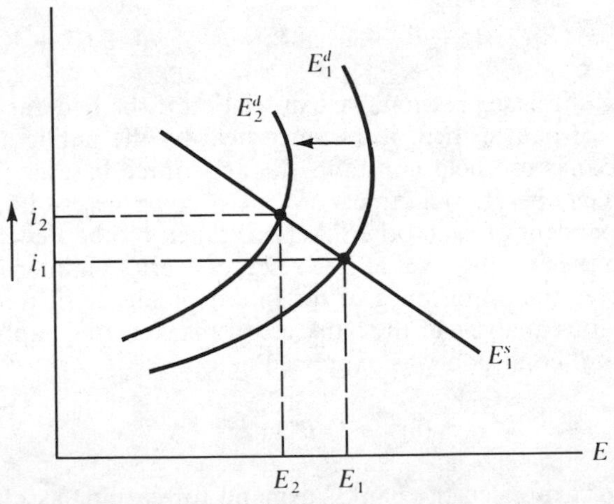

Figure 9.2 Bank Credit Market: Decrease in the Banks' Demand for Earning Assets

---

[3] The change in bank credit depends upon where E^s cuts E^d. If banks are constrained by Regulation Q, then an upward shift in E^s may result in a rise in market interest rates, a *decrease* in bank credit, and an expansion of money.

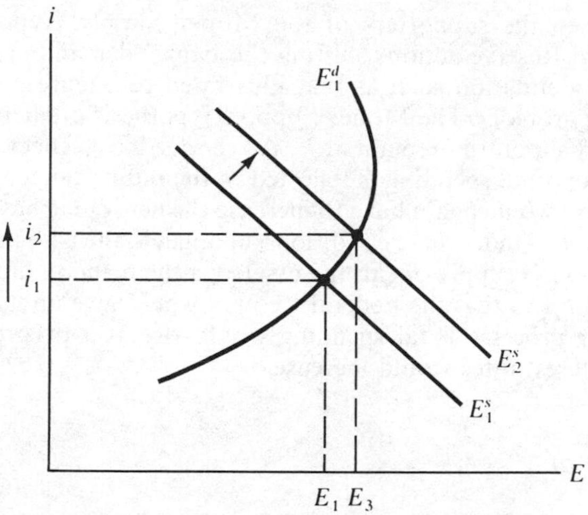

Figure 9.3 Bank Credit Market: Increase in the Public's Supply of Earning Assets to Banks

raise the level of free reserves. If the rise in market rates to i_2 reflected a shift in E^d, then this policy action would shift E^d to the right from E_2^d to E_1^d and market rates would fall from i_2 back toward i_1.

If, however, the rise in the interest rate resulted from a shift in the public's supply of assets curve (E^s), then the result of the Federal Reserve's policy is to shift the banks' demand curve to E_3^d as shown in Figure 9.4. Bank credit does not return to E_1 as interest rates fall to i_1, but expands to E_4. The Federal Reserve's actions exert a very expansionary influence on the money supply process.

If the rise in market rates reflected a change in the public's supply of

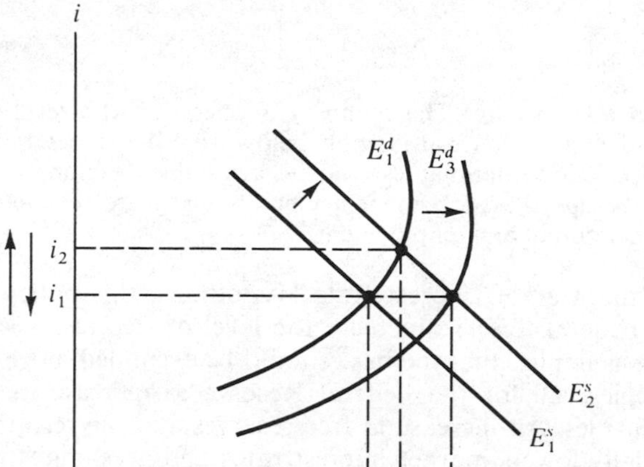

Figure 9.4 Bank Credit Market: Effect of an Increase in B^a To Offset the Interest Rate Effects of an Increase in E^s

earning assets, then the supporters of the Money Supply Hypothesis would assert that Federal Reserve actions shifting the banks' demand curve would be self-defeating. In a situation such as that illustrated by Figure 9.4, the money stock expands very rapidly. The Money Supply Hypothesis predicts that market rates would only temporarily remain at i_1. As the feedback effect of the rise in the money stock on total spending is reflected in the public's demand for credit, the Federal Reserve would again have to increase the net source base to maintain the market yield at i_1. Under these conditions, changes in the base are determined by shifts in the public's supply of earning assets via the reaction of the monetary authorities. This implies that the Federal Reserve would give up its control over the money supply process. Total spending would rise at a progressively more rapid rate and interest rates would increase.

Implementation of Policy under Different Economic Conditions

The framework developed in this book is used in this section to illustrate how alternative policy prescriptions can arise in response to changing economic conditions. To make the exposition easier for the reader to follow, the process has been broken into several stages. At each stage a state of the economy is specified, and the monetary policymakers are assumed to make a policy decision based upon their information about the state of the economy. The stages are chosen to illustrate that the likelihood of a divergence between the information transmitted by interest rates and growth of the money stock—and correspondingly the prescribed operating strategies—is greatest at turning points in economic activity. In the following analysis the money stock (M^1) is chosen as the monetary aggregate. Therefore, instead of referring to the Monetary Aggregate Hypothesis, we shall refer to the Money Supply Hypothesis.

Stage 1

> *State of the economy:* The economy is operating at a level of real output and employment considerably below what the monetary policymakers decide is an optimal level. Prices are stable or falling.
> *Policy decision:* Pursue a monetary policy that increases the growth rates of real output and employment.

Under the Market Interest Rate Hypothesis, this policy objective requires that the Federal Reserve increase the level of free reserves. The Money Supply Hypothesis implies that the base should be expanded more rapidly. Both operating strategies call for the Federal Reserve to increase its purchases of government securities. An increase in free reserves and the resulting expansion of the base initially lowers market interest rates and accelerates the growth of the money stock. Both indicators transmit to the policymakers information that the expansionary monetary policy is proceeding as planned.

As total spending rises, and real output and employment recover from low levels, the expected rate of return on real capital increases and this feeds back to the credit market in the form of a rise in the public's supply of earning assets to the credit markets. Hence, upward pressures develop on credit market interest rates. If policymakers use market interest rates as their indicator, the slowing in the decline of interest rates informs them that policy actions are now having less of an expansionary effect on their ultimate policy objectives. To maintain the same degree of expansionary influence, it appears that the Federal Reserve should follow an operational target policy of increasing free reserves to a higher level than previously.

Assuming that the policymakers adjust their purchase of securities to raise the level of free reserves, the growth rate of the base accelerates, the money stock grows more rapidly, and the growth of total spending accelerates, resulting in a further upward surge in the demand for real output and a greater demand for labor services. The increase in total spending is now reflected partly in a rise in the price level, as well as increases in real output. The further rise in real output, and now also the increase in price expectations, feed back to the credit market in further upward pressures on credit market interest rates, offsetting much of the base-induced decreases in interest rates.

The banks' desired excess reserves and borrowings from Federal Reserve Banks are partially dependent upon market interest rates. A rise in interest rates increases the opportunity cost of excess reserves for banks and hence reduces the amount of excess reserves banks desire to hold. Also, if the discount rate is not adjusted upward along with market interest rates, then borrowings from the Federal Reserve become an attractive source of funds, and the level of member bank borrowings increases. Therefore, under these conditions, free reserves would be expected to decline.

We now begin to see the problems that can arise from the choice of different indicators. Credit market interest rates are transmitting information that the Federal Reserve System's policy actions are becoming progressively less expansionary. At the day-to-day operational level, the Trading Desk must increase its purchases of government securities to continue to maintain the previous level of member bank free reserves.

Economists who use the growth rate of the money stock as their indicator would reach an opposite conclusion about the thrust of policy. They would assert, contrary to the supporters of the Market Interest Rate Hypothesis, that the Federal Reserve was exerting a progressively more expansionary influence on the future movements of total spending and hence on the demand for real output, the demand for labor services, and the rate of change of prices.

Stage 2

> *State of the economy:* The economy is operating at full employment. An increasing proportion of total spending is reflected in rising prices. Commercial banks have raised their offering rates on time deposits to Regulation *Q* ceiling rates.
>
> *Policy decision:* Policymakers shift the focus of their attention from real output and employment to the growth rate of prices.[4]

---

[4] This shift in focus of attention does not mean the policymakers now ignore the growth rate of real output and employment. As discussed earlier, the ability of the policymakers to achieve a definite value for the ultimate objective ($\dot{p}$) is conditioned by the influence of their policy actions on real output and employment.

Using the Market Interest Rate Hypothesis, policymakers may reason that, although credit market rates have risen sharply, interest rates must be pushed even higher to slow total spending and bring aggregate demand in line with the productive capacity of the economy. Consequently, the Federal Reserve adopts an operating strategy designed to further raise market rates. This involves, in the framework of the Market Interest Rate Hypothesis, using policy instruments to reduce the level of free reserves. The Trading Desk is instructed to "pursue open market operations with a view to obtaining tighter money market conditions." The result of these open market actions is to decrease the growth rate of the base, which results in a slowing in the rate of expansion of the money stock.

Although the growth rate of the money stock slows, total spending continues to expand, reflecting the lagged effects of the previous periods of more rapid monetary expansion. The continued increase in total spending is now translated mostly into price increases, and only a small amount of the increase reflects gains in real output and employment. Credit market interest rates soar upward, reflecting the impact of a slower growth rate of the base superimposed on the upward pressures of rising price expectations.

Banks can no longer compete for time deposits and disintermediation begins. Consequently, the amount of earning assets banks desire to hold declines. In restructuring their portfolios, banks rationally first attempt to reduce their holdings of lowest-yielding assets. The time sequence of this process would probably be declines in holdings of short-term government securities first, followed by declines in holdings of municipal securities. As long as possible, banks try to reduce holdings of securities in order to continue to acquire business loans.[5] The impact in the credit market is a sharp decline in the prices of municipal bonds and government securities. Cries of a liquidity crisis or "credit crunch" may arise in the financial community.

Other financial intermediaries, especially those that borrow on a short-term basis and then use these funds to extend long-term loans, such as savings and loan associations, are also affected by the rapidly rising credit market interest rates. Added to the outcry from the securities markets may be an asserted danger of the failure of some savings and loans. In an attempt to avert such a crisis, the Federal Reserve may now decide to lower Regulation *Q* ceiling rates and raise reserve requirements on time deposits. This causes further disintermediation and reduces the growth rate of bank credit, causing additional upward pressures on credit market interest rates.

The scenario outlined in stage 2 corresponds, in rough form, to monetary policy in 1966. In late 1965 and early 1966, the monetary policymakers moved to a more restrictive monetary policy aimed at reducing the "emergence of inflationary pressures." During the summer of 1966 the Federal Reserve pursued a progressively more restrictive policy. As market interest rates rose above Regulation *Q* ceiling rates, the Board of Governors did not raise Regulation *Q* rates. As funds flowed out of banks and nonbank savings institutions,

---

[5] The rise in the share of loans in bank assets during periods when banks must reduce the total volume or growth rate of bank credit also reflects the long-run profitability of bank-customer relationships. See Edward J. Kane and Burton G. Malkiel, "Bank Portfolio Allocation, Deposit Variability, and the Availability Doctrine," *Quarterly Journal of Economics*, LXXIX (February 1965), 113–134.

these institutions faced a costly period of portfolio adjustment. The result of these policies culminated in August 1966 in a relatively short-lived liquidity crisis, called the "Credit Crunch of 1966."[6]

Stage 3

> *State of the economy:* Liquidity pressures have developed in the financial markets, and there are preliminary signs of slowing in real economic activity.

Under these conditions, the Federal Reserve policymakers face a very difficult decision. Using interest rates as indicators, the information transmitted to them is that they are following very restrictive policies. Reinforcing this view is a slowdown in the growth of bank credit and almost all information transmitted to them directly from financial markets and the financial intermediaries. The correct operating strategy now appears to be to quickly reverse open market operations and ease the pressures in the financial markets.[7]

We will denote the policy decision based on this analysis as policy alternative A.

> *Policy alternative A:* Reduce the liquidity pressures in the financial markets. Engage in a more expansionary policy that will exert a less restrictive influence on the financial sector.

If the money stock is being used as an indicator, the reduced growth rate of money resulting from the slowing in the rate of increase of the base also signals that the policymakers have begun to exert a less expansionary influence on the ultimate policy objectives. However, within a broader framework of analysis, the sharp rise in credit market interest rates and the above-average liquidity pressures in the financial market are not necessarily a sign for a drastic reversal of operating strategy. Banks are forced to reduce their rate of production of bank money and reduce the credit they extend to the rest of the economy; these are the key elements of a less expansionary monetary policy. This is the necessary preliminary to the desired policy objectives of reduced aggregate demand and hence a reduced rate of increase of prices.

We will denote the policy decision based on this analysis as policy alternative B.

> *Policy alternative B:* Continue to maintain the slower growth rate of the base.

Let us now examine, in terms of the analysis we have developed, some of the implications of pursuing either of these two policy alternatives. First, let us assume that the policymakers adopt policy alternative A.

If the Federal Reserve pursues policy alternative A, an expansion of the base may begin. Initially, credit market interest rates fall. The fall in interest

---

[6] See Albert E. Burger, "A Historical Analysis of the Credit Crunch of 1966," Federal Reserve Bank of St. Louis *Review*, September 1969, pp. 13–30.

[7] It should also be noted that the Federal Reserve does not make policy decisions in a vacuum. At such times the Federal Reserve may be under great pressure to ease its policy.

rates results in a decline in the money multiplier and, therefore, initially offsets much of the effect of the renewed expansion of the base on the money supply process. Time deposits may begin to increase rapidly; hence, the fall in interest rates has less of a dampening effect on bank credit, and the growth of bank credit is renewed before that of the money stock.

The lagged effects of the previous periods' slower growth of money on total spending now appear in the real sector, resulting in a fall in the rate of growth of real output and an easing in the rate of price increases. The slowing in real output growth lowers the expected rate of return on real capital, the demand for credit eases, and credit market interest rates continue to decline.

As the monetary aggregates begin to respond to the renewed expansion of the base, total spending begins to accelerate, the quantity of real output demand begins to rise and there are renewed upward pressures on prices. These results in the real sector begin to feed back to the credit market in the form of a rise in the public's supply of earning assets, and the fall in credit market interest rates comes to a halt.

Another phase of expansion now begins where the outline follows closely that described previously. Market interest rates transmit information that the Federal Reserve is becoming progressively less expansionary. The money supply signals that the Federal Reserve is becoming progressively more expansionary. If the Federal Reserve follows credit market interest rates as its indicator and follows an operational target of trying to maintain the existing level of member bank free reserves, the base expands more rapidly, the growth of money and bank credit accelerate, and progressively more and more of the resulting rise in total spending is converted into price increases.

This process bears a similarity to monetary developments in 1967 and 1968. From April 1966 to January 1967 there was essentially no growth in the money stock. Responding to the effects of this policy, interest rates, prices, and employment eased during the first quarter of 1967.

In late August and early September of 1966, the monetary policymakers engaged in substantial open market operations to offset the asserted liquidity crisis. During the latter part of 1966 the monetary policymakers decided to move toward a less restrictive policy. Over the next two years, the money stock grew at an annual rate of about 7 per cent. In the second quarter of 1967 the growth rate of prices began to increase, and interest rates began to move upward. By the end of 1968, prices were rising at a 4.3 per cent annual rate, and market interest rates had reached new peaks. During most of this period the majority of the members of the FOMC appear to have interpreted the rising market interest rates as an indication of monetary restraint.[8] The growth rate of the money stock, however, indicated a decidedly expansionary influence of monetary policy on the ultimate objectives of policy.

Now let us suppose that the policymakers accepted policy alternative B rather than policy alternative A. An analysis based on the Money Supply Hypothesis agrees that a continued operational policy of restricting the growth rate of the base would, in the short run, lead to higher levels of market interest rates. Over the intermediate term, however, the resulting slower growth of the

---

[8] See Jerry L. Jordan and Charlotte E. Ruebling, "Federal Open Market Committee Decisions in 1968—A Year of Watchful Waiting," Federal Reserve Bank of St. Louis *Review*, May 1969, pp. 6–15.

money stock would exert a dampening influence on total spending. The slowdown in total spending would exercise a dampening influence on the upward pressures on prices and also lead to a reduction in the demand for credit. Hence, pursuing such an operational target would, according to this hypothesis, lead to lower market interest rates and the desired ultimate policy objective of a decrease in prices.

Stage 4

Let us now assume that the policymakers have continued a set of policy actions that resulted in a slowing of economic activity. This permits an analysis of the implications of different methods of implementing policy in a cyclical downturn.

> *State of the economy:* The growth rate of real output has been reduced well below its long-run potential of 4 per cent. The level of unemployment has risen above 5 per cent.
>
> *Policy decision:* Pursue a monetary policy that results in an increased growth rate of real output and hence a decreased level of unemployment.

This stage might be labeled the "Let us turn it around stage." The choice of an indicator and operational target have important implications for the Federal Reserve's ability to achieve this goal within the time period desired by the policymakers.

As real economic activity continues to slow down, market interest rates begin to decline. The fall in interest rates raises the bank's desired excess reserve ratio. Also, if the downturn in economic activity was preceded by a "crunch" in the financial markets, this may also operate a raise in the banks' desired *e*-ratio. As market rates approach or fall below the discount rate, borrowing from the Federal Reserve Banks becomes an unprofitable source of funds. As loans are repaid, banks use the funds to repay borrowings at the Federal Reserve Banks rather than to extend new loans. If during the crunch the Federal Reserve exercised relatively strict administration of the discount window, this factor would also act to lower the banks' desired ratio of borrowings to deposits.

If the Federal Reserve follows the Market Interest Rate Hypothesis, it may decide that the falling market rates indicate that its policies are exerting less of a contractionary influence on the future course of economic activity. A sharp decline in the volume of member bank borrowings and a rise in excess reserves may be taken as an indication that banks are in a very easy reserve position. Hence the Federal Reserve may be reluctant to pursue a more aggressive policy of open market purchases.

In terms of the money supply process, however, the fall in the *b*-ratio and rise in the *e*-ratio operate to reduce the money multipliers and hence reinforce the slowing in the growth of money, bank credit, and M^2 resulting from the slower growth of the base. Hence the money supply indicator transmits opposite information, that policy actions are exerting a progressively more restrictive effect on the future course of economic activity.

Credit and Money

Because rising market interest rates and a slower growth of money do not always occur together, there may arise conflicting interpretations of the influence monetary policy is exerting on the future course of economic activity. Indeed, near turning points in economic activity, times at which it is most crucial that the Federal Reserve correctly interpret the influence of policy, money and interest rates move together.

If shifts in the public's supply of earning assets to the credit market (E^s) dominate movements in market interest rates, then the disagreement about the influence of policy may reflect a confusion between money and credit. During periods of economic expansion, an increase in interest rates may reflect an increase in the demand for *credit*. The statement that "credit is tight" means the cost of credit is rising. Unfortunately, the word "credit" is sometimes replaced with the word "money." The above statement may then appear as "money is tight." A confusion of credit and money can be fatal for the conduct of monetary policy. As illustrated in the preceding sections, such a confusion can result in policy that reinforces, rather than dampens, swings in economic activity.

To analyze the influence of policy on the economic system we must isolate the reason for the increased demand for credit. The increase in the demand for credit may reflect the influence of the acceleration in total spending resulting from an acceleration in the growth of money. Interest rates may be rising, not because money is tight, but because the money stock is growing at too rapid a pace. Likewise, in an economic downturn, falling interest rates may not signal that money is easier, but that the growth rate of money has been sharply reduced. It is credit, not money, that is easier (cheaper).

Empirical Evidence on the Choice of an Indicator

In this chapter, the proposition that the Federal Reserve should use market interest rates as its indicator has fared rather poorly. We have shown, within an analytical framework, how market interest rates could fail to provide reliable information to the policymakers about the thrust of monetary policy. Also, it was shown that following an operational strategy to control market rates by controlling free reserves (or any of the other money market factors for which free reserves act as a surrogate), could lead to movements in the money stock that have effects on economic activity which are opposite to those desired by the policymakers.

A considerable amount of empirical evidence has been presented by other authors that supports the proposition that the money stock is a more reliable indicator for monetary policy than interest rates. In the first chapter the work of Milton Friedman and Anna Schwartz, Leonall Andersen and Jerry Jordan, and other economists was cited as providing evidence that changes in the money stock have strong and predictable effects on economic activity. In the Appendix at the end of Chapter 7, a summary of the work of Richard Zecher was presented. Among his conclusions, based on a study of four large-scale econometric models, was the following one.

> A constant interest rate policy has the following characteristics according to these models: (a) control of demand deposits is forfeited the quarter the policy is instituted, (b) control of time deposits is forfeited after the first quarter, and (c) the sharp reversal of the response to B^a after the first quarter, and the resulting shift in the relative influence on the short-term interest rate of the initial changes in B^a and income, make the conduct of an interest rate policy in succeeding quarters increasingly complicated.

Further empirical evidence has been presented in separate articles by Michael Keran and Manfred Willms. In a study based on U.S. economic history from 1919 through 1969, and on the experience in five other countries (Canada, Germany, Japan, South Africa, and the United Kingdom), Keran investigated the question, "Which of the two variables (money stock or interest rates) has been observed to have the closest association with economic activity?" The results of his study were:

> 1. Of the eleven test periods—six from the United States and five from other countries—only in two periods did changes in interest rates have a statistically significant negative value (U.S., 1929–39 and Canada in post-World War II). In the other nine periods, the change in the interest rate coefficient was significantly positive in one period (U.S. 1947–52), and statistically insignificant in the eight other periods.
>
> 2. The money stock, on the other hand, had a positive relationship with economic activity in all eleven periods and was statistically significant in all but one period, World War II (U.S., 1939–1946). In spite of the wide diversity of institutions and economic circumstances represented in the different time periods and different countries, changes in the money stock have almost always led to a predictable change in economic activity in the direction consistent with economic theory.[9]

In a study of monetary indicators in Germany, Professor Willms concluded that:

> As the analytical discussion of the relationship between total spending and the five monetary indicators has shown, the most unambiguous relationship can be expected if the extended monetary base or the money stock is used as an indicator. This conclusion was supported by statistical tests, where the liquidity ratio, the bank lending rate, the extended monetary base, the money stock, and bank credit together with some fiscal variables were related to nominal GNP by regression analysis. The "*t*" value, which measures the confidence of the association between an independent and a dependent variable, is statistically

---

[9] Michael W. Keran, "Selecting a Monetary Indicator—Evidence from the United States and Other Developed Countries," Federal Reserve Bank of St. Louis *Review*, (September 1970), pp. 8–19.

> significant with respect to the sum coefficient only for the extended monetary base and the money stock. Consequently, changes in the extended monetary base and the money stock had the most predictable influence on changes in total spending.[10]

A recent study by William Gibson of the relationship between interest rates and current and past rates of change of money for the 1947–1966 period further emphasizes the difficulty in using market interest rates as indicators.

> These results make clear the dangers inherent in using interest rates to read either the thrust or the effect of monetary policy. Properly interpreted, interest rates can, of course, be useful for both purposes. But if one watches rate movements, keeping in mind only the negative relationship given by liquidity effects, one is liable to reach incorrect conclusions. Monetary acceleration will indeed cause interest rates to fall, but the acceleration will also soon thereafter cause rates to rise again as the rate of change of income adjusts. A conventional interpretation would call this later rise in rates an indication of a tightened policy, yet rates rose because income began increasing faster than before. And it seems inappropriate to label as "tight" a policy which causes income to rise faster than otherwise.[11]

Accepting the money stock as an indicator of monetary policy does not involve accepting the proposition that interest rates are unimportant in the transmission of the influence of monetary policy. The acceptance of the money stock as an indicator is based on the fact that empirical evidence has shown that there is a more predictable relationship between money and economic activity than between interest rates and economic activity.

---

[10] Manfred Willms, "An Evaluation of Monetary Indicators in Germany," *Proceedings of the First European Conference of Monetary Policy at Konstanz*, Karl Brunner, ed. (Goettingen, West Germany: Vandenhoeck and Ruprecht, 1971).

[11] William E. Gibson, "The Lag in the Effect of Monetary Policy on Income and Interest Rates," *Quarterly Journal of Economics* (May 1970), 288–300.

Chapter Ten

A Schema for the Implementation of Monetary Policy

Suppose the Federal Reserve would decide to attempt to control one of the monetary aggregates or bank credit. What information does our hypothesis provide about the actual nuts and bolts of implementation policy? In order to answer this question, we will review a few major conclusions reached in the first seven chapters and then present a schema for the implementation of monetary policy.

A basic result developed earlier was:

> I. A well specified connection was derived between the net source base (B^a), the monetary aggregates (M^1 and M^2), and bank credit (E).

The derived quantities expressing the relationships between B^a and M^1, M^2, and E were called multipliers. The multiplier–base relationships take account of the way the monetary policy instruments affect the money and bank credit processes, and how portfolio actions by the banks and the public, Treasury deposit decisions, and institutional factors modify the influence of policy actions on the stocks of money and bank credit.

To this major result, two further conclusions are added based on empirical studies of the relationship between the base and the monetary aggregates, and on close analysis of the institutional structure within which day-to-day monetary policy actions are taken.

> II. The Federal Reserve System can exercise close *short-run* control over the magnitude or rate at which base is supplied to the public and banks.

Conclusion II asserts that very close short-run (weekly) control over the stock of base money is not only possible but also feasible given the existing structure and information within which open market operations are carried out by the Trading Desk at the New York Federal Reserve Bank.

Given the present means of data collection, the time lag within which the Federal Reserve receives accurate information on the source base is much shorter than the time lag for money stock data. Today the Federal Reserve has only "reasonably accurate" information about the effects of its actions on the money stock two weeks earlier. Also, on a weekly basis short-term technical factors may exercise an important influence on movements in the money stock. For example, the money stock on a seasonally adjusted basis was reported to have risen from \$200.2 billion in the week ended March 25, 1970, to \$206.8 billion in the week ended April 1, 1970. An important contributory circumstance in this large weekly jump in money was that banks in Europe were closed for a four-day Easter holiday during this reporting period, whereas most banks in the United States remained open on Friday and Monday. Consequently, the portion of cash items in process of collection which arose from transactions between U.S. banks and so-called Edge Act Corporations decreased sharply. Since cash items in process of collection are deducted from gross demand deposits to obtain the demand deposit component of the money stock, the reported weekly figure for money was biased upward.

However, today the Federal Reserve has accurate information about the effects on the net source base of the actions it took yesterday. From the sources side, the information on the net source base comes from the books of the Federal Reserve Banks and from the Treasury.[1] If the Federal Reserve makes an error in predicting today's net source base, it knows about this error the next day.

If the Federal Reserve had accurate daily information on the money stock and the factors influencing the money supply process, the monetary authorities could aim for daily money stock control. However, because they lack this information, the base is introduced as an operational target. The purpose of controlling B^a is to control the money supply process. The period of control for M^1 is not daily but a longer period, such as a quarter.

III. Changes in the magnitude of the base over an intermediate period of time dominate changes in the magnitudes of the monetary aggregates.

Figure 10.1 illustrates the relationship between annual rates of change on a quarterly basis[2] of the money stock, net source base, and net monetary base (NMB). The net monetary base is equal to B^a plus a reserve adjustment magnitude which takes account of the effect of changes in reserve requirements.[3] Examining Figure 10.1, we see there is a close relationship, on a quarterly basis, between the growth rate of B^a and the money stock. Using the net monetary base, we see that in those periods where there is a noticeable divergence between B^a and M^1, this can be largely accounted for by changes in reserve requirements. For example, the growth rate of the net monetary base shows a sharp decline in 1966, reflecting reserve requirement increases in July and September. The growth

---

[1] Again, the distinction between sources and uses of net source base must be emphasized. The Federal Reserve has accurate daily information about the sources, not the uses such as bank reserves and currency held by the public.

[2] For example, the annual rate of change for

$$\text{I/70} = \frac{\text{I/70} - \text{I/69}}{\text{I/69}}.$$

[3] See Appendix I at the end of Chapter 3.

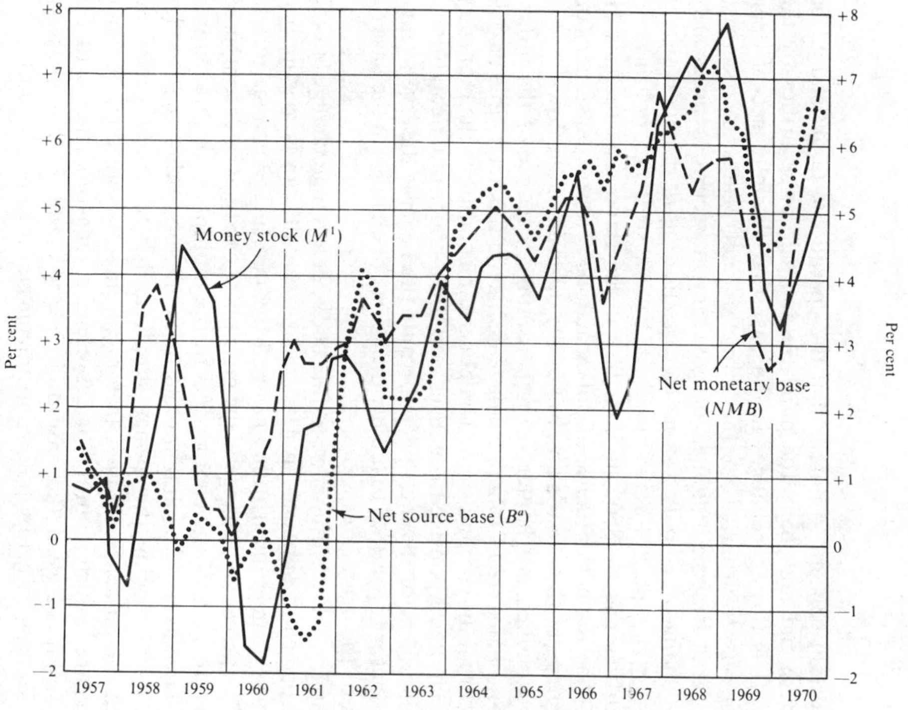

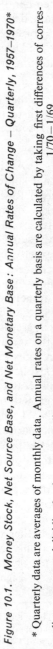

*Figure 10.1. Money Stock, Net Source Base, and Net Monetary Base: Annual Rates of Change – Quarterly, 1957–1970**

* Quarterly data are averages of monthly data. Annual rates on a quarterly basis are calculated by taking first differences of corresponding quarters and dividing by the corresponding quarter in the previous year. For example: $1/70 = \frac{1/70 - 1/69}{1/69}$

of the net monetary base begins to accelerate in the last half of 1960, while B^a does not begin a marked upward growth until about mid-1961. The difference between the NMB and B^a is explained by the decrease in reserve requirements in September 1960. Again, in 1958, the acceleration in the net monetary base is explained by the progressive lowering of reserve requirements that occurred in the February through April period of 1958.

Using these results, the following major conclusion about the implementation problem of monetary policy results.[4]

> If the Federal Reserve wants to control one of the monetary aggregates (M^1, M^2) or bank credit, then the best operating target is the net source base (B^a).

An important concept to note is that the operational target should be the net source base and not solely the purchase and sale of securities by the Federal Reserve. It is through changes in the base that the influence of open market operations is transmitted to the monetary aggregates. A decrease (increase) in Federal Reserve holdings of government securities necessarily involves an equal change in B^a only if other factors affecting B^a remain constant or exactly offset each other. For example, if Federal Reserve holdings of government securities rise by $500 million, but at the same time there is an outflow of gold, then the net influence of policy actions is less expansionary on the monetary aggregates than in the absence of the offsetting gold flows.

As was explained in Chapter 7, the percentage response of the monetary aggregates and bank credit to a percentage change in the net source base is not the same under all initial conditions. Under certain conditions the monetary aggregates will be more responsive to changes in B^a than under other conditions. The explicit development of the multipliers permits the Federal Reserve to take into account the factors operating to modify the effects of changes in the base on the growth rates of the aggregates.

Using the framework presented in this book, percentage changes in the money stock, or percentage changes in M^2 and bank credit, can be partitioned into the percentage change due to the base and the percentage change due to the multipliers. The percentage change in the multipliers can then be decomposed into the parts due to each of the components of the multiplier. In this manner the monetary policymakers can pinpoint the major factors, other than policy actions, which are influencing the money supply and bank credit processes. Having examined the influence of other factors, an analysis can then be made of whether these are only temporary or represent a long-run change in the prevailing relationship between the base and M^1, M^2, and E. The pressure exerted on the operating target by policy intruments can then be altered.

Figure 10.2 shows one possible decomposition of the change in the

---

[4] There may be some disagreement as to exactly which form of the base concept—net source base (B^a), source base (B), or monetary base (MB)—should be used. To avoid going into the finer points of the relative merits of these three base concepts, the conclusions shall be expressed in terms of net source base which is the base concept used in this book. The reader may note that one of the other base concepts might also be used.

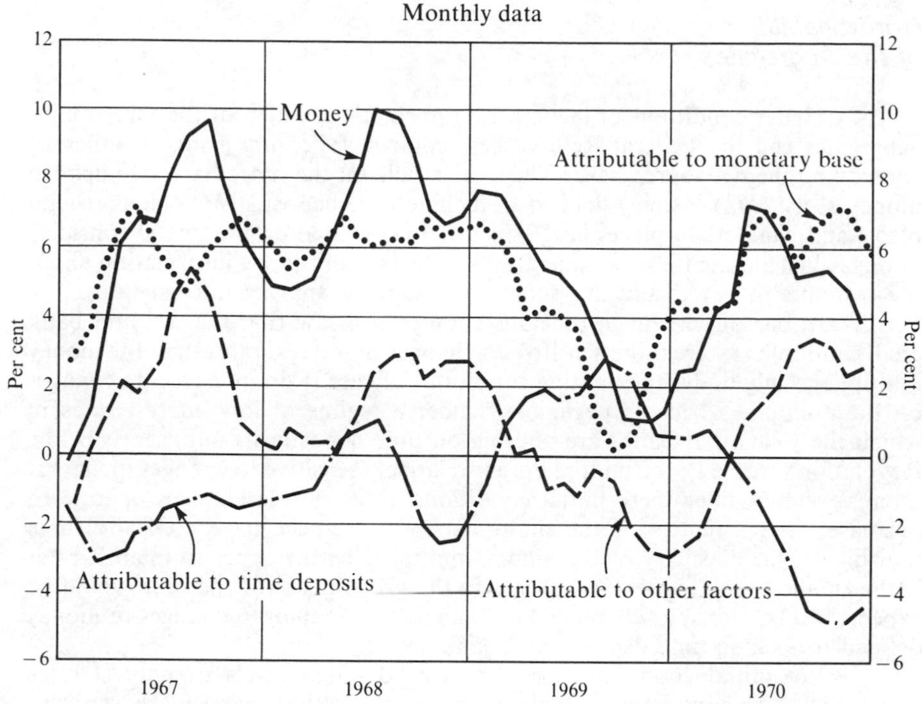

*Figure 10.2 Decomposition of the Growth of Money**

* For an explanation of this procedure see footnote 5 page 191.

money stock.[5] The percentage change in money is divided into (1) the percentage change due to the influence of Federal Reserve actions (open market operations, reserve requirement changes, and discount window lending to member banks); these influences are summarized in the monetary base.[6] The second factor is the influence of the *t*-ratio on the money supply process. The third line summarizes the influence of all other factors on the money supply process.

---

[5] The data in Figure 10.2 are computed as percentage changes between averages of adjoining three-month periods. These percentage changes are in annual rates and are plotted on the last month of the most recent three-month period. For example, The annual rate for June =

$$\left[\frac{\text{Avg. (Apr. through June)} - \text{Avg. (Jan. through Mar.)}}{\text{Avg. (Jan. through Mar.)}}\right]^*$$

* Converted to a compound annual rate.

[6] Some economists would contend that the Federal Reserve, at an operational level, cannot control the volume of member bank borrowings. Other economists would contend that, since the Federal Reserve sets reserve requirements, controls the discount rate, and because of the dominance of Federal Reserve holdings of securities in the base, it can control the monetary base. Regardless of whether one accepts that the Federal Reserve can control the monetary base, it provides a useful summary measure of the influence of Federal Reserve policy actions on the money supply process.

Relative Controllability of the Aggregates

Under conditions of incomplete information, which of the three major aggregates can the Federal Reserve best control, following a target policy of controlling the net source base? The choice falls on the more narrowly defined money stock (M^1). Money defined to include time deposits (M^2) takes second place, and bank credit places last. This ranking is based on pragmatic considerations. Chief among these considerations is the lack of precise information about the response of banks and the public to changes in market interest rates.

In our discussion in previous chapters we saw that the M^2 and bank credit multipliers were more sensitive to changes in interest rates than the money multiplier. Only under the limiting conditions of case II do interest rate changes on the multipliers become negligible. Under a regime of low interest rates, in which the yields that banks are offering on time deposits are sufficiently below Regulation Q (case I), the multipliers are relatively sensitive to changes in market interest rates. Under these initial conditions, interest rate changes operate to decrease the elasticities of the multipliers with respect to B^a. Of the three multipliers, the elasticity of the money multiplier with respect to interest rates is the smallest. Consequently, changes in the growth rate of the base would be expected to be more closely related to changes in M^1 than to changes in money defined to include time deposits and bank credit.

For initial conditions such as case III—high levels of interest rates and the effective constraint of Regulation Q—the t-ratio is particularly sensitive to changes in interest rates. Changes in levels of market interest rates resulting from open market operations or changes in other policy instruments result in sharp inflows and outflows of time deposits to commercial banks. This process of disintermediation and reintermediation may result in significant changes in the values of M^2 and bank credit multipliers. Although the money multiplier is also affected by changes in the t-ratio, the $\varepsilon(m^1, t)$ is less than the $\varepsilon(m^2, t)$ and $\varepsilon(m^2 - 1, t)$.

Also, as was discussed under case IIIb conditions, if a continued expansion of B^a results in rising interest rates (via feedback effects) then an expanding supply of base money may be accompanied by a reduction in the growth rates of M^2 and bank credit. As banks are forced to accept large runoffs of CDs, the rate of increase of M^2 and bank credit slows, but the growth of money (M^1) accelerates.[7]

If we had complete information about the response of the components of the multipliers to changes in interest rates and about $\varepsilon(i, B^a)$ the central bank, by controlling B^a could equally well control M^1, M^2, or bank credit. However, since the information about these factors is far from complete, the conclusion follows that the Federal Reserve can control movements in M^1 better than movements in M^2 or bank credit by controlling the net source base.

---

[7] Under such conditions, a reduction in the growth rate of bank credit does not necessarily imply a decrease in total credit. For an example of the process by which, under certain conditions, disintermediation in the banking system is potentially expansionary on total credit, see Jerry L. Jordan, "Elements of Money Stock Determination," Federal Reserve Bank of St. Louis *Review*, October 1969, pp. 17–19 (also available as Reprint No. 46).

Control of the Money Supply Process

Let us assume that the monetary authorities pick the money stock as their indicator.[8] We shall not present a simplified exposition of the manner in which the Federal Reserve could operate to control the money supply process. Perhaps the best way to illustrate the nuts and bolts of the process is to actually go through a simplified schema taking the implementation process a step at a time. Therefore, let us now turn to such an example.

Suppose that at the end of December the monetary policymakers meet to determine policy. The following sequence of steps outlines a possible procedure for implementing policy decisions.

> *Step I:* Determine the values or rates of change of the ultimate objectives the policymakers desire.

This step involves some intermediate-term planning. Policy actions such as a change in open market operations that alters the growth rates of B^a have a lagged effect on the ultimate objectives of policy that is distributed over time. The policy actions taken at the first part of the year probably will not show an effect on the ultimate objectives until at least the end of the second quarter of the year. At the end of December, the policymakers are planning policy to affect real output, employment, and prices over the last half of the coming year.

> *Step II:* Translate the policy goals for the ultimate objectives into a desired growth rate for money.

Having sorted out their preferences with regard to ultimate objectives, the policymakers then must translate these goals into a growth rate for money. As the year proceeds, the policymakers use the rate of change of money as an indicator of whether their policy actions are exerting the desired degree of ease or restraint on the future rates of change of the ultimate objectives.

> *Step III:* Translate the desired growth rate of money into a desired growth rate of net source base. Communicate this in the form of a directive to the Trading Desk.

Step III moves the policy decision to an operational level. The net source base is chosen as the operational target. The policymakers then issue operating instructions to the Trading Desk at the Federal Reserve Bank of New York, whose duty it is to carry out day-to-day market operations for the Federal Reserve System.

For example, let us assume that step II resulted in a choice of a 4 per cent growth rate for money; in the operating instructions this is translated into a 4 per cent growth rate for the net source base. Let us further assume that B^a equals \$60 billion on average for December. To permit a 4 per cent annual

---

[8] Prior to the start of 1970 this kind of assumption would have been considered an exercise in sheer fantasy. However, since early 1970 this is no longer so far from reality.

growth rate (ignoring compounding problems) the Trading Desk is to allow B^a to rise to an average of $60.2 billion for January. As an example of the operating procedure, let us assume the following composition for B^a.

December Data for B^a

Federal Reserve holdings of government securities (S^G)	$45.00 billion
Float	2.00
Other items net in sources of B^a	13.00
Total B^a (sources side)	$60.00 billion

The Desk must now plan how to achieve an average of B^a in January that is $200 million higher than in December. In making this plan, changes in the items in the net source base must be estimated. Let us, for simplicity, assume that the Desk estimates that:

1. Other items in B^a will average $13 billion in January as in December.
2. Based on past seasonal patterns of float, the average level of float will decline to an average of $1.85 billion for January.

The operating plan might appear as follows:

Source base components	Average, first half of January	Average, second half of January	Average, month of January
S^G	$45.20	$45.50	$45.35
Float	1.85	1.85	1.85
Other	13.00	13.00	13.00
B^a	$60.05	$60.35	$60.20

Over the first half of January, the Desk plans to buy securities so that the System's average holdings rise by $200 million. Given the predictions for the other items and float, the average for B^a over the first half of the month rises to $60.05 billion. During the last half of the month, the Desk plans to follow operations designed to increase the average security holdings of the System by $300 million. If all goes according to plan, the average for B^a in January rises to $60.20 billion. Federal Reserve holdings of government securities average $45.35 billion in January compared to $45.0 billion in December.

However, all may not go exactly as planned. The Desk has complete control only over S^G, but movements in the other components of the base must be estimated. As a simple illustration, let us take float. Over the first half of January, float was predicted to follow its usual seasonal pattern and decline. However, suppose that instead of declining to an average of $1.85 billion, float averages $2 billion over the first half of January. If the Desk follows its plan, B^a averages $60.2 billion over the first half rather than $60.05 billion.

The plan for open market operations must now be revised for the second half of the month. Since B^a averaged \$60.2 billion over the first half, the Desk does not want to operate so that it averages \$60.35 billion over the last half. Operating strategy must be revised so that, on the average, B^a equals \$60.2 billion in the last half of the month.

In revising its plan, the Desk might predict that, since float did not show its usual seasonal decline in the first half of January, unless special circumstances have developed, the seasonal decline will occur in the last half of the month. Indeed, it is possible that the decline may be to an average of less than \$1.85 billion for the last part of the month. In adjusting open market purchases, the Desk would take these factors into consideration and adjust the Federal Reserve's average holdings of securities so that an average of \$60.2 billion for B^a would be achieved for its operating target.

An important point about this method of operations should be kept in mind; the Desk does not need to make instantaneous adjustments every time B^a moves off its desired average. To illustrate, suppose due to prediction error, B^a averaged \$60.2 billion over the first week of the month and \$60.4 billion over the second week. This does not mean that at the end of the second week \$1,400 million of government securities must be sold on the last day of the statement week to place that week's average base figure exactly on the desired value.

On average over the first two weeks of the month, B^a equals \$60.3 billion. What this implies is that, over the second half of the month, the Desk must ensure that B^a averages \$60.1 billion. Open market operations can be spread over the last two weeks of the month to reach the monthly average of \$60.2 billion. The goal is a monthly average figure, not that the net source base has to equal \$60.2 billion every day of the month or every week of the month.

Let us assume that the Desk, operating in the above manner, is able to keep the growth rate of net source base very close to the rate desired by the policymakers. The purpose of operating to control B^a was to ensure a 4 per cent growth rate of M^1. What change in the implementation procedure or in the directive should be made if M^1 does not grow at an average rate of 4 per cent?

For example, suppose that in the past the prevailing relationship between B^a and M^1 was such that if the Federal Reserve manipulated its holdings of government securities so as to achieve a 4 per cent growth rate of B^a, then the growth rate of money was held at a 4 per cent rate. Now in a short period of time, say during a tax payment period, there is a large shift of publicly held demand deposits (D^p) into Treasury deposits at banks (D^t). The result is that the *d*-ratio rises; this alters the relationship between M^1 and B^a, which is reflected in a fall in the money multiplier. The growth rate of M^1 associated with a 4 per cent rate of increase of B^a is smaller than before. However, this change in the *d*-ratio is probably only a temporary factor and will be reversed in a short time. Using the framework presented in this book, the temporary character of this influence on the money supply process can be isolated; hence there is no necessity to alter the basic operational target policy of maintaining a 4 per cent growth of the net source base to continue a long-run 4 per cent growth rate of M^1.

On the other hand, suppose that because of an increased competitiveness of banks for time deposits, the public is induced to alter its desired allocation of bank deposits between demand deposits and time deposits. The rise in the t-ratio lowers the value of the money multiplier and hence alters the relationship between B^a and M^1. The Federal Reserve observes that maintaining a 4 per cent growth rate of its operational target no longer results in a 4 per cent growth rate of M^1. Close analysis of the problem reveals that the change in the money multiplier is due to the t-ratio. An examination of the causes of the change in the t-ratio reveals that it represents a basic change in the public's desired ratio of time to demand deposits. Hence, the monetary policymakers now know that to continue to maintain a medium-term 4 per cent growth rate of money they must instruct the Desk to use open market operations to insure a growth rate of B^a that is greater than 4 per cent.

Empirical Evidence

In this section some preliminary evidence is presented concerning the degree of control the Federal Reserve could expect to exercise over the money supply process using the schema outlined in this chapter. After choosing the growth rate of money consistent with the Federal Reserve's ultimate objectives, this growth rate of money must be converted into a daily-average monthly value for the net source base. This requires that the Federal Reserve predict the money multiplier. Having predicted the value for the money multiplier, and given the desired level for the money stock in any month, the average monthly value for B^a necessary to achieve the desired growth of money is determined.

Next month's multiplier might be predicted by any one of the following methods:

1. predict the value of each of the parameters of the multiplier,
2. predict the value of some of the parameters of the multiplier, and assume that the remaining parameters will have the same values next month as in this month,
3. predict the total multiplier.

In this section, the third method is used, and the procedure for forecasting the multiplier is based on a method used by Lionel Kalish.[9] These results are preliminary, and should be taken as a measure of the smallest degree of money stock control the Federal Reserve could be able to attain.

Therefore, the following procedure has been used:

1. It was assumed that the policymakers chose a 4 per cent growth rate for money over the period 1967 through 1969.
2. Beginning in January 1967 the policymakers each month attempt to achieve the level of the money stock consistent with a 4 per cent growth rate of money over this period.

---

[9] Lionel Kalish, "A Study of Money Stock Control," *Journal of Finance* (September 1970), pp. 761–776.

3. Each month the money multiplier is forecast. The forecasting equation includes (a) six month moving average of past values of the multiplier, (b) last month's commercial paper rate, (c) a three month moving average of Treasury deposits at commercial banks, (d) a three month moving average of the spread between the commercial paper rate and the discount rate,[10] and (e) dummy variables to account for seasonal factors.

4. Having forecast the multiplier for any month, the Federal Reserve then supplies the amount of net source base necessary to achieve the desired money stock level.

5. If, in the preceding month, the actual money stock was unequal to the desired money stock, then the Federal Reserve aims policy actions in the present month to get back on the original 4 per cent growth line.

TABLE 10.1

ACTUAL COMPARED TO DESIRED QUARTERLY AVERAGES OF THE MONEY STOCK: 1967–1969 (BILLIONS OF DOLLARS)

Quarter	Actual Achieved by the Control Process	Desired	Difference Between Actual by Control Process and Desired	Percentage Difference Between Actual by Control Process and Desired
I 67	171.69	172.58	−0.88	0.5%
II 67	174.43	174.29	0.14	0.1
III 67	176.76	176.01	0.76	0.4
IV 67	178.03	177.72	0.31	0.2
I 68	180.72	179.43	1.29	0.7
II 68	181.65	181.15	0.50	0.3
III 68	182.27	182.86	−0.59	0.3
IV 68	184.52	184.58	−0.06	—0—
I 69	187.68	186.29	1.39	0.7
II 69	188.52	188.01	0.52	0.3
III 69	189.15	189.72	−0.57	0.3
IV 69	191.20	191.43	−0.23	0.1

Mean value of deviations:	Absolute	.601
	With Sign	.214
Variance of deviations:	Absolute	.163
	With Sign	.479

Each month, the actual money stock level is obtained by taking the level of the net source base determined by our operating strategy and multiplying it by the value of the multiplier that actually prevailed in that month. To the extent that the forecast multiplier is different from the one that actually prevailed in that month, the achieved level of money is different from the desired one.

Table 10.1 presents the results of this procedure on quarterly averages for the money stock. From this table we can see that the quarterly averages obtained by this control procedure do not deviate by a wide margin from the desired levels.

[10] The last month in each of these moving averages is the month that is being predicted.

It must be emphasized that the forecasting equation for the multiplier and the data for this section are taken from the preliminary stages of an ongoing study of money stock control and its implications for the ability of the monetary authorities to achieve their desired policy objectives. This example is used to illustrate one possible means of implementing policy using money stock control. The procedure used for forecasting the multiplier is a very simple forecasting equation. It does not use information about changes in the individual parameters and multipliers.[11] This evidence is presented to illustrate that even using what many economists would consider a very naive forecasting technique for the multiplier, the Federal Reserve could still expect to exercise fairly close control over the growth of money.

Selection of an Operational Target

The discussion in the previous chapters implies that accepting the desirability of controlling money is not a sufficient condition for actually achieving such control. The Federal Reserve must also adopt an operational strategy that is appropriate for insuring intermediate-term (quarterly) control over the growth rate of money.

To illustrate this point, let us assume that although policymakers accept the growth rate of the money stock as their indicator, policy is still implemented at an operational level using the operational target of the Market Interest Rate Hypothesis. When judging the impact of day-to-day open market operations on the growth rate of money, the Trading Desk uses free reserves or with equivalent results, the Federal funds rate.

Under this situation, the FOMC decides upon some desired growth rate for money, as in the procedure we outlined. However, instead of converting this growth rate of money into a growth rate of the base, it is converted into a level of free reserves or range for the Federal funds rate. The Desk is given a directive stated in these terms, instead of in terms of the base.

At turning points in economic activity this type of operating strategy can create difficult problems for the operation of monetary policy. For example, in a period of economic downturn (stage 4 in the previous chapter) the monetary authorities may not be able to achieve the growth rate of money they desire if they follow this operational strategy. As free reserves rise and the Federal funds rate falls, the Federal Reserve may be unwilling to pursue an aggressive enough open market policy to increase the base rapidly enough to achieve some desired monetary growth. The policymaker's failure to achieve some announced growth rate of money *does not mean* the Federal Reserve cannot control money. The failure to reach the desired monetary growth path, under this procedure, results from using an inappropriate operational target.

---

[11] For example, this procedure does not explicitly account for the effect of possible base-induced changes in interest rates on the money multiplier.

Use of Other Policy Instruments

The Federal Reserve has several other policy instruments besides open market operations; the major ones are legal reserve requirements, the discount rate, and Regulation Q ceiling rates. The analysis in Chapters 5 and 7 provides information on the effects of using these other policy instruments. Under some conditions, changes in these other policy instruments can reinforce the effects of an operating strategy using the base as an operational target, but under other initial conditions they can operate to dampen the effects of changes in B^a on the monetary aggregates and bank credit.

Consider initial conditions in case IIIa; interest rates are at high levels, and the yields banks are offering on time deposits are near Regulation Q ceiling rates. Suppose that the Federal Reserve chooses to follow a policy of reducing the growth rates of the monetary aggregates and bank credit. The System would follow an operational target of reducing the growth rate of B^a and hence effect a reduction in the growth rates of M^1, M^2, and bank credit. However, assume that the monetary policymakers decide to supplement their operational policy by lowering Regulation Q ceiling rates. This would dampen the contractionary effects of the operational policy on the money stock but reinforce the contractionary effects on bank credit.

Under conditions of incomplete knowledge, these other policy actions—such as reserve requirement changes and lending through the discount window, along with splintering, lagging, and selective use of reserve requirements—increase the difficulty of controlling the growth of the monetary aggregates and bank credit.

Comparison with the Present Method of Operations

The schema for money supply control presented in this chapter does not require any drastic change in existing institutional conditions. Also, it does not require any major change in the information already available to the Trading Desk, or a major change in the technique by which the Trading Desk operates. It does require that this information be organized in a specific way and viewed from a different direction than it is currently. Particularly, emphasis should be placed on the *sources* side of the base, rather than on the *uses* of the base.

The operational procedure in our implementation strategy is defined in specific terms; the Desk is directed to achieve a precisely given monthly average value for the base. Historically, the directive issued to the Desk has not precisely defined the operational strategy. The translation into an operational strategy of the many factors considered by the FOMC in its policy decisions has depended upon the Trading Desk being able to correctly interpret the "consensus" of the members of the FOMC. Rather than being precise, such a translation has been more of an art.[12] Although, since May 1966 the directive has included a proviso clause, the actual operational strategy still lacks precision.[13] For example, there is still room for interpretation as to just when the proviso clause should be invoked.

The operating strategy discussed in this chapter does not require that the Federal Reserve completely abandon its traditional concern for viable financial markets. The Federal Reserve could continue to use open market operations to smooth short-run pressures in the financial markets arising from situations such as Treasury financings or a Cambodian crisis. However, to control the growth rate of the money stock, it must consider the effect of these actions on the growth of the base which dominates the intermediate-term growth rate of the money stock.[14]

The discussion in this book implies that a continued attempt by the central bank to determine the levels of market interest rates may result in an extremely large cost in terms of instability in the growth rates of the monetary aggregates and hence real variables and prices. Therefore, the goals of controlling the growth rate of money and insuring smoothly operating financial markets free of sharp increases and decreases in interest rates should not be in conflict. Preventing excessive expansions and contractions of the money stock would avoid major fluctuations in prices, income, and employment which are the root cause of much of the instability that occurs in financial markets.

One should not leave this chapter with the impression that control of money is a rote procedure involving only the consideration of the growth of the base. Under present conditions, the Federal Reserve would maximize its control over the money supply process by using the base as its operational target. This procedure does not imply a complete disregard of other factors. The fact that other factors influence the money supply process does not imply that the Federal Reserve must "look at everything" or that it cannot control money. The analytical framework of this book isolates these factors and explains how changes in these factors influence the money supply process.

Conclusions

The Federal Reserve System, under the terms of the Federal Reserve Act, is given the authority to manipulate aspects of the economic environment. This authority was delegated to the Federal Reserve because Congress believed

---

[12] For a discussion of the operational strategy of the Federal Reserve see Jack M. Guttentag, "The Strategy of Open Market Operations", *Quarterly Journal of Economics*, Vol. LXXX, February 1966, pp. 1–30.

For a statement by the Federal Reserve about the method by which policy is implemented see "Monetary Aggregates and Money Market Conditions in Open Market Policy" Federal Reserve *Bulletin*, February 1971, pp. 79–104.

[13] The proviso clause until late 1969 generally stated that open market operations between FOMC meetings should be based on a specific set of money market conditions, provided that a specific monetary aggregate behaved in a prescribed manner. See Elaine R. Goldstein and Leonall C. Andersen, "1966—A Year of Challenge for Monetary Management," Federal Reserve Bank of St. Louis *Review*, April 1967, pp. 17–18.

[14] For a further discussion of this point, see Allan Meltzer, "Controlling Money," Federal Reserve Bank of St. Louis *Review*, May 1969, pp. 16–24.

it would be in the public interest to have a central body of policymakers, removed as far as feasible from political considerations, who could take actions which promoted certain "desirable economic goals." Since the inception of the Federal Reserve System in 1914, the general view of what are desirable economic goals of monetary policy has undergone considerable change and broadening. From the early view that the monetary authorities should be concerned primarily with insuring a smooth, orderly functioning of the financial system, the goals of policy have been broadened to include such ultimate objectives as real output, employment, and prices.

With the broadening of the concept of the Federal Reserve System's responsibility, the complexity of the implementation of monetary policy has also increased. If the Federal Reserve is going to direct policy toward real output, employment, and prices, then a more developed understanding is necessary of the process by which policy actions filter through the financial system, are modified by other factors, and finally reach the policy objectives. These questions relate to the transmission mechanism of monetary policy. Basic questions arise over whether market interest rates, one of the monetary aggregates, or bank credit best summarizes the total thrust of the financial system on the real sector. Also, it becomes very important to have an explanatory framework and confirming empirical evidence on how these economic variables are interdependent.

A large and growing body of empirical evidence supports the proposition that changes in the money stock are the best summary measure of the effect of monetary policy actions on the economy. However, a relationship between M^1 and the spending decisions of the public has only limited appeal to policymakers until they can be shown how the money supply process operates and where their policy instruments fit into the process.

Policymakers have been, and correctly should have been, leery of approaches which put policy instruments at one end of a process feeding into a black box, with the money stock coming out of the other end of the black box. The monetary policymakers, being practical men from the area of finance, knew from their own experience that policy actions by the Federal Reserve were not the only factor determining the amount or rate at which money and credit are supplied to the economy. Also, they were not satisfied with a peek inside the black box that showed that money and bank credit were related to the reserves held by the banking system.

This book removes the black box and replaces it with a fully developed explanation of the money supply and bank credit process. Policy instruments and existing institutional conditions, actions by the banks and the public, and Treasury actions that are relevant to the process have been explicitly incorporated. Also the explanatory framework makes explicit the interrelationships of the monetary aggregates (M^1 and M^2), bank credit, and credit market interest rates.

The analysis presented in this book does more than forecast changes in the money stock, bank credit, and credit market interest rates. It explains the money supply process and hence permits monetary authorities to analyze the effects of other factors on the process and adjust their policy actions to take these changes into account.

This analysis is not the only possible framework. Other economists have organized the basic relationships in a different manner. However, it permits a very detailed development and analysis and permits the derivation of many important consequences of policy actions, changes in institutional factors, and portfolio decisions by the banks and the public.

Much work remains to be done on the exact form and specification of the basic underlying behavioral relations. Also, the proposed hypothesis must have its derivable consequences continually exposed to empirical evidence and hence to potential falsification. However, the money supply and bank credit processes and their relationships with credit market interest rates are no longer enshrouded in mystery. If the monetary authorities decide to control the money stock, the explanatory framework presented in this book gives them a clear blueprint of the process.

It may be appropriate to end with a paraphrase of a quotation from the Swedish economist Bent Hansen:

> Bad policies are not necessarily due to bad policymakers; the policy makers can do no better than that picture of the economy which is drawn for them by economists and statisticians permits. That, on occasion, they continue to fare worse than should be necessary is another kettle of fish which can only be remedied by a better appreciation on the part of policymakers as to how a rational policy should be designed.[15]

[15] Hansen, p. 3.

References

Andersen, Leonall C., and Jordan, Jerry L. "Monetary and Fiscal Actions: A Test of their Relative Importance in Economic Stabilization." Federal Reserve Bank of St. Louis *Review*, November 1968, pp. 11–24.

———, and Jordan, Jerry L. "The Monetary Base—Explanation and Analytical Use." Federal Reserve Bank of St. Louis *Review*, August 1968, pp. 7–14.

Benston, George J. "Interest Payments on Demand Deposits and Bank Investment Behavior." *Journal of Political Economy*, LXXII, October 1964, pp. 431–449.

Brunner, Karl. "Institutions, Policy and Monetary Analysis." *Journal of Political Economy*, LXXII, April 1965, pp. 197–218.

———. "Monetary Analysis and Federal Reserve Policy." *Targets and Indicators of Monetary Policy*. Karl Brunner, ed., San Francisco: Chandler Publishing Company, 1969, pp. 269–271.

———. "The Role of Money and Monetary Policy." Federal Reserve Bank of St. Louis *Review*, July 1968, pp. 8–24.

———. "A Schema for the Supply Theory of Money." *International Economic Review*, January 1961, pp. 79–109.

———, and Meltzer, Allan H. "A Credit-Market Theory of the Money Supply and an Explanation of Two Puzzles in U.S. Monetary Policy." *Essays in Honor of Marco Fanno*. Padova, Italy: 1961.

———. "Liquidity Traps for Money, Bank Credit and Interest Rates." *Journal of Political Economy*, LXXVI, January/February 1968, pp. 1–37.

———. "Predicting Velocity: Implications for Theory and Policy." *Journal of Finance*, XVIII, May 1963, pp. 319–354.

———. "Some Further Investigations of Demand and Supply Functions for Money." *Journal of Finance*, XIX, May 1964, pp. 240–283.

———. "The Meaning of Monetary Indicators." *Monetary Process and Policy: A Symposium*. G. Horwich, ed., Homewood, Ill.: Richard O. Irwin Inc., 1967, pp. 187–217.

———. "The Nature of the Policy Problem." *Targets and Indicators of Monetary Policy*. Karl Brunner, ed., San Francisco: Chandler Publishing Company, 1969, pp. 1–26.

Bryan, William R. "Bank Adjustments to Monetary Policy: Alternative Estimates of the Lag." *American Economic Review*, September 1967, pp. 855–864.

Burger, Albert E. "An Historical Analysis of the Credit Crunch of 1966." Federal Reserve Bank of St. Louis *Review*, September 1969, pp. 13–30.

———. "Revision of the Money Supply Series." Federal Reserve Bank of St. Louis *Review*, October 1969, pp. 6–9.

———, and Andersen, Leonall C. "The Development of Explanatory Economic Hypotheses for Monetary Management." *Southern Journal of Business*, IV, October 1969, pp. 140–164.

Cagan, Phillip. *Determinants and Effects of Changes in the Stock of Money, 1875–1960*. New York: Columbia University Press, 1965.

———. "The Demand for Currency Relative to the Total Money Supply." *Journal of Political Economy*, LXVI, August 1958, pp. 303–328.

Cohen, Morris R., and Nagel, Ernest. *An Introduction to Logic and Scientific Method*. New York: Harcourt Brace Jovanovich, 1934.

Dewald, William G., and Dreese, Richard G. "Bank Behavior With Respect to Deposit Variability." *Journal of Finance*, XXV, September 1970, pp. 869–879.

Fand, David I. "Some Issues in Monetary Economics." Federal Reserve Bank of St. Louis *Review*, January 1970, pp. 10–27.

"Fast on His Feet in Philadelphia." *Business Week*, February 14, 1970, p. 76.

Federal Reserve *Bulletin*. All issues.

Frazer, William J., and Yohe, William P. *The Analytics and Institutions of Money and Banking*. New York: D. Van Nostrand and Co., 1966.

Friedman, Milton, and Schwartz, Anna. *A Monetary History of the United States: 1867–1960*. Princeton, N.J.: Princeton University Press, 1963.

Frost, Peter. "Bank's Demand for Excess Reserves." Unpublished Ph.D. dissertation, University of California, Los Angeles, 1966.

Gibson, William E. "The Lag in the Effect of Monetary Policy on Income and Interest Rates." *Quarterly Journal of Economics*, LXXXIV, May 1970, pp. 288–300.

———, and Kaufman, George G. "The Relative Impact of Money and Income on Interest Rates." Staff Economic Studies, No. 26. Federal Reserve Board of Governors, 1966.

Goldfeld, Stephen M. *Commercial Bank Behavior and Economic Activity*. Amsterdam: North-Holland Publishing Company, 1966.

Goldstein, Elaine R., and Andersen, Leonall C. "1966—A Year of Challenge for Monetary Management." Federal Reserve Bank of St. Louis *Review*, April 1967, pp. 17–18.

Guttentag, Jack M. "The Strategy of Open Market Operations." *Quarterly Journal of Economics*, LXXX, February, 1966, pp. 1–30.

Halberstadt, William H. *Introduction to Logic*. New York: Harper & Brothers, 1960.

Hansen, Bent. *Lectures in Economic Theory: Part II, the Theory of Economic Policy and Planning*. Lund, Sweden: Studentlitteratur, 1967.

Hempel, Carl G., and Oppenheim, Paul. "The Logic of Explanation." *Readings in the Philosophy of Science*. Herbert Feigl and May Brodbeck, eds., New York: Appleton-Century-Crofts, 1953, pp. 319–324.

Horwich, George, and Hendershott, Patric H. "The Appropriate Indicators of Monetary Policy (Part II)." *Savings and Residential Financing, 1969 Conference Proceedings*. Donald P. Jacobs and Richard T. Platt, eds., Chicago: U.S. Savings and Loan League, 1969, pp. 32–52.

Jordan, Jerry L. "Elements of Money Stock Determination." Federal Reserve Bank of St. Louis *Review*, October 1969, pp. 10–19.

————. "Relations among Monetary Aggregates." Federal Reserve Bank of St. Louis *Review*, March 1969, pp. 8–9.

————. "The Market for Deposit-Type Financial Assets." Unpublished Ph.D. dissertation, University of California, Los Angeles, 1969. (Available as Working Paper No. 8, Federal Reserve Bank of St. Louis.)

————, and Ruebling, Charlotte E. "Federal Open Market Committee Decisions in 1968—A Year of Watchful Waiting." Federal Reserve Bank of St. Louis *Review*, May, 1969, pp. 6–15.

Kalish, Lionel. "A Study of Money Stock Control." *Journal of Finance*, XXV, September 1970.

Kane, Edward J., and Malkiel, Burton G. "Bank Portfolio Allocation, Deposit Variability, and the Availability Doctrine." *Quarterly Journal of Economics*, LXXIX, February, 1965, pp. 113–134.

Keran, Michael W. "Monetary and Fiscal Influences on Economic Activity—The Historical Evidence." Federal Reserve Bank of St. Louis *Review*, November 1969, pp. 5–24.

————. "Selecting a Monetary Indicator—Evidence from the United States and Other Developed Countries." Federal Reserve Bank of St. Louis *Review*, September, 1970, pp. 8–19.

————, and Babb, Christopher T. "An Explanation of Federal Reserve Actions (1933–68)." Federal Reserve Bank of St. Louis *Review*, July 1969, pp. 7–20.

Leftwich, R. H. *The Price System and Resource Allocation*. Revised Edition, New York: Holt, Rinehart and Co., 1960.

Meltzer, Allan H. "The Appropriate Indicators of Monetary Policy (Part I)." *Savings and Residential Financing, 1969 Conference Proceedings*. Edited by Donald P. Jacobs and Richard T. Platt. Chicago: U.S. Savings and Loan League, 1969, pp. 10–31.

———. "Controlling Money." Federal Reserve Bank of St. Louis *Review*, May 1969, pp. 16–24.

———. "The Demand for Money: The Evidence from the Time Series." *Journal of Political Economy*, LXXI, June 1963, pp. 219–246.

Mill, John Stuart. *Principles of Political Economy* (first ed. 1848). New York: Augustus M. Kelley, 1961.

"Monetary Aggregates and Money Market Conditions in Open Market Policy." Federal Reserve *Bulletin*, February 1971, pp. 79–104.

Mundell, Robert. "Inflation and Real Interest." *Journal of Political Economy*, LXXI, June 1963, pp. 280–283.

Nagel, Ernest. *The Structure of Science*. New York: Harcourt, Brace and Company, Inc., 1961.

Poindexter, Carl J. "The Currency-Holding Behavior of the Public and the Strength of Monetary Controls." *The Bulletin*. New York University Graduate School of Business Administration, No. 67, November 1970.

Poole, William. "Optimal Choice of Monetary Policy Instruments in a Simple Stochastic Macro Model." *Quarterly Journal of Economics*, LXXXIV, May 1970, pp. 197–216.

Roosa, Robert V. "Monetary and Credit Policy." *Economics and the Policy Maker*. Brookings Lectures, 1958–1959, Washington, D.C.: Brookings Institute, 1959, pp. 89–116.

Ruebling, Charlotte E. "The Administration of Regulation *Q*." Federal Reserve Bank of St. Louis *Review*, February 1970, pp. 29–40.

Saving, Thomas R. "Monetary-Policy Targets and Indicators." *Journal of Political Economy*, LXXV, August 1967, pp. 446–456.

Schwartz, Anna. "Why Money Matters." *Lloyds Bank Review*, October 1969, pp. 1–16.

Tarski, Alfred. *Introduction to Logic and to the Methodology of the Deductive Sciences*. 3rd. ed. Translated by Olaf Helmer. Galaxy Books. New York: Oxford University Press, 1965.

Teigen, Ronald L. "An Aggregate Quarterly Model of the U.S. Monetary Sector." *Targets and Indicators of Monetary Policy*. Edited by Karl Brunner. San Francisco: Chandler Publishing Company, 1969, pp. 175–218.

Thornton, Henry. *Two Speeches of Henry Thornton, Esq. on the Bullion Report, May 1811. An Enquiry into the Nature and Effects of the Paper Credit of Great Britain* (*1802*). Edited by F. A. V. Hayek. New York: Augustus M. Kelley, 1962, pp. 323–361.

Tinbergen, Jan. *Economic Policy: Principles and Design*. Amsterdam: North-Holland Publishing Co., 1966.

Toulmin, Stephen. *Foresight and Understanding*. Bloomington: Indiana University Press, 1961.

Willms, Manfred. "An Evaluation of Monetary Indicators in Germany." *Proceedings of the First European Conference of Monetary Policy at Konstanz*. Edited by Karl Brunner. Goettingen, West Germany: Vandenhoeck and Ruprecht, 1971.

Yohe, William P., and Karnosky, Denis S. "Interest Rates and Price Level Changes, 1952–69." Federal Reserve Bank of St. Louis *Review*, December 1969, pp. 18–38.

Zecher, Joseph R. "An Evaluation of Four Econometric Models of the Financial Sector." Dissertation Series Number 1. Federal Reserve Bank of Cleveland *Economic Papers*, January 1970.

———. "Implications of Four Econometric Models for the Indicators Issue." *American Economic Review*, May 1970, pp. 47–54.

Zwick, Burton. "The Adjustment of the Economy to Monetary Changes." *Journal of Political Economy*, LXXIX, January/February 1971, pp. 77–90.

Index